Military thought in the
French army, 1815–51

Also in the series

The army, politics and society in Germany, 1933–45
Klaus-Jürgen Müller

Troubled days of peace: Mountbatten and SEAC, 1945–46
Peter Dennis

The politics of manpower, 1914–18
Keith Grieves

The Commonwealth armies: manpower and organisation in two world wars
F.W. Perry

Kitchener's army: the raising of the New Armies, 1914–16
Peter Simkins

The Spanish army in the Peninsular War
Charles J. Esdaile

Paddy Griffith

Military thought
in the French army, 1815–51

Manchester University Press
Manchester and New York
Distributed exclusively in the USA and Canada by St. Martin's Press

For Tom Pickard

Copyright © Paddy Griffith 1989

Published by Manchester University Press
Oxford Road, Manchester M13 9PL, UK
and Room 400, 175 Fifth Avenue,
New York, NY 10010, USA

Distributed exclusively in the USA and Canada
by St. Martin's Press, Inc.,
175 Fifth Avenue, New York, NY 10010, USA

British Library cataloguing in publication data
Griffith, Paddy
   Military thought in the French army, 1815–51.
   ——(War, armed forces and society).
   1. France. Military policies, history
   I. Title   II. Series
   355'.0335'44

Library of Congress cataloguing in publication data
Griffith, Paddy.
   Military thought in the French army, 1815–51 / Paddy Griffith.
      p.   cm. — (War, armed forces, and society)
   Bibliography: p.
   Includes index.
   ISBN 0-7190-2882-5
   1. Military art and science—France—History—19th century.
2. France. Armée—History—19th century.   I. Title   II. Series.
U43.F8G75   1989
355'.00944—dc19   89-2810

ISBN 0 7190 2882 5 *hardback*

Typeset in Monotype Garamond
by Megaron, Cardiff, Wales

Printed in Great Britain by
Courier International, Tiptree

Contents

	List of maps, figures and tables	*page* vi
	Acknowledgements	vii
Part 1	**The French army, 1815–51**	1
Chapter 1	The army and the nation	3
Chapter 2	Small wars and big riots	21
Part 2	**The nature of military thought**	51
Chapter 3	The makers of military thought	53
Chapter 4	The impact of military thought	68
Part 3	**Military thought within the regiment**	83
Chapter 5	Regimental life	85
Chapter 6	Regimental education	101
Chapter 7	Tactical training	114
Part 4	**Higher military thought**	131
Chapter 8	The military schools	133
Chapter 9	National strategy and the ministry of war	149
Conclusion	**A mature yet innovative army**	167
Appendix I	The military budgets	170
Appendix II	Military crime	172
Appendix III	Bibliographical note on secondary sources	173
	Bibliography	176
	Notes	190
	Index	229

Maps, figures and tables

Maps

1	Spain 1823	*page*	23
2	Greece 1828		26
3	Antwerp 1832		29
4	Rome 1849		31
5	Algeria		34–5
6	The North-Eastern Frontier		162

Figures

1	Principal education establishments in the French army, 1815–51	134
2	Higher Organisation of the French army, 1815–48 (schematic)	152

Tables

1	Rank at which military writers first wrote	66
2	Authorship of projects, 1830–33	78

Acknowledgements

This book is the end product of my second exposure to armies and 'the military mind'.

My first exposure came at school – both through the generally militarised post-war society into which I was born, and in that more specifically 'CCF' ambiance of the Fifth and Sixth Forms which has been so well captured in the film *If*.

My second exposure came when I was a postgraduate student researching this book between 1968 and 1973, while I was wrestling simultaneously with four – properly separate – alien worlds: namely those of *Historical Research*, *France*, *Armies*, and that *Particular Era of History* which happened to fall, uncomfortably and unresolvably, between Vietnam's Tet Offensive and Northern Ireland's Bloody Sunday.

My third exposure – and in some ways the consummation of my life as an armchair strategist – came only after that . . .

This book started its life as a doctoral thesis for Oxford University. It was initiated in 1968; largely written by 1974, and accepted in 1976. At the invitation of Manchester University Press I have now extensively revised, updated and condensed it without, I hope, radically changing its thrust.

I am very grateful indeed to everyone who has helped me in researching, visualising and writing the text, particularly Professor Norman Gibbs, who supervised my original thesis and unfailingly gave me sound advice and real moral encouragement.

Among those whom I consulted I especially wish to thank John Naylor and Drs George Gandy, Gordon Anderson, Ian Beckett, Christopher Duffy, Richard Holmes, Tony Clayton, John Lynn, Douglas Porch and my *beauffre* – who is, as it happens, appropriately the son of a *Chasseur* – Réné Mouriaux. I am also indebted to Andrew Wheatcroft, Lt. Com.

Tony Thomas and Professors Richard Cobb, Sir Michael Howard and John Shy – all of whom offered valuable advice.

For an unforgettable insight into the way that military thought can be formed, my special thanks go to the late Carroll L. Wilson and his staff in the European Security Study of the American Academy of Arts and Sciences.

I also owe a particular debt of gratitude to the librarians of the Corpus Christi College, History Faculty, and Codrington libraries in Oxford; of the RMA Sandhurst Central Library, of the *Bibliothèque Nationale* in Paris, and particularly of the *Archives Historiques de la Guerre* in Vincennes. Equally to Sylvie Overs for her typing, no less than to all the many friends and family members who made my life as a researcher almost bearable – in Oxford, Paris, Rouen, Brixton, Camberley and the two Aughtons. Outstanding among these is my great uncle the late George Griffith – a former lobby correspondent during the Asquith government who bequeathed me six months of research time that I had absolutely no right to expect.

Finally, I wish to make it clear that none of the above persons, nor the British Government or Ministry of Defence, are in any way responsible for the views which I express in these pages. These are all entirely my own.

Paddy Griffith
Owlsmoor, September 1988

Part 1

The French army, 1815–51

I

The army and the nation

The 'best army in the world' and its internal debate

Historians have not been charitable to the French army of the constitutional monarchies and Second Republic. They have portrayed it as a 'blind and silent'[1] mercenary force – unengaged in genuine political debate since the overthrow of the first Napoleon, yet heavily involved in the repression of working class dissent: uninterested in the art of war, but dedicated to the tinsel glitter of Napoleonic *gloire*. As its crowning achievements, say the historians, this army helped to overthrow a second republican experiment in favour of a second Empire; it initiated an endless, unwinnable war in Algeria and – most damningly of all – it prepared the ground for a still more humiliating repetition of Waterloo at Sedan in 1870.[2]

There is a certain sense in which this comprehensive indictment is perfectly justified. The army was indeed the heir to many of Napoleon's abuses and even crimes, and it did unquestionably lose the Franco-Prussian War. It did take part in numerous anti-liberal counter-insurgency operations; nor was there anything remotely accidental about the social inequalities of its recruiting structure. It played a less than totally impartial role in the street battles of 1830 and 1848 (not to mention the Commune of 1871, and it even issued commemorative campaign medals for its bloody role in Louis Napoleon's coup d'état of 1851. The makers of Parisian opinion naturally regarded all these events as matters of very great significance indeed – and it is scarcely astonishing if they have inserted some deeply anti-military views into the historical record.[3]

This process ran out of control, however, during the witch-hunt which followed the *Débâcle* of 1870, when any weakness in the military machine that anyone had ever noticed, at any time since 1815, was hastily catalogued as yet more evidence of a malaise which was deemed to extend even beyond the army, into the moral fabric of society itself. A few pre-war military critics, such as Trochu, Castellane or de Vigny, were seized upon – normally out of context – as prophets of great insight and clairvoyance who had been ignored and rejected by a generation in which 'Military thought was moribund'.[4] The broader intellectual climate in which such critics worked – which was actually one of very widespread questioning and debate, and which also often fed them their very best lines – was studiously overlooked.

The existence of a sophisticated body of military criticism in the post-Waterloo French army has thus been seen not as evidence of a lively and modern army but rather – mistakenly, wilfully, and paradoxically – as evidence of an army that was devoid, precisely, of any mental activity whatsoever. Every sign of institutional health or efficiency in the pre-1870 army has been strenuously denied or down-graded. The old army has been denigrated in its entirety, while laughably mythological phenomena such as the 1870 *Franc-Tireurs* have been piously evoked as the true standard-bearers of French military values.[5]

Neither the makers of nineteenth-century Parisian opinion nor more recent historians appear to have broken through this wall of propaganda to a more properly balanced view of the pre-1870 army and its intellectual life. We should remember, for example, that this was an army which inherited not only Napoleon's odium but also much of his prestige – as well as many of his best generals and best ideas. It also conducted many carefully calculated – and entirely successful – operations in support of national policy. In 1823 it reversed the verdict of the 'first' Peninsular War, even capturing the fortress of Cadiz that had for so long eluded it before. Other small wars included Greece in 1827–29; Madagascar in 1829 and again in 1845; Senegal at various times; Belgium in 1831–32; The Vendée from 1831; Rome from 1849, and of course the difficult – but ultimately complete – occupation of Algeria which started in 1830. Still more impressive were to be Napoleon III's victories, using this same army, over Russia in the Crimea and over Austria in Italy.

It may even be suggested that the defeat of 1870 was itself no more than a temporary aberration. We need not necessarily attribute it to a multitude of deep-seated institutional problems, but may perhaps apply Occam's razor and reduce our explanation to a tiny number of personal and contingent causes. It is quite conceivable that a full, complete and sufficient explanation of the disaster may be provided merely by reference to the Emperor's sickness and his rashness in declaring war at the wrong moment, taken together with a few poor decisions made by Marshal Bazaine between 16th and 18th August. If this is in fact the case, we need no longer slavishly follow those who insist on some generalised corruption throughout the military machine – let alone a fatal moral degeneracy afflicting France as a whole.

It is perhaps unfashionable to trace the fate of nations and continents to so trivial an influence as one man's fleeting whim on one particular day; but in this case it is an argument that can be well sustained. Besides, even if we prefer alternative interpretations we must at least confront the fact that Bazaine had actually won the decisive battle of Gravelotte at the moment when he conceded it to the enemy. Hence even if we accept that his army was ultimately not quite as good as the German army, we still have to recognise that it must have been at least reasonably competent in modern warfare, in order to get as far as it did.[6] However much we may sympathise with the sentiment that 'France deserved a happier outcome', we are scarcely compelled to accept all of the dire allegations of inefficiency variously levelled against her military institutions.[7] If we do accept them at face value and in their entirety, indeed, it is difficult to see how the troops could have managed to leave their barracks at all.

It is not without reason that the mid-nineteenth-century French army was generally considered by contemporaries to be the best in the world.[8] It was an efficient yet relatively cheap and unintrusive instrument of national policy, and within the metropolis it fitted perfectly into the social, economic and political requirements of its day. Despite several changes of régime, frequent revolutionary upheavals and some inevitable internal stresses of its own, it usually managed to remain responsive to its political masters. It did almost everything that was asked of it, and can legitimately be seen as a model for the armed forces of a non-militarist democracy in times of 'cold war', 'crisis management' and domestic unrest.

On the strictly military plane, the army of these years was already immensely experienced from Napoleonic times, and it continued to fight more combats and sieges than practically any other army outside British India. It was by no means technically inert, but was busy building new fortresses, designing new weapons and tactics, and keeping well abreast of the times. Its deterrent value was demonstrated by major mobilisations during the diplomatic crises of 1831, 1840 and 1848; and – of central interest to us in the present volume – its practical actions were always accompanied by a lively internal discussion.

France was and is above all a nation of debaters; and we should not in any way be surprised to find that this applies to her army as much as to her political and literary circles. With Guibert and the encyclopaedists towards the end of the eighteenth century it even seemed for a moment as though all these groups of orators and writers might eventually become merged into a single debate. Then the Revolutionary and Napoleonic Wars threw theoretical military speculation into the background for a while; but once *La Grande Guerre* was over, the army found itself free once again to renew discussion with redoubled enthusiasm. It discovered a wonderful opportunity to reflect upon its recent experiences; to re-define its contemporary self-image, and to take a confident peep into the future. The result was a sizeable production of military books, journals and pamphlets such as was probably unmatched by any other nation.[9]

It is unfortunate that historians have largely overlooked this debate, preferring instead to characterise it as simply 'the age of Jomini and Clausewitz'. With the benefit of hindsight, and with their enthusiasm boosted by 1945 no less than by 1870, they have often explained how the Prussian Clausewitz managed to outpoint the Swiss Jomini – at least in depth of perception, if not in clarity of style. Nevertheless their analysis has not ventured very far into the specifically French literature of the day.[10] Since the French army was the 'best in the world' at the time, this surely makes a very strange omission indeed.

It is an omission, however, which it is the aim of this present volume to correct.

A national but professional army

It is not our purpose to look deeply into civil-military relations, which have already received the attention of a whole generation of French historians,[11] but rather to consider the military debate on its own terms. Before we turn to the military writers, however, it will be useful to set the scene by taking a brief overview of the place of the army in society.

Perhaps the most significant feature of the constitutional monarchies and their armies was that they almost unanimously rejected the 1792 Republican doctrine of 'The Nation in Arms' – the idea that all healthy males of military age should serve for a spell in the peacetime army, and that practically every citizen – regardless of age or sex – should serve in some militarily-related capacity during wartime. Instead of this, Restoration France was determined to enlist only a relatively small proportion of its manpower in normal times; to fight only limited wars in support of a relatively cautious foreign policy; and if possible to avoid *La Grande Guerre* altogether. It was only if the worst came to the absolute worst – in the highly unlikely event that a major coalition of Teutonic or Slavonic hordes from the East should succeed in penetrating deep into France herself – that recourse should be made to the Nation in Arms. For all practical purposes, therefore, the army was to be kept 'small but good', while the mass of citizens would be unarmed, untrained, but decisively vengeful and patriotic if the unthinkable should ever occur.

The idea of a small army was initially an anti-Bonapartist and anti-democratic reflex on the part of the returning monarchy. In the 'White Terror' of 1815–16 the Bourbons tried to root out the 'Brigands of the Loire' at the same time as they rewarded their own long-suffering followers. For three years the army was cut back to a small all-volunteer force organised as 'Departmental Legions' – quasi-local units intended to give some expression to the legitimist faith in a decentralised rural society based on *noblesse oblige*.[12]

Stringent cut-backs in army size were also a necessity born of demographic exhaustion. A quarter-century of warfare had drained the manpower pool and led to great resentment among the conscripted groups. Any arrangement which lightened the general burden of service, especially as it affected the politically powerful middle classes, would be more than welcome. This was, after all, a period of *La Grande Bourgeoisie au Pouvoir*,[13] when suffrage was extremely limited and members of 'a good family' felt entitled to more privileges than is usual even in French society. In military terms this meant easy exemption from conscription – an underlying consideration of great importance which was scarcely changed by either the July Revolution or, indeed, by the advent of more populist politics in 1848.

A degree of conscription was reintroduced in the *Loi St Cyr* of 1818, but it was designed to be applied to only a relatively small proportion of the fit population. This selective, and therefore apparently inequitable, system was advertised as fair and 'national' mainly because it depended on a blind lottery. Only the unlucky numbers would be assigned to the annual contingent, and then only a part of the contingent would eventually be called to the colours. The 'fairness' of the system would be further demonstrated by the fact that exemption could be bought by anyone who could find a fee – usually around 2,000 francs, or twice a labourer's annual wage – sufficient to provide a replacement to serve in his stead. Once called to the colours, on the other hand, a conscript might not expect to see his family again during most of his six-year term of active service. Even after returning home, he would face a further six years' liability as a 'veteran' in his departmental reserve.[14]

A quarter-century of warfare had also exhausted France's monetary reserves, especially after Napoleon's heady adventurist expansions had ceased, and war could no longer be made to pay for itself. Throughout the constitutional monarchies there was to be a very parsimonious approach to defence spending, with army pay scales among the lowest in Europe. The army's budget was also kept very strictly and consistently at between around 20% and 25% of a total governmental expenditure which was itself very tightly controlled. Even in years of national emergency there was to be relatively little change in this pattern. The crises of 1831-32 and 1840-41, for example, each led to increases of only around a quarter in what the army could spend. The Spanish war of 1823 saw the biggest cash increase, with 53% extra being spent in the year.[15]

In military terms, also, there were many arguments put forward in favour of a 'small but good' army. By the later years of the Empire it had become obvious that large, shambling, unwieldy forces were militarily far less effective than small, concentrated bodies of well-trained regulars. Whereas the *Levée en Masse* had been an unavoidable stop-gap for Carnot in the 1790s, Napoleon increasingly found that he was successful only with his tightly-knit, manoeuvrable armies of Italy and the Boulogne camp. When he expanded his forces, most notably for the 1812-14 campaigns, he started to suffer astronomical march losses and a diminishing combat edge.[16]

Many of Napoleon's generals complained of the evils of his 'corrupt gigantism', and longed to return to more professional practices. They believed there was an optimum size for a mobile army, beyond which additional numbers became unmanageable, un-feedable and generally counter-productive. This doctrine stood in flat contradiction to the republican tradition of big battalions – and incidentally also to the liberal Prussian school of Clausewitz and Scharnhorst. It was nevertheless widely held by French officers who looked back either to the orderly small wars of the *Ancien Régime* or to the relatively small-scale but virtuoso rapier-thrusts of Marengo, Ulm, Austerlitz and Jena.[17]

The generals were all too well aware that – in these days before the railway – overland mobility depended largely upon the resilience of the soldiers' legs and the cohesion of their units. With close-order tactics, survival in battle depended upon a steadiness that came only from long drilling. In the days when travelling ten miles from home was a rare adventure for most of the population, furthermore, they knew that young peasants torn from their familiar surroundings would suffer mass epidemics of 'nostalgia' unless they were very carefully inducted into their new military families.[18]

A similar pattern was later to be seen in Algeria, where an initial deployment of a mass of unacclimatised troops led to horrific casualties from disease and on the march.[19] Small, tough and manoeuvrable columns came to be preferred, which were familiar both with the theatre of operations and with each other. Their vital qualities as cohesive fighting units were recognised as the embodiment of what was called 'military spirit' – a quality much prized in the metropolitan army no less than in the colonies.

The need for military spirit was greatly reinforced, in the eyes both of military officers and of bourgeois politicians, by a fear of its opposite – armed anarchy. The 'dangerous classes' had shown their power too often in recent times, and continued to do so at all-too-frequent intervals, for there to be any illusions about the depredations that civil disturbance could entail. One of the army's primary roles was therefore to maintain internal order, and it was generally felt that military institutions should be structured accordingly. This in turn implied that soldiers and civilians should not be allowed to mix too closely in their everyday lives, since the germs of anti-militarism could spread quickly among troops who became too familiar with the local population. One could scarcely be expected to open fire on one's café companions of the night before, after all.

The national army therefore had to be 'professional' and 'regular', living a self-contained life in barracks rather than billets – preferably with each regiment rotated to a different town every two or three years. It was found that subversion spread fastest among troops who had remained longest in the same place, or who had the closest social links with the civilian community. For many officers, in fact, the best military spirit was to be fostered only when the soldiers lived in large-unit drill camps, well outside the towns and away from civilians altogether. In extreme cases an infected body would be sent still further afield, for a spell of service in Algeria or Guadeloupe.[20]

A small professional army generally seemed to be ideal – but difficulties emerged as soon as the number of troops available started to be set against the tasks that had to be performed. In days of internal tension the propertied classes often felt they needed to reinforce the army with their own National Guard units, to give sustained protection in each street. In days of major international crisis the field army, numbering around a third of a million men, had to be released from routine garrison duties for service on the frontier. Once again there was a need for a National Guard or some other form of active reserve. If the crisis became catastrophic, moreover, as it was to become after Sedan, a second reserve would have to be mobilised – the genuine *Levée en Masse*.

The problem for the constitutional monarchies was therefore a matter of finding these large numbers of reserve and auxiliary soldiers without infringing the principles of either economy or of 'military spirit'. There was felt to be a danger that even the territorially-based National Guard, let alone a *Levée en Masse*, might quickly turn into an armed mob and go over to the forces of disorder. This nearly happened in Paris in 1827, and when the Guard was promptly abolished it lent extra recruits to the revolutionary circles that were to overthrow the régime just three years later. The July Monarchy revived the National Guard in 1831, restricted membership to taxpayers only – but omitted to give most of them the vote. This, once again, helped dispose them to topple the monarchy in the revolution of 1848. A not dissimilar sequence was to recur for a third time during the Commune of 1871, giving yet another argument to the opponents of mass militias.[21]

There were always a few soldiers and socialists, both inside and outside Parliament, who would have preferred an all-militia mass army, of a million men or more, to the few-yet-disciplined long-service regulars beloved by the establishment. This opposition was not politically very significant, however, and even most liberals felt that it could be ignored. Generals Foy and Lamarque, for example, were both leading liberal spokesmen during the early Restoration. They argued strongly (albeit vainly) for an increased National Guard on the Prussian pattern; but they both still accepted that the regular army alone should be used for the first battle on the frontier. A more rabid opponent of poorly trained troops than Lamarque, indeed, would have been exceedingly difficult to find.[22]

During the crisis of 1831 there were many spontaneous patriotic demonstrations by the National Guard against any threatened invasion from the East. Provision was even made – in theory although not in practice – for 'detached' units that might march with the field army, as the 'Mobiles' were to do in 1870. This went some way towards reassuring strategists that there would always be a natural safety net for the regular army in case of disaster – a deterrent force of free citizens who, if all else failed, could be depended upon to maintain the spirit of 1792. In more technical language, however, it meant that the army saw no particular need to organise its own reserves in depth. If reserves would arise spontaneously whenever *La Patrie* was seriously in danger, then what was to be gained by organising them on a permanent basis?[23]

The army did nevertheless possess certain organised reserves of its own. The process of mobilisation, somewhat clumsily referred to as 'passing from a peace to a war footing', was intended to include an expansion of the infantry by about one third. The additional troops could be found either by adding completely raw drafts to veteran units and 'training them on the march',[24] or by using an already trained reserve. The former method was administratively far simpler and had often worked in the past; but the latter involved less improvisation and was favoured by many reforming generals of the centre, notably the War Ministers Gouvion St Cyr in his law of 1818 and Soult in his of 1832.

We have seen how Gouvion St Cyr made provision for veterans to remain liable for service for six years after leaving the colours. They were originally intended to maintain their training by occasional parades, but this was widely suspected of being a hidden form of local militia, and generally remained a dead letter. St Cyr's veterans were nevertheless activated for the war of 1823, although the measure proved so unpopular and unworkable that it was shelved in legislation the following year.[25]

An alternative possible approach was to give basic training to that part of the contingent which was not called to the colours. Soult attempted to include this arrangement in his new recruiting law of 1832, but was forced to abandon it when the opposition once again consolidated against the hint of a local militia that it seemed to contain. All he could achieve was to shorten the period actually served by conscripts to four or five years out of the new legal obligation of seven, while still maintaining their liability during the remaining time. This enabled around a quarter more men to be rotated through the ranks, without expanding the numbers serving in the peacetime army.[26] It was not an ideal solution and did not provide a really sizeable trained reserve; but it was the best that could be achieved in face of the government's aversion to territorial militias.

On the other hand it is also worth noting that not even Soult's preferred, but defeated, solution would have allowed for a mobilised army of more than around half a million men, which was not a really radical improvement over the existing numbers. There thus seems to be little evidence supporting the idea that Soult was a champion of a mass militia army. Instead, he ultimately shared in the majority opinion that was dead set against such an uncontrollable monster.

It was entirely reasonable, in the circumstances of the day, to suppose that an attack by any one European power could be defeated, or at least held in check, by a French army of around a third of a million men. A larger force would be required only if France took on several hostile powers allied together in a coalition, or in other words she would require parity with the rest of the world only if she wanted to fight against the rest of the world.

After Waterloo, there was no-one in a position of authority in France who believed that taking on the rest of the world was either a rational or a desirable policy. It was specifically renounced in numerous official statements, and when Thiers seemed to be toying with the idea during the crisis of 1840, he was swiftly deprived of support. Even in 1870 it is doubtful that war would have been accepted if the full extent of the German coalition – and the corresponding diplomatic isolation of France – had been properly understood by the Emperor.

The army in the state

After a disastrous series of military coups and attempted coups during the Revolutionary and Napoleonic eras, it was to be expected that the political establishment of the Second Restoration would be exceptionally suspicious of the army. This suspicion was reinforced by a number of military plots and subversive incidents – especially between 1815 and 1823, but continuing until the revolution of 1830 when the army signally failed to maintain the Bourbon monarchy. Nor did the change of régime succeed in allaying the turmoil, since republican agitation was actively maintained within the army until around 1836.[27]

Official suspicion of the army was expressed most obviously in the control of appointments, which suffered from some severely politically-motivated interference. There were savage anti-Bonapartist purges of the officer corps in the early years, which were later repeated on a smaller scale by successive waves of dismissals and appointments. For example the demobilisation cuts of 1824, following the Spanish war, presented a new setback. Bonapartists did nevertheless start to trickle back into positions of authority from 1818 onwards, and it was notable that the legitimist government always gave them the lion's share of command whenever there was serious military work to be done.

After the revolution of 1830 the Bonapartists became dominant in the army for a time, displacing many royalists and ex-émigrés in their turn. Then by 1848 the ageing remnants of the Imperial generation could be shouldered aside by new men who had won their spurs in the African campaigns. The new cohort was itself soon split, however, as the right wing reaction gathered strength from the summer of 1848. Following the coup of 1851 the more republican generals were arrested or exiled, while their more conservative colleagues seized the opportunity to consolidate their position with the new emperor.[28] Thus two of the leading groups that had pulled together at the start of 1848 – the followers of Bugeaud and Lamoricière respectively – found themselves on opposite sides of the political divide by 1852. Bugeaud's heir St Arnaud received his baton and commanded in the Crimea, while Lamoricière was exiled and took service in the Papal States.

Apart from purging appointments, civilian authority over the army was further expressed by tight control over the minister of war. Although he would always be an officer drawn from the army's own ranks, and would enjoy considerable autonomy within the strictly military sphere, in politically significant matters he was usually very much a puppet of the government – quite expendable and often changed. Indeed, there were to be some twenty-seven appointments as minister between 1815 and 1851, making an average term in office of but sixteen months. Only Soult, with a total of nine years at various times during the July Monarchy, stood a chance of establishing anything like a true continuity of policy.[29]

In 1840 even the details of military affairs were themselves effectively usurped by a civilian, Thiers, although his rare enthusiasm for the subject made this intervention tolerable to the army. In normal years it was only the princes of the blood who lent much support to military reform, and then with only mixed success. While Angoulême was mocked in 1823 for his resistance to the political police, and for a less than crisp military bearing, Orleans became very popular with the army of the July Monarchy and helped launch many innovations before his untimely death in 1842.[30]

Of considerable importance to civilian control of the army was the systematic blocking of all attempts to allow a more independent military voice to be established in the shape of a General Staff, or *Conseil Supérieure de la Guerre*. It was the minister, as the government's mouthpiece, who was seen as the natural centre of authority – not some committee of generals that might win a separate identity by the continuity and depth of its doctrines. Thus the Dauphin's experiment with such a staff in 1828 had originally been conceived as a means for him to exercise greater personal control over appointments, but when it became clear that the generals wanted a greater say in wider issues of policy, he hastily disbanded them.[31]

Military men were of course naturally inclined towards obedience and respect for authority, and would express at least a public distaste for political intrigue. If they served in a governmental role, it was often out of a sense of duty and subordination to the appointed cabinet. They would also almost always serve in relatively unimportant ministries such as War, the Navy or Foreign Affairs. It is true that Soult was thrice President of the Council of Ministers during the July Monarchy, but even that illustrious position was somewhat peripheral to the real centre of power. Apart from Cavaignac's exercise of full executive powers in Paris during the crisis of 1848, only Lauriston penetrated to the 'inner ring' of truly sensitive portfolios, when he was Minister of the Interior in 1821.[32]

The case of Cavaignac is especially revealing, since his sense of loyalty to the civil authorities made him step back from the military coup that was within his grasp. He allowed power to be transferred legally to Louis Napoleon in the presidential election at the end of 1848, and it was under the latter's leadership, not that of a soldier, that the military coup of 1851 was to be conducted.

Active and retired officers participated in the two chambers of Parliament to a surprising degree, with captains or higher ranks often providing between 10% and 20% of the Deputies, and generals furnishing between 30% and 40% of the Peers.[33] These men, especially the more senior among them, usually voted for the government of the day. In 1824 the minister of war specifically indicated that this was expected of them, although in the 1834 law on officers' status any sanctions were prohibited. The army did produce a number of opposition figures – most notably Foy and Lamarque in Parliament, no less than adventurers like Fabvier outside it.[34]

Possession of sufficient wealth to qualify for a vote in parliamentary elections also seemed to lead to a certain independence of spirit. Such riches were rare in the army, however, until the Second Republic introduced universal suffrage. This measure was intended to give private soldiers as great a stake in the state as only their most privileged officers had previously enjoyed. To many it appeared to represent the end of all hierarchy, since the ncos who stood for Parliament in opposition to their generals could not be prevented from taking their seats, nor could the great mass of soldiers be prevented from voting against General Cavaignac for the presidency of the Assembly.[35] The advent of the Second Empire, however, saw a reversion of the mass military vote towards support for the government, and its exercise continued to be tolerated, albeit in a somewhat restricted form.

Much emphasis was laid upon the officer's oath of loyalty to king and constitution and the classic 1791 formulae whereby 'discipline makes the principal strength of armies' and the army is 'essentially obedient' to the civil power.[36] It was expected to do what it was bidden; not to play a role on its own behalf. However, the very fact that there were so many changes of régime is itself eloquent of the limited confidence that could be placed in such provisions. No one who had to change his cap-badges every few years – from eagle to *fleur de lys* and then to gallic cockerel, to *tricolore* and eventually back again to eagle – could seriously be expected to show equally unswerving devotion to each one at all times. With so many changes in régime, and such a strong official interest in the army's opinions, it was natural that most officers should keep their own counsel, while carefully observing the outward rituals of loyalty.[37]

For most officers the true centre of loyalty had to be the army itself, backed by an abstract notion of 'France' and perhaps also an awareness of a special relationship with the person of the monarch. Towards the end of the Restoration, for example, the officers who asked for higher pay scales explained that they were serving not for profit but because they saw themselves as a type of 'nobility of service'. They had to maintain their social status relative to civilians only in order not to dishonour their king.[38]

Unlike that of the *Ancien Régime*, this army drew relatively few of its officers from the nobility of birth – although the 'particule' still held a potent *cachet*, and especially the Restoration was anxious to attract aristocratic cadets.[39] The majority nevertheless felt that the army itself was a noble institution which conferred distinction upon its members. Hence woe betide any régime that appeared to be cutting too deeply into those things that the army held most dear – its pay, promotion, privileges and general prestige! The First Restoration had done this, and had paid the penalty in the coup of March 1815. The Second Restoration and July Monarchy learned more wisdom; but the Second Republic was less well advised. It failed to see the need to woo as well as to command its army, and it too ended in a Napoleonic coup.[40] We can perhaps conclude that the mass of the army was essentially apolitical throughout this period, apart from those moments when its own interests and honour seemed to be centrally threatened.

The army's upper echelons normally enjoyed considerable social prominence, mixing in the best circles and participating in the cultured life of the *salon* and the *spectacle*. Far from being isolated from civilian life, as they wanted their men to be, they were fully open to current patterns of thought and anxious for the army to be seen as a 'microcosm of society'.[41] They kept abreast of such fads as Phrenology, Prison Reform or

Orientalism. Some generals took the lead in agricultural reforms or even advanced industrial techniques – although his penchant for the latter was to lead Marmont into bankruptcy.[42]

For much of the officer corps, however, such civilised luxuries were very much a closed book. For subalterns who had to live on their pay there was all too little money left over after simple living expenses had been met, and debts were a major occupational hazard. In the mess there was a different table and a different menu for each rank, finely calculated according to the level of expenditure that rank could afford, and to some extent also the level of refinement, or lack of it, that could be expected.[43]

As time went by the officers were recruited increasingly from the business, functionary and even working classes rather than the landed gentry, and promotion from the ranks was running at easily the highest level in Europe. In 1818 one third of the sub-lieutenancies had been guaranteed to men rising in this way; but the figure had in practice soon risen to no less than three quarters. Few of the ex-rankers won high promotion, being less favoured than graduates of the military schools, although in each generation there was at least one representative, from Soult through Gérard and Reille to Randon and Bazaine, who did succeed in reaching the very top of his profession. Admittedly some of the officers rising from the ranks were sons of the aristocracy who had joined specifically to win a commission 'by the back door', without having to attend a fee-paying military school. Nevertheless it is clear that the bulk of officers came from relatively lowly social backgrounds with correspondingly lowly educations, and had to live entirely on their pay.[44]

A career open to talent

'The career open to talent' was simultaneously the glory and the shame of the French army: an institution so different from the practice in other countries that it has been notoriously difficult to characterise. On one hand it was splendidly democratic and modern – a showpiece for 'the spirit of 1789', and a century ahead of its rivals. On the other hand it has been identified as yet another of the 'primary' causes of defeat in 1870; a focus of deadening egalitarianism which promoted the illiterate[45] and forced the nation's élite into a mould of the most squalid bureaucratic mediocrity.

In military terms there was much to be said for maintaining a class of subalterns who made up in professional commitment and knowledge of soldier life for what they lacked in education, general culture and ambition. This was to some extent a circular argument, however, since the French failed to retain a strong class of long-service senior ncos, such as might have fulfilled a similar role, precisely because the best men passed quickly through to become subalterns. In these circumstances there could not be quite that social gulf between officer and man that existed in most other armies, and the French found it necessary to stress the need for aloof behaviour as a substitute.[46]

One result was that in times of revolutionary ferment it was noticeably the senior ncos who were most active in denouncing their officers for dubious political opinions or professional inefficiency – in order to create vacancies into which they might themselves be promoted.[47] Thus General du Barail described their role as '. . . the weak point of our military organisation. The nco lives nearer to the soldiers than the officer. He knows their mood, shares their passions, and it would not be astonishing if he should take a decisive influence over them on a day of rioting.'[48]

The various disturbances within the army, especially those of 1830–31, usually had more to do with personal ambition among senior ncos than any deeply held political beliefs. In general the ordinary soldiers were entirely neutral in politics, and took sides only when given a strong lead. Despite police suspicions, for example, their veteran societies established around 1840 had no ulterior political purposes.[49]

Another consequence of the 'career open to talent' was a widespread obsession with promotion and with the pecking order of the *annuaire*. Something similar may doubtless be identified in any large organisation, but perhaps the French army suffered from it more than most. There were many shady intrigues to bypass regulations, and the dossiers of generals reveal that it was not considered servile to bombard the minister with flowery self-advertisements and recommendations from important people. Most of the brightest careers appear to have been launched under the patronage of some name of high standing either inside or outside the army.

None of this should surprise us, however, in a time of demobilisation and peace when the supply of officers far outstripped demand. It was not uncommon for lieutenants and captains to stay in the same rank for well over a decade. Especially during the early Restoration, the cafés of every garrison town also contained the débris of the *Grande Armée*, waiting on half pay for a recall to duty that often came only after the revolution of 1830. By that time many of these men had passed their prime of usefulness, and were quickly retired. Only towards the middle of the July Monarchy did a more normal promotion market start to apply, whereby a greater proportion of gifted officers could rise relatively quickly to the top.[50]

Contrary to common opinion, the French promotion structure was actually rather less open to irregularity and abuse during this era than it had been in the eventful decades before 1815. One of the strongest movements in the army of the constitutional monarchies was a general multiplication of regulations and an insistence on uniformity; a reaction both against the chaos of the Revolutionary and Napoleonic epoch, and against the personal and regimental idiosyncrasies of the *Ancien Régime*. In the promotion field this found expression in new laws, passed in 1818, 1831, 1832 and 1834, which defined career and pension structures, limited the role of arbitrary ministerial choice in promotions, and guaranteed half-pay officers in their rank.[51]

One incidental aspect of all this was that it led to a particular type of promotion-related journalism. A certain part of the military press was devoted to watching for – and denouncing – abuses. This had the beneficial effect of helping to reform the system and create an atmosphere of regularity: but it also unfortunately left a trail of strident denunciations which subsequent historians could only too easily invoke as evidence of widespread corruption. Paradoxically, it was precisely a mechanism for reform which helped convince the army's post-1870 denigrators that there had been no reform. Worse – the debate became so lively that Maison in 1835 and Soult in 1841 attempted to regulate its wilder forays. They introduced official censorship for the public writings of officers, thereby allowing historians to find still further spurious evidence of alleged military anti-intellectualism.[52]

Conditions of employment did gradually improve in this army, although the graduates of military schools could not be prevented from seeing themselves as members of a superior class to those who had risen through the ranks.[53] Inspectors continued to report regimental messes which were seriously split into factions, either on this basis or by age, experience, patron, political conviction or even region of origin.[54] The various purges continued to create tension and insecurity as much as they were a spur to the ambitious and a wholesome mechanism for shedding the inefficient.[55]

Officers also continued to exhibit certain clique-ish and even anti-social attitudes towards the civilian population. They married late, and then only with official permission. Many of them passed their copious free time in drinking houses or brothels.[56] They were often also personally violent men, among whom the tradition of duelling was by no means dead. This might easily spill over into attacks on civilians which could subsequently be defended as 'protecting the army's honour'.[57] They also frequently held anti-industrial, anti-commercial and anti-urban beliefs, the moreso as junior officers were shamefully underpaid. It was only natural that they should be envious of the fabulous fortunes that were increasingly being amassed by less 'noble' civilians in the newly scientific age. Officers were also being drawn increasingly from the rural population, and regarded cities as notoriously unhealthy for armies – both as recruiting grounds and as battlefields. During revolutionary *Journées* in a city the risk of soldiers becoming infected by socialist subversion was as high as that of officers being denounced by the press. It is scarcely surprising that but few of them relished the prospect of duty in such an environment.[58]

By the end of the nineteenth century these attitudes were to merge into a virulent brand of military anti-semitism; but it has been claimed that this did not yet exist in the decades with which we are concerned.[59] It is true that there was nothing remotely comparable to the scale and vehemence of the 1890s' anti-Dreyfus feeling; but there were at least a number of elements already at hand which would later help to fuel such prejudices. The writers of memoirs did sometimes express anti-semitism, just as the officer corps was always profoundly suspicious and contemptuous of any and all foreigners. The army's interest in horse-breeding also kept it – worryingly – well abreast of modern speculations about bloodstocks and the evolution of races. Finally, the army had suffered from poor supply services in its Polish and Algerian campaigns – and in both cases it had been forced back on the strong local Jewish merchant classes, not always with happy results. On the other hand, however, a truly Bonapartist officer would typically respect an anti-clerical and pro-Masonic tradition much more readily than he would an anti-semitic one. He was far more likely to look for an internal enemy among those who took their orders from Rome – and who in the Restoration had used army chaplains as political spies – than among the Children of Israel.[60] It was therefore particularly ironic that in most of its many wars between 1815 and 1851 the French army was to find itself aligned strongly on the side of the Roman Catholic against the Infidel.

We may today find the social attitudes of the average post-Napoleonic officer deplorable, and his general level of culture primeval. We may be outraged that a career open to talent was apparently also open to numbing mediocrity. However, we must understand that there is ultimately little in all this which points to a serious undermining of French military efficiency, particularly if we remember that with some 20,000 officers the army was the largest of all the professional groups in a nation that was culturally the most sophisticated in the world – but which by 1860 could confer a grand total of only 1,400 university degrees per annum.[61] In no serious army, even today, is the average officer supposed to be a professor of military theory – and even in the Prussian army of Carl von Clausewitz there were many notorious defects and inefficiencies, just as in the Pan-Germanic army of the two von Moltkes there were some disastrously inefficient appointments.

Despite political interference in promotions, talented French officers did normally rise to the top, sooner or later, while notorious incompetents were removed. Divisions within the officer corps were habitually overcome in moments of crisis. Neither humble social origins nor frustration with riot control duties in the cities necessarily debarred officers from fighting effectively in the open spaces on the European frontiers or in North Africa. Personal ferocity, a belief in military honour and a habit of deference to military authority must also, surely, if anything be accounted as positive advantages. Finally – albeit only as a point of pure logic – we can perhaps accept that even a readiness to move against any government which seems to be seriously threatening the army's own fundamental interests need not necessarily imply a loss of military efficiency.

France was generally well served by its army in these years; an army whose internal debate was concerned not with rescuing it from a deep malaise, but with finding ways of making a good army better still. Of course it suffered from many institutional and personal weaknesses, just as every other army in history has suffered; but we do a severe injustice to the spirit of those constructive and optimistic times if we are too ready to stress the difficulties, while dismissing the many concrete achievements. Above all, we should emphatically reject that widespread brand of hindsight which sees everything that happened between 1816 and 1869 as merely an overture to a new age of 'typically French incompetence and muddle'.

Small wars and big riots

Continental operations

The French army between 1792 and 1815 conducted more military operations and fought more battles than any other. Its commanders acquired an expertise in 'march manoeuvres' and battle-management that quickly became the envy of the world. Much ink was to be spilt in attempts to analyse these techniques and distil them into a new science of 'strategy' for *La Grande Guerre* – and nowhere was this process to be more actively pursued than in France itself. It was to remain a purely theoretical exercise in the years between Waterloo and the Crimea, however, since the French did not fight against any of the major European powers.

This is not to say that the French army did not fight, for it did. It gained a wide variety of practical experience in several different types of conflict, and elaborated its doctrines in a number of novel directions. Let us therefore pause to look into these diverse campaigns, which we may divide roughly into three categories – a comparatively familiar type of limited intervention in Europe; the new techniques of pacifying and colonising Algeria; and the equally evolving art of counter-insurgency within France herself.

Within Europe, the chief French operations in our period were in Spain 1823–24; Greece 1827–29; Belgium 1831–32, and Rome from 1849 onwards. None of these amounted to major warfare as practised by Napoleon, although the Spanish expedition did come quite close. Each of them involved certain aspects of large-scale operations but, like many of our own 'Cold War' deployments since 1945, they were all essentially limited or 'peace-keeping' missions which succeeded without the need for a great battle. Nevertheless they 'imposed harsh fatigues and real dangers upon the soldiers who took part',[1] and in the eyes of at least one participant they gave an essential leavening of regularity and military bearing to new regiments that had been unsettled since their creation soon after Waterloo.[2]

The Spanish War, 1823

Since 1820 Spain had been in the grip of political ferment, with the bulk of the army forcing King Ferdinand to observe the liberal constitution, and later holding him a prisoner in his own palace.[3] This had led to a strong royalist or 'white' reaction, and eventually the outbreak of civil war. Towards the end of 1821 France used the excuse of a yellow fever epidemic in Barcelona to impose a 'sanitary cordon' along the Pyrenean frontier – but this was more to prevent infection by liberal ideas, one suspects, than by more physical maladies. There were soon some cross-border raids, in which the liberals accused the French of actively protecting fugitive bands of royalists, while the French accused the liberals of attempting to subvert the frontier garrisons.

Tension continued to mount until, supported by all the powers except Britain, the French began to organise an expedition in February 1823. Some 100,000 men and ninety-six guns, in five army corps, were assembled under the Duc d'Angoulême. Political circles were surprised to note the large number of Bonapartist veterans to whom he allocated commands – men who had but recently been proscribed[4] – although this did not prevent scores of others, such as Colonel Fabvier, from plotting against the expedition. This in turn caused the minister of war, Marshal Victor, to scrutinise the ranks of the expeditionary force with redoubled zeal – his suspicions even rising as high as the Chief of Staff, General Guilleminot. Only Angoulême's personal intervention allayed the furore, and the campaign went ahead with its original staff. On 6th April, the eve of the Bidassoa crossing, the outposts were hailed by Fabvier's 150 armed French and Piedmontese liberals and carbonarists, dressed in Napoleonic Imperial Guard uniforms and waving the *Tricolore*. However a whiff of grapeshot dispersed them with over a dozen casualties, and there was no 'about turn' in the Bourbon ranks.[5]

More serious was the ministry's failure to provide adequate supplies for the army in good time, leading it to a last-minute acceptance of the scandalously extortionate terms offered by a private contractor, Monsieur Ouvrard. He was an effective operator, however, and after a difficult start the French march into the interior of Spain was provided with at least a minimum of necessary supplies. Contrary to the Napoleonic experience,

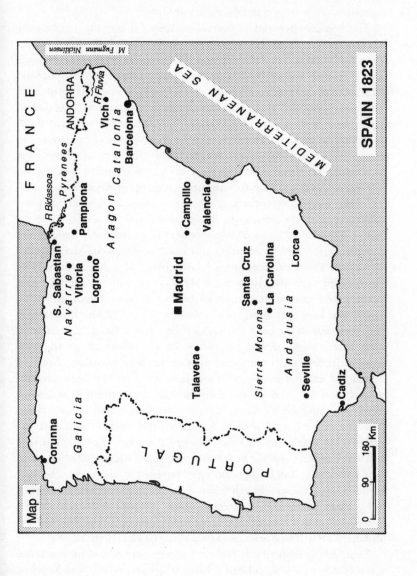

Map 1

SPAIN 1823

FRANCE

R Bidassoa

Pyrenees

ANDORRA

R Fluvia

Vich

Barcelona

Aragon

Catalonia

S. Sabastian

Pamplona

Navarre

Vitoria

Logrono

Campillo

Valencia

Madrid

Santa Cruz

La Carolina

Lorca

Sierra Morena

Andalusia

Seville

Cadiz

Talavera

Galicia

Corunna

PORTUGAL

MEDITERRANEAN SEA

M Fügmann Nicolinson

Km
0   90   180

furthermore, the French quickly found that they could rely upon the co-operation of the priests and the rural populace.[6]

The French advanced in several columns, skimishing occasionally against supporters of the constitution, and investing the fortresses on their way such as San Sebastian and Pamplona. Logroño was stormed, and a Spanish square broken in the cavalry pursuit which followed. The route to Madrid from Vitoria was left open when Ballasteros, with 20,000 men, decided not to try conclusions with the invader. Angoulême gave chase with a part of his army, but detached a series of hard-marching columns westwards along the Biscay coast and eastwards to sweep into Catalonia from Aragon. This division of forces was potentially dangerous, although the French were confident that any one of their columns could destroy any opposition by an immediate assault.[7]

In the eastern Pyrenees a corps under Moncey experienced great difficulties with the terrain, the heavy rainfall and the wily old guerilla leader Espoz y Mina – who manoeuvred unpredictably around the mountains for several months, and effectively delayed the siege of Barcelona. The city fell only on 4th November.[8] Meanwhile Madrid had surrendered very quickly on 23rd May, almost without a fight. From Madrid the French were anxious to press on in two columns to Seville, where the king was being held prisoner. The Alberche bridge near Talavera, and Santa Cruz and La Corolina in the Sierra Morena were each spectacularly cleared of enemy by the advanced guard, with many prisoners and trophies taken. General Bourdesoulle's 'Army of Andalusia' entered Seville on 22nd June after yet another successful assault, and followed up the constitutional government – and King Ferdinand – to their last refuge in Cadiz. Meanwhile Molitor had entered Valencia, dispersed the army of Ballasteros and captured well over 100 cannon. He later completed this victory by storming Lorca, winning a battle at Campillo, chasing and capturing General Riego – who was hung by the royalists – and finally winning a Marshal's baton. At the other end of the country General Bourk stormed the outskirts of Corunna on 15th July, easily scattering a defence which included Fabvier's French renegades[9] and a sympathetic English deputation under Colonel Sir Robert Wilson. The fortress was then invested and fell in August.

There is little more to tell. The war had been narrowed to the pursuit of a few beaten columns, and half a dozen sieges around the peripheries of Spain. Of these the essential one was Cadiz, where a regular sapping approach was required, leading to a formal storming of the Trocadero island outwork before dawn on 31st August. This was entirely successful, suffering only 145 total casualties as against ten times that number on the enemy side. Following this capture the way was open for a naval bombardment of the city, but it was to be unnecessary. On 28th September the mere threat was enough to secure the capitulation of the place and the liberation of the king.[10]

Total French combat casualties cannot have exceeded 2,000 in the whole of this seven-month episode, and the apparent ease with which every enemy force was dispersed may lead us to conclude that the campaign was merely a 'military promenade'. Nevertheless there were some twenty combats and more than six hard sieges of varying sizes. In Catalonia the French were led a merry dance by Mina, and everywhere the troops were pressed to the limit by protracted march manoeuvres in difficult climatic conditions. If the Spanish war was a promenade, it was by no means an easy one.

Greece, 1828

The next continental operation came four years later, when the Russians, British and French determined to take a hand in the Greek war of independence. This war had been spluttering along since 1822, with the help of liberal West European adventurers such as Lord Byron and the ubiquitous Colonel Fabvier. Now an allied fleet attempted to demilitarise the area; but despite a totally successful sea battle at Navarino on 20th October 1827, it was unable to stop the cruel Turco-Egyptian campaigns on land. When the Russians launched a campaign through Moldavia, therefore, the Western allies felt they should intervene in Greece itself. At London in July 1828 it was agreed that a French military expedition should be sent.

Unlike the 1823 expedition to Spain, the new enterprise was uncontroversial within France. General Maison was appointed to command 14,000 men with some thirty-two guns. He was meticulously briefed by the Minister of War, de Caux, and in contrast to 1823 his supplies were carefully organised in advance. Also unlike 1823, however, was his worrying awareness that he was being sent to a devastated and disease-ridden land with an uncertain maritime supply line, against an enemy who disposed three times his numbers.[11]

Maison was instructed to proceed cautiously and avoid military action until all diplomatic means had been exhausted, but in that event to act with the greatest possible rapidity and vigour. On arrival on 30th August in the Gulf of Messini, therefore, he sent his deputy Chief of Staff, Colonel Trézel, to negotiate with Ibrahim Pasha, commander of the main

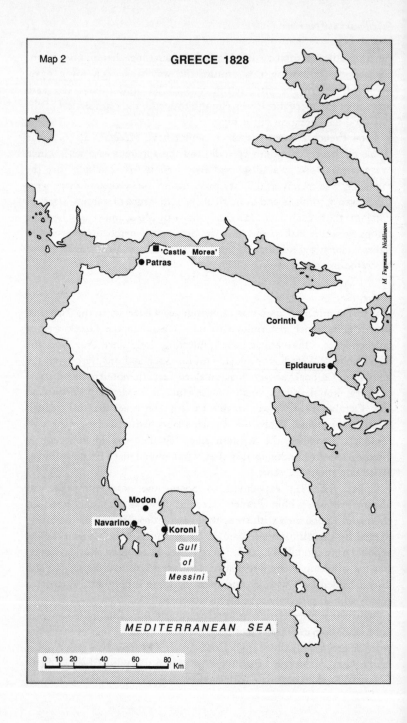

Map 2   **GREECE 1828**

'Castle Morea'

●Patras

●Corinth

●Epidaurus

●Modon

Navarino●

●Koroni

Gulf

of

Messini

MEDITERRANEAN SEA

M Fugmann Nicklinson

0   10   20   40   60   80 Km

Turco-Egyptian army in the Peloponnese. But far from receiving a rapid reply from a bilateral interview, Trézel found himself involved in a complex six-sided international conference, with Greek, British and Russian participation including the French ambassador from Constantinople – the same General Guilleminot who had been Chief of Staff in Spain. The bellicose (and Anglophobe) Maison rapidly grew impatient with all this, and sent General Schneider to exercise more direct leverage by blockading the nearest Egyptian garrison, at Koroni. This unfortunately served only to prolong the diplomatic negotiations still further, so Maison next tried to hasten them by investing Navarino. There matters rested for a time while storms, bad water, fever and dysentery began to make themselves felt throughout the tented camps and bivouacs. Ships were wrecked and major deficiencies started to appear in the supply arrangements.

At the start of October Schneider was sent to confront the forts in the Gulf of Lepanto – just as Ibrahim finally sailed home with his Egyptian field army, leaving only scattered forts in the Peloponnese. These were then summoned and escaladed by columns of troops who were under orders not to be the first to open fire. Navarino and the exceptionally strong Modon offered no resistance; Koroni repelled the first attempt by throwing rocks, but opened its gates on 9th October.[12]

Schneider was meanwhile applying the same technique at Patras, where he secured the governor's agreement to surrender both that town and the nearby 'Castle Morea'. The latter, however, refused to recognise the order and opened fire on officers sent to negotiate. The French, helped by some British warships, then opened a regular siege of the castle. A week's sapping and counter-battery fire confined the 500-strong garrison to their casemates and prepared the way for a crushing four-hour breaching bombardment on 30th October, which quickly produced the unconditional surrender of the place. Total French casualties in this siege were a mere twenty-two soldiers, as compared to a total for the whole campaign of around 2,000 sick, including some 400 who died of fever and a few of plague.

The fall of 'Castle Morea' marked the complete reduction of the Peloponnesian garrisons and the attainment of the allied aim. Despite the almost complete lack of a Greek army, Maison – now promoted Marshal – was certain the Turks were quite unable to mount a counter-offensive, and this proved to be accurate. By February 1829 he was able to withdraw with half his force, leaving only Schneider and 6,000 men to maintain a presence and urge the Greeks to reform their own defences.[13]

As the French army's first 'oriental interlude' since Napoleon's Egyptian campaign, this operation can be seen as a rehearsal for the Algerian campaign that was to start little over a year later. With its long line of supply, rigorous winter in fever-laden tented camps, and its culminating siege, it may also in some ways be seen as a miniature preview of the Crimean War. But closer to the conditions of the Sebastopol siege, perhaps, was to be the 1832 attack on Antwerp.

Antwerp, 1832

Belgium declared its independence from Holland in 1830, but the French had been too preoccupied at home to prepare Marshal Gérard's *Armée du Nord* for an intervention. In August 1831 the Dutch launched their 'ten day invasion', and were pleasantly surprised to find the Belgians, too, had failed to prepare an army for their own defence. Elation soon turned to dismay, however, when Gérard instantly responded to a request for help from Brussels. The telegraphs wagged furiously; the frontier garrisons were gathered and 50,000 French soldiers force-marched forward, to be followed later by their supplies and newly-appointed generals. This was an improvised offensive from which lessons might have been drawn in 1870!

The movement was completely successful and the Dutch retreated hastily without a clash of arms. The *Armée du Nord* let them go and retired to its start line, before the British should have time to become convinced that Louis Philippe entertained dynastic or territorial ambitions in the region.[14]

The Dutch did not abandon the citadel of Antwerp in their withdrawal, however, but maintained it as a key to Scheldt navigation and a symbol of the sovereignty which they claimed. It was manned by a strong garrison commanded by the ferocious General Chassé, who had already fired into the insurgent city and now had instructions to resist any siege to the bitter end. The French were more than happy to oblige him, and once the necessary diplomatic underpinning had been agreed with the British, Gérard was free to return with 70,000 men. He set up his camps outside the citadel in late November 1832, and set about reducing this final Dutch presence on Belgian soil.

The siege was a very stylised, 'classical' event, displaying all the choreography and etiquette that Vauban might have wished.[15] Geometrically-designed saps and parallels were dug; batteries built at precise angles to the enemy bastions; pontoons emplaced over moats to allow mines to be set in position. Chassé humanely insisted that the French

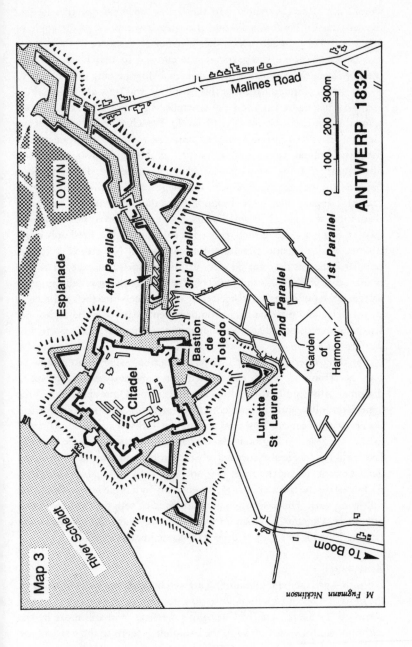

Map 3

River Scheldt

Esplanade

TOWN

4th Parallel

Citadel

Bastion de Toledo

3rd Parallel

Lunette St Laurent

2nd Parallel

'Garden of Harmony'

1st Parallel

Malines Road

To Boom

0   100   200   300m

ANTWERP 1832

M Fugmann Nicdinson

should not allow overshots into the city – the same city that he had himself already bombarded – and this greatly complicated the angle of attack.[16] Finally, on 24th December when every resource of the defence had been exhausted, the garrison was allowed to march out with its weapons and to the applause of onlookers, before passing into captivity.

The strictly limited nature of this operation was only appropriate to a 'war' that had started as a somewhat symbolic gesture, and which no one wanted to spread more widely. From the French point of view it gave General Haxo's engineers a chance to practise their art on a scale greater than the annual 'simulacra' of sieges at Metz. It also offered an opportunity for the 'state of the art' to be assessed. From General Neigre's gunner perspective, too, this siege was valuable. The breech-loading rampart rifles were disappointing, although they did point the theoretical way ahead in small arms design. A massive new Paixhans mortar, firing a 1,000 lb shell, proved equally unreliable, fired only a few rounds, and did not penetrate the casemates. Nevertheless it was popularly seen as the 'star' in a conventional mortar barrage, of 20,000 bombs, that was terrible in its effects. The barrage dismounted the guns, flattened the buildings and forced the garrison deep into their shelters. It was the size and power of this bombardment, especially the occasional Paixhans' explosions, that most impressed contemporaries as a portent of warfare yet to come.[17]

The three operations which we have described were by no means the only occasions on which the French felt sufficiently strong to make diplomatically-significant deployments in Europe. Quite apart from three general mobilisations at moments of great national crisis, the Spanish border was once more 'observed' during the Carlist wars of the 1830s and in 1835 the Foreign Legion itself was handed over bodily to the Spanish. Events in Italy were also successively monitored and moulded – first by a garrison sent to Ancona from 1832 to 1838; then by an *Armée des Alpes* mobilised on the frontier in 1848;[18] and finally by a force sent to Rome the following year. This last originally purported to support the new liberal government against Austrian intervention – but was soon revealed to be helping Pius IX to extirpate those very same liberals instead.[19]

Rome, 1849

On 30th April General Oudinot *fils* arrived beneath the walls of Rome at the head of 6,000 men with twelve guns. Expecting an easy entry, he was surprised by the tenacity of Garibaldi's defences, and still more by the dashing counter-attack through the Pamphili gardens to the south of the

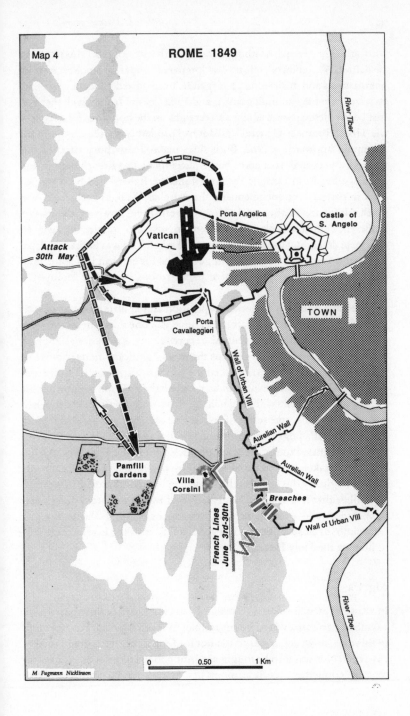

Map 4

ROME 1849

River Tiber

Porta Angelica

Castle of
S. Angelo

Vatican

Attack
30th May

TOWN

Porta
Cavalleggieri

Wall of Urban VIII

Aurelian Wall

Aurelian Wall

Pamfili
Gardens

Villa
Corsini

Breaches

French Lines
June 3rd-30th

Wall of Urban VIII

River Tiber

0   0.50   1 Km

M Fugmann Nicklinson

Vatican. The French withdrew hurt, with the loss of almost 1,000 casualties. A renewed effort was prepared under a smokescreen of negotiations and misleading propaganda, until on 3rd June they returned to seize the same Pamphili gardens and Villa Corsini from which they had just been evicted. Not wishing a street fight on the populous East bank of the Tiber, Engineer-General Vaillant had prudently chosen this point for a sapping approach *en règle*. Both sides realised that possession of this ground was capital, so a fierce battle developed. The French won it, and the siege began in earnest. By 22nd June the Italians had been pushed back in panic to retrenchments on the Aurelian Wall; but they held firm on that line for a further week. Early on 30th June, however, the French made their final assault, with orders to give no quarter to such an obstinate defending force. By 3rd July the whole city was in Franco-Papal hands and Garibaldi had fled. Altogether the French had lost something like 2,750 casualties out of a total of 30,000 troops eventually deployed to the papal states.

In technical terms the Roman expedition added little that was new to the body of French doctrine. It represented just one more successful siege on foreign soil. In its eventual repercussions on national morale, however, it may be seen as perhaps the most significant military move of the whole period 1815–51. It paved the way for Napoleon III's nineteen years of Italian involvement and then – when the garrison supporting the Pope was disastrously withdrawn in the crisis of 1870 – produced much of the breast-beating and sense of moral malaise that was to characterise Louis Veuillot's pilgrimage movement in the 1870s.[20]

We are entitled to see the triumphant Virgin of Le Puy, forged from 113 cannon taken at Sebastopol, as the most prominent of the monuments erected to glorify this army's achievement in limited warfare. But we must remember that it is mightily overshadowed by the expiatory *Sacré Coeur de Montmartre* – a monument expressing everlasting shame not for Gravelotte or Sedan, but for the eventual failure of the brushfire crusade to liberate the Holy Father.

Algeria

In 1827 the French entered a 'small war' in North Africa that started with a symbolic gesture even more trivial than the Dutch defiance at Antwerp. In this case, however, it was to last not for four weeks but a grand total of 135 years. Nor was it to be fought according to the niceties of eighteenth-century etiquette – as Bourmont, its first ground commander, had hoped[21] – but often with an ingenuous unconcern for human rights and civilised values that was to show all too little diminution as the 1830s passed painfully into the 1950s.

The Dey of Algiers believed he was owed money by France. In 1827, in heated debate with the French consul, he chose to flick the unfortunate functionary in the face with his fly-whisk. This was taken as an insult by Charles X and his government, and a naval squadron was sent to impose a blockade. After a number of sea fights, however, purely naval action was deemed to have been insufficient; so in 1830 the decision was taken to send ground forces as well.

Despite some resistance by 'refractory' soldiers, 37,000 troops were assembled, including many of the units that had served in Spain or Greece. Supplies were scrupulously organised, and the contractor Seillère engaged to provide food. General de Bourmont, a favoured royalist who had deserted Napoleon on the eve of Waterloo, was given the command.

The first landing took place on 14th June at Sidi Ferruch, just west of Algiers.[22] There was some fighting in the dunes, and a most worrying storm at sea; but a fortified logistic base was soon built and the army was ready to fight the defensive-offensive Battle of Staouëli on the 19th. This became the biggest French battle of the whole period 1815–51, with at least 30,000 troops assembled on the enemy side from Algiers, Médéah, Constantine and Oran. In common with many other colonial battles, however, almost everything depended on the initial shock of impact. The African attack was firmly held and then quickly repulsed. Rockets, and the new-system Valée field and mountain guns worked wonders. The infantry charged in formation at the *pas de course* with high élan, and took the Dey's camp for the loss of only some 500 casualties – one tenth of the enemy figure.

The French next moved forward and consolidated, although almost every day saw an attack by mounted guerrillas against isolated detachments, or infantry sniping from subtly-utilised cover. As the drain of casualties steadily mounted, the French began to glimpse the true nature of a North African form of warfare that would face them for decades yet to come. It was scarcely a reassuring insight.[23]

Finally, between 29th June and 4th July, the French invested and fiercely bombarded the dominating 'Emperor' fort on the outskirts of Algiers. Rather than surrender, the Turkish commander ordered evacuation and then blew the magazine, flattening the work completely. It was yet another example of the decisive French use of artillery – and especially mortars – in the culminating siege of a campaign. We may also speculate

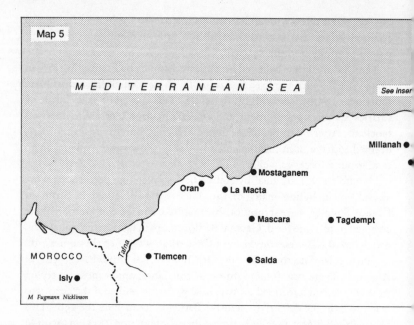

Map 5

MEDITERRANEAN SEA

See inser

Millanah ●

● Mostaganem

Oran ●   ● La Macta

● Mascara   ● Tagdempt

MOROCCO   ● Tlemcen

Isly ●   ● Salda

M Fugmann Nicklinson

that it was perhaps no coincidence that the guns were commanded by General de la Hitte, a veteran of both the Cadiz and Greek sieges.

The campaign was effectively over, and Bourmont duly received his Marshal's baton. Many of the Turks were forcibly shipped home; the Dey's treasure, worth well over fifty million francs, was appropriated to pay for the war; unsightly town houses were demolished to improve the defences; and the despised Moors and Jews were placed in positions of authority over the Arabs. To set against these civilising achievements, however, the French found that disease was ravaging their troops while the metropolitan population, now in full revolution, was totally indifferent to the army's fate. Nor were the Beys who ruled the Algerian provinces especially keen to pay their homage. Outside the city of Algiers, sniping continued. Various columns were sent forth to make a show of force and occupy the provincial centres of Oran and Bône – but some of them were attacked, and Arab leaders were able to perceive that their new conquerors were anything but invincible. The campaign may well have been over, but the war had scarcely begun.

Bourmont was personally outraged by the July revolution, and plotted to march on Lyon to topple the new government. The navy would not help him, however, so he hastily made good his escape to Spain.[24] His

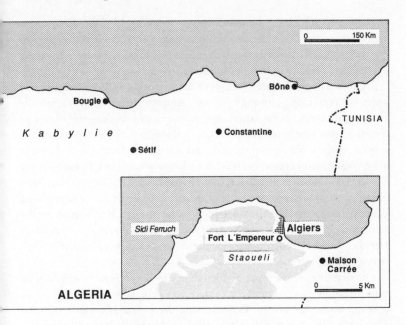

successor was the imperturbable but aggressively erratic Clauzel, a noted Napoleonic veteran who now had to face the problem of just how far the occupation should be pushed. The army was anxious to improve and develop its hard-won conquests, and it saw that the coastal towns of the *Tell* were easy of access. The key strongholds in the towering mountains, even a few miles inland, nevertheless posed a much more intransigent problem. Clauzel's expedition to sack Médéah turned into a shambles, and he soon had to abandon it as well as Blidah and Bône. In Oran he became involved in a dishonest treaty to appoint a Bey from the Tunisian royal house, while in the Algiers area he seemed to be enthusiastically presiding over a destructive orgy of speculation and land-grabbing.

Clauzel was forced by scandal to resign, and was replaced by Berthezène – formerly a solid and successful subordinate to Bourmont. As Commander in Chief, however, Berthezène had the thankless task of reversing his predecessor's adventurism with drastic retrenchments. His forces were reduced to around 16,000, with low morale among both civilian and military personnel. In Oran General Boyer further discredited the French name by a personal reign of terror, while Berthezène's new expeditions to Médéah and Bône were both failures. Nor was the situation helped by continued guerrilla attacks, fever, and 'the disease particular to soldiers' – homesickness or 'nostalgia'.[25] Like many of his contemporaries, Berthezène could see no clear way forward for the war. He was replaced in turn by the sinister Savary, Duke of Rovigo – formerly Napoleon's chief of police – at the end of 1831.

By this time the French element of the garrison had been reduced to a mere 11,000 men, although it was supplemented by a variety of indigenous units, penal battalions, refugees and freebooters – not to mention the newly-formed Foreign Legion.[26] Administration in the coastal enclave was strengthened, and settlement from the metropolis encouraged. However there was also notorious corruption, exacerbated by several gratuitous massacres, to such a point that the first general Arab rising was provoked. Savary suppressed this easily at Boufarik and occupied Bône for the third time; but he won no friends by subjecting the latter town to the arbitrary misrule of the renegade Moslem ex-interpreter Captain Yusuf. When he died of cancer in April 1833, the Duke of Rovigo was mourned by few.

Opinions were now more divided than ever about how North African policy should proceed, and the subject was debated several times in the metropolitan Parliament. On one side were the advocates of total evacuation, or at best minimal occupation of a walled coastal entrepôt. Berthezène, Guizot, the economists and ultimately the government itself inclined towards this view. On the other side were those such as Clauzel, Thiers, the settlers and the Marseille commercial lobby, who wanted energetic expansion, or even the extirmination of indigenous populations. Within this wider debate, furthermore, there were bitter arguments over the degree to which native hierarchies should be respected; the degree to which colonisation should be state-subsidised or controlled; the degree to which the army should lead civil policy, and the degree to which French law and religion should be superimposed on existing Islamic structures. In military terms there were equally strong differences between the advocates of small or large columns; many or few outposts; steady low-key expansion or violent thrusts forward. The army's role in Africa thus provided a whole new subject area in military literature, which has maintained much of its interest and volume right up to the present day.[27]

Savary's 'temporary' successor, Voirol, had some expansionist plans but was forever finding himself short of both troops and political authority. He therefore placed particular emphasis on 'native politics' or, in more classical colonialist terminology, the technique of 'divide and rule'. Further to this goal he reinstated Arabs to positions of authority in local government, and set General Trézel to developing Savary's intelligence network to encompass more wide-ranging responsibilities. The much vaunted *Bureaux Arabes* were created, as agencies for the military supervision of civil affairs.[28] In this atmosphere also – although actually beyond Voirol's control – General Desmichels in Oran concluded a controversially generous treaty with the up-coming young Arab chieftain Abd-el-Kader.

The authorities in Paris were also at this time thinking more in terms of retrenchment than of expansion. In an ordinance of 22nd July 1834, inspired mainly by Soult, the first clear long-term policy was spelled out. It was decided that there should be firm military control; firm supremacy of French over native institutions; but only a slow and restricted expansion of territory. Few extra resources were made available, either in cash or in troop strength.

To implement this policy the post of 'Governor General' was instituted – although the first appointee turned out to be the near-senile D'Erlon, a major architect of the defeat at Waterloo. In common with his predecessor, D'Erlon wanted to expand faster – especially in the Mitidja – than Paris would support. The result was a hesitant advance around Boufarik which served only to increase the Arabs' guerrilla attacks. In Bougie and Bône, on the other hand, there were ill-conceived attempts at conciliation; but they produced little concrete advantage, either. As for Oran, D'Erlon at first agreed with the metropolitan government that Desmichels' treaty with Abd-el-Kader should be renounced, and that Desmichels himself should be replaced by the more aggressive Trézel. This was a major mistake, however, since the young Emir had greatly increased his influence since the previous year – just as he was to do every year for at least the next five. D'Erlon saw this too late, and back-pedalled hastily – but Trézel's punitive column had already been decimated, on 28th June 1835, in the La Macta swamps. In the ensuing public outrage D'Erlon was brusquely replaced by the more demonstratively 'colonialist' Clauzel, for his second term in command.

Now promoted Marshal, Clauzel was excellently placed to obtain the reinforcements and political support that he needed. At the end of 1835, in a wet and ill-supplied campaign accompanied by the Duke of Orleans, he took 11,000 men to sack – and then immediately evacuate – Mascara. At the start of 1836 he descended on Tlemcen, taxed it extortionately, and left 500 men under Captain Cavaignac – an energetic Polytechnician, republican and ex-carbonarist agitator[29] – to hold out against the counter-attacks that were often repeated during the following fourteen months.

The fact that Cavaignac survived at all was enough to rehabilitate his name in army circles, and paved the way for his accession to supreme office in 1848.

These operations may be taken as 'the end of the beginning' of the war in North Africa, in that initial uncertainty in Paris was at last starting to evaporate. France was emerging from her revolutionary turmoils, and now felt sufficiently confident to ignore British reservations and stake her prestige at least upon avenging La Macta, if not on anything more ambitious. Among the troops on the ground, furthermore, there was an increasingly urgent feeling that the sacrifices so far endured made it imperative that the whole of the country should be brought to heel. In Spain, Greece and Belgium an entire nation had been created, or saved, within a few short months. There seemed to be no particular reason why a similar outcome should not be expected from a major French effort in Africa, too.

After a successful start, however, Clauzel's campaigning soon ran into serious trouble. He met a check first at his staging camp at the mouth of the Tafna, which was blockaded, then at Médéah, which had to be abandoned. In Bône he supported the dire Captain Yusuf, who persuaded him to advance into the interior against the mountain stronghold of Constantine. Denied reinforcements from France, this adventure went ahead at the end of 1836 without either a siege train or adequate manpower. Thus when the Arabs closed the gates of the town there was nothing the French could do to break in. They had to retreat in very adverse conditions, harried all the way and suffering 1,000 casualties. Total catastrophe was averted only by Changarnier's energetic rearguard action, although it was paradoxically Yusuf who stole the popular imagination and won promotion. His exotic appeal in the Parisian salons seemed to exonerate him from all his many crimes.

Clauzel's failure at Constantine stood in clear contrast to General Bugeaud's minor triumph further to the west, which marked the start of what was to be an epic career in Africa. In a short campaign Bugeaud imposed a new, more mobile concept of operations, winning the miniature 'battle' of Sikkak in fine style and successfully relieving first the Tafna camp, and then Tlemcen. The way seemed open for further French advances into the interior. By February 1837, however, Bugeaud had returned to the Oran area to make huge concessions to Abd-el-Kader in the 'Tafna' peace treaty – very much in the spirit of Desmichels, and with equal dishonesty surrounding the secret clauses. In effect the Tafna treaty recognised Arab sovereignty everywhere that was not already occupied by the French, although several official efforts were made to conceal this fact.

Clauzel had by now been replaced by Damrémont as Governor General, and the African army had reached a strength of 43,000 – its highest to date. Within it were already many of the brightest names of the rising generation: Captains Le Boeuf and Niel – the ministers of war in 1868–70; de Saint-Arnaud – the foxy acolyte of Bugeaud who was to assist Louis Napoleon to power; de Ladmirault, MacMahon and Canrobert – all energetic and innovative light infantrymen with brilliant futures; Changarnier the resourceful duellist and snob; the Zouaves Bourbaki and Cavaignac; the intellectual Duvivier; Bedeau the meticulous puritan diplomat,[30] and – above all – Lieutenant Colonel de Lamoricière.

Lamoricière was an imaginative engineer who had arrived with the first invasion, learned Arabic and made his name with the Zouaves. The Zouaves in turn owed much of their fame to him, as the embodiment of the *Armée d'Afrique's* unconventional and colourful style. They gained a reputation as something akin to our modern SAS or Green Berets – ruthlessly single-minded raiders who could move fast, exploit every possible means of living off the land, and who set the international trend in military fashions. Lamoricière adapted many Arab habits to French use, including such diverse items as the Zouave dress itself (actually borrowed from the Turkish janissaries), *Couscous* and the *Razzia*. He corresponded with Catholics, Positivists and St Simonians at home: in fact with anyone who seemed to offer a 'radical but corporate' alternative to parliamentary egalitarianism.[31] Such a politico-religious philosophy was very much the fashion in the African army right from the start, and we do not have to wait for the generation of Boulanger, Lyautey or the *Ligue des Patriots* to find it at work, let alone the era of the military 'Maoists' of the 1950s.[32]

Petulant and eccentric, Lamoricière was always a potential rather than an actual force at the top of the army. He was briefly Acting Governor General of Algeria in 1845, and briefly Minister of War in 1848; but when he was proscribed by Napoleon III in 1851 his underlying Catholicism came to the fore, and he suffered an unexpected conversion to legitimism. He took service in the papal army, where he fought and lost the battle of Castelfidardo in 1860.

The 'Africans' of 1837 were soon to be joined by many others – the young cavaliers du Barail and Bosquet; the meticulous Pélissier; Forey, Randon, Le Flô, Charras and many more besides. These men were far from unanimous in their views on important questions of policy, and often bitterly divided by personal differences. They nevertheless formed the main group of energetic and successful officers who were destined to make history between 1840 and 1880, just as it had been the widely-experienced 'Napoleonic veterans' – helped during the Restoration by a few of their former émigré opponents – who had made the running between 1815 and the 1840s.

In October 1837 Damrémont eventually besieged and sacked Constantine at the head of an expedition of over 16,000 men – but he was killed in the process. Marshal Valée took up the poisoned chalice of African command, combining wide ambitions for expansion with a certain failure to make doctrinal or governmental innovations. In common with his predecessors he was baffled by the poor medical state of his command, and many of his efforts were devoted merely to resupplying his bases by convoys. In the Constantine area he staked out a system of vassal chieftains, but found that it led to a series of local revolts that could be suppressed only by constant expeditions. Late in 1839 he mounted a prestigious demonstration of force further afield than usual, through the 'Iron Gates' south-west of Bougie; but this too led to unexpected consequences. Abd-el-Kader interpreted it as a deliberate infringement of the Tafna treaty that had been concluded with Bugeaud, and unleashed a concerted attack on the Mitidja in retaliation.

There was a massacre of settlers and an outcry in Paris. Valée's defences were denounced for being too thinly spread – although the retributive expeditions that were demanded would have spread them more thinly still. More troops were sent from France – but the European diplomatic crisis meant that many of them were soon recalled. In the spring of 1840 the Marshal did progress to Cherchell, Médéah and Milianah – but disease and guerrilla warfare took a heavy toll, and many of the garrisons were soon blockaded. In five months some 4,200 soldiers died in hospital, and in twelve months forty-four officers were killed – the worst casualties of any year between 1830 and 1847. Valée was made a scapegoat for all this, but at the same time there was a strengthening of Parisian opinion behind a more active 'colonial' view. It was felt that the setbacks could be redeemed only by a total occupation of the whole area, which now became a fully-fledged colony to be known as *Algérie*.[33]

The voluble and restless Bugeaud took command in December 1840. He had served with distinction under Suchet in the Peninsular War and in the Alps during the Hundred Days, but had not been re-employed under the Restoration. With the 1830 Revolution he had quickly returned to favour, however, and played a prominent role as a 'political general' closely associated with Thiers in the troubled early years of the July

Monarchy – first acting as gaoler to the troublesome Duchesse de Berry; later commanding the troops responsible for the 'massacre of the Rue Transnonain' in Paris, 1834.[34] Now he shook up the African army in its entirety – constantly seeking new methods while moulding a devoted circle of top-class officers.

One tactical method that was already being used was the classic Arab *Razzia* – a means of exerting pressure upon an unseizable nomadic enemy at the same time as revictualling one's own troops. In a nutshell, the procedure was to set out with a column of anything between 500 and 7,000 men – horse, foot or a mixture – with pack animals but without wheeled vehicles. Marching far and fast with empty knapsacks, and acting on intelligence, the force would manoeuvre to a position from which the enemy's camp could be surprised. As the raiders swept in, they would seize anything useful they could carry or drive back with them, and destroy whatever – and often whomever – was left. This deprived the enemy of his only economic resource – his flocks – and terrorised him through his womenfolk and children.

In his thrust for 'absolute domination' of Algeria, Bugeaud was to apply the policy of scorched earth far more systematically, and for longer, than any of his predecessors. Admittedly he did try to stop the practice of paying native auxiliaries for the human heads they brought in, just as other attempts had been made by Valée and Changarnier to 'moralise' the *razzia*; but in the buccaneering atmosphere of the African army this made little practical difference. The war became ever more cruel and wasteful. As Canrobert put it, in an unconscious echo of another great nineteenth-century *ravageur,* William T. Sherman; 'It will be barbarous, but one doesn't make war by philanthropy.'[35]

In 1841 Bugeaud's force stood at 63,000; a figure that he was to increase to 118,000 within five years. The deployment of such large numbers – a third of the French army – reflected a major change in political will. This was a larger force than Angoulême had commanded in Spain; larger than Napoleon had commanded at Waterloo, about the same as was later to be put into line at Gravelotte and Sedan – although rather less than was fielded at Solferino. It at last allowed a systematic advance on a wide front: a luxury that had been denied to Bugeaud's predecessors. Indeed, it has been persuasively argued that it was simply this material advantage, rather than his own much-vaunted new tactics, that swung the balance in his favour.[36]

Be that as it may, Bugeaud first consolidated his hold on the low-lying coastal regions, closing down Valée's smaller posts and converting the larger ones into major depots. Then he started to send out a succession of light columns deeper than usual, to towns loyal to Abd-el-Kader such as Mascara, Tagdempt, Boghar, Taza and Saïda. The Emir thereby lost both his granaries and the reassurance of a firm territorial base. By 1843 the *razzias* were probing deeper still, aiming at the ambulant centre of the Arab main force, the *Smala*. Aumale managed to surprise and disperse this near Boghar in May – an incredibly lucky victory of 500 against 30,000 which finally set the seal on Abd-el-Kader's doom.

Bugeaud himself, now a Marshal, first ravaged Kabylia and then turned back to pursue the beaten Emir into Morocco. In August 1844 he won the battle of Isly, setting a famous first precedent for what was to become a long-term habit of unauthorised 'hot pursuit' incursions into neighbouring territories. Obviously the French army was already deeply worried by the sanctuary that could be offered to a mobile enemy by a neutral frontier.

Abd-el-Kader nevertheless remained unsubdued for a further three years, moving from one valley to the next and animating the Algerian nation wherever he appeared. The Moroccans also sponsored a *Mahdi* of their own, in the shape of the youthful Bou Ma'za. Bugeaud reacted by multiplying the number of his columns – sometimes to as many as eighteen active at one time – in order to close the net ever tighter around his elusive prey. Most expeditions were successful, and there were some notable demonstrations of French resolve – not least Pélisier's exemplary asphyxiation of 700 civilian refugees in the Dahra caves. There were nevertheless still some heroic French disasters in the grand tradition, such as the combat of Sidi-Brahim in 1845 – an epic 'last stand' from which but fourteen soldiers out of 423 survived.

The total submission of Algeria north of the Sahara was not to be achieved until well into the 1850s. In the meantime the strain of intensive activity took a heavy toll on French shoe-leather, manpower and, especially, horseflesh. It was reckoned that after two operations the average battalion would have shed about a half of its men, but the rest would be acclimatised and battle-worthy. All the horses, however, would have been effectively used up.[37]

These years also saw the elaboration of Bugeaud's egregious ideas on colonisation, supporting a right-wing and military version of precisely that Saint Simonism which in Paris or Lyon was considered the army's greatest enemy. It was perhaps no coincidence that an ideologically anti-colonial press was also starting to appear in Paris. Nothing like the required number of French volunteer settlers ever come forward to 'civilise' the new lands, so the authorities had to make do with a motley collection of convicts, East European refugees and old soldiers. Despite much rhetoric – and even idealism – these could not be expected to make an entirely happy blend with the already very mixed Algerian population. Nor could civilian primacy over the army ever be established. Bugeaud himself did much to make Algeria a military enclave that was to be forever beyond the full control of the government in Paris.

At least the army was able to make considerable strides in the administrative organisation of its provinces, and in 1847 even Bou Ma'za and Abd-el-Kader were compelled to surrender – followed the next year by Ahmed, the veteran Bey of Constantine. By this time Bugeaud had finally gone home, however, and the Republican Cavaignac had succeeded to the governorship. Cavaignac was in his turn recalled to command all the forces in Paris during the 1848 June days, where with the 'Africans' Lamoricière, Changarnier, Charras and Bedeau he was to engineer the stern *reprise en main* of both the metropolitan population and its army.

Days of revolutionary violence

If most officers felt that their noblest vocation lay in warfare on the frontier or in North Africa, many civilians believed the army's chief role was to uphold order within France itself – to suppress the street rioting and rural insurgency that were all too common at this time. Such operations held a fundamental importance for the survival of the régime and for the protection of private property, in a way that limited external adventures did not.

There were many different battlefields. Between 1828 and 1832 there were widespread grain riots throughout the country, not to mention the 1830 revolution itself in Paris. This in turn led to a wave of urban uprisings in the years until 1834, and then again in 1840. From 1831 to 1833 the legitimist Vendée rose for the fourth and last time, while the Duchesse de Berry made an abortive coup in the south, and was imprisoned in Blaye – just as Louis Napoleon was later to be in Ham. In 1831 and 1834 the disturbances of the Lyon silk workers made their city into a miniature version of revolutionary Paris. The 1840s were generally more peaceful – but the nationwide explosion of 1848 was as violent as anything that had been seen before. The army was at first caught off guard, but there was then a continuing cycle of riot and repression in the cities until the riots were bloodily extinguished soon after the coup d'état

of 2nd December 1851. In its own way the countryside was affected just as
much. In 1848 a total of more than 48,200 troops (including 5,300 cavalry)
were deployed to deal with approximately 250 incidents of rural unrest, in
a 'war of cabbage stalks', of grain taxes and of forestry rights. If we make
allowance for some fifty occasions on which the number of troops is
unknown, the average deployment to each of these incidents appears to
have been approximately 240 soldiers.[38]

Counter-insurgency was always expensive in manpower. Since at least
the notorious siege of Sarragossa in 1808[39] it had been recognised that
street-to-street fighting was especially intense, and no troops could be
expected to stand its strain for many days. Marmont, whose 12,000-
strong Paris garrison had been quickly overwhelmed in July 1830, later
stressed the need for reinforcement and relief if the action became
protracted.[40] Obviously the problem would become bigger in proportion
as the city to be controlled was bigger. In the seemingly endless rabbit-
warren backstreets of Paris or Lyon this made for a very heavy drain on
manpower indeed, since every street might have several barricades that
could be covered by fire at close range from upper stories, and every
block could become a deadly citadel. It was a drain, furthermore, which
was made far far worse if – as happened to Marmont and others in a
similar position – significant numbers of units and individuals defected to
the insurgents. The risk of this happening made it doubly important to
bring in fresh troops who had not been contaminated by the mob's
sedition during the weeks leading up to the outbreak.

Marmont's 1830 experience was traumatic enough, but it was to be
repeated, in essence, by Roguet *père* at Lyon in November 1831 and again
by Bugeaud himself in Paris during February 1848. In each of these three
cases the army was taken by surprise and suffered a major defeat on its
home ground, leading to intense self-doubt and recriminations. In Lyon
1831, for example, it lost 11% of its 3,500 men in killed or wounded, and
28% as deserters or 'prisoners' of the National Guard and the mob. In
February 1848 three-quarters of the twenty regiments in Paris were
disarmed and one-eighth deserted.[41] No self-respecting army could
possibly contemplate such a scale of loss with anything like equanimity.

The result was that there were two distinct phases during which the
army reviewed its methods and tightened up its determination to resist.
The first of these came in 1831–34; the second extended from the June
Days of 1848 to the final coup d'état of 2nd December 1851. It is
from these two periods of *reprise en main* that we can date the birth
of both a systematic doctrine of counter-insurgency and a new toughness

in attitude. The essential point was that military units should be uncompromising in keeping civilians at bay, and unhesitating in attacking provocative mobs. This, however, opened the way to a less tolerant general comportment. During heavy street fighting in 1830 St Chamans had shrunk from setting fire to buildings in Paris; but by 1850 Roguet *fils* was reluctantly accepting that this might sometimes be necessary. Equally in 1848 Lamoricière tried to stop the National Guards from shooting their prisoners – but he refused to accept that such prisoners enjoyed any right to clemency.[42] By this time too much blood had been spilt on each side[43] – and too much promotion awarded to ambitious peacetime officers – for all the conventional restraints to be automatically observed.

The philosophical attitude of Napoleonic veterans who were accustomed to fighting an external enemy – men like Marmont or Roguet *père* – was gradually slipping out of fashion. We must remember that the dominant generation in 1848 was composed of the single-minded careerist 'Africans' of the *razzia* and the Dahra caves. They were led by a Bugeaud who, although he may have been wrong-footed in February 1848, was nevertheless still the author of the 1834 Rue Transnonain massacre. Taking a wider view of the century, we can say that the lessons learned in 1848 led not only to Haussman's opening of wider fields of fire in the Paris boulevards, but directly to the unprecedented savagery of the suppression of the Commune in 1871.

In technical terms urban counter-insurgency was more tricky even than counter-guerrilla operations in Algeria. Within France the army naturally had a much higher political profile, and careers could be made or broken almost at the whim of any passing journalist. It was certainly no accident that Bugeaud himself had a deep-rooted hatred of the press.[44] On a day of riot an officer would often be faced with an agonising choice between his professional inclinations towards activity and firmness, and the diverse and often unpredictable decisions of his theoretical superiors – the local political authorities. He would have to decide for himself which way he should move, and how far he could afford to break his 'essential obedience' by acting alone. At the local level this decision could and did go either way, depending on the particular mixture of personalities and forces in play in each different riot. It was only at the higher political level – especially in Paris – that a more consistent record of obedience to the civil power could be maintained.

On some occasions a single misplaced or unplanned musket shot could alienate an entire suburb, and premature fusillades were far from unknown. On 9th September 1841 at Clermont Ferrand the troops fired while National Guardsmen were still mixed with the crowd, leading to the concerted fury of the whole city and the army's rout. Something similar turned the scale against the July Monarchy on the Boulevard des Capucines in Paris, 23rd February 1848.[45]

On other occasions fusillades and energetic assaults might be the only possible way of retaining the loyalty of the troops at the same time as making the necessary point to the insurgents. Clearly a delicate line always had to be drawn between firmness and restraint – requiring both an accurate assessment of the underlying political balance, and quick-thinking leadership of a high order. As General Roguet *fils* stated in 1850, in his splendid book on street fighting: 'No (*battlefield*) demands so much latitude and spontaneity of action, within certain limits, from each rank, fraction of troop or position occupied.'[46]

A considerable amount of study was put into the question of how a city could be prepared in advance against riots, and a consensus emerged which stressed both moral and physical aspects. Mental preparation included the careful preliminary police intelligence that had already been well understood in the eighteenth century;[47] but to this were now added some specifically military measures. The selection of resolute leaders, invested with undisputed unity of command, was important – as was the strict supervision of the soldiers' loyalties and a general dissemination of warning instructions intended to avert surprise. In 1833 Bugeaud felt that three quarters of the psychic shock of a riot could be averted by these means, which would also help to build national confidence and remove any ambiguities that might surround the army's likely attitude.[48] Once battle had commenced, furthermore, one should turn surprise to one's own advantage by striking the enemy's flanks with several converging columns.[49] In attacking barricades a turning attack, through the buildings on either side of the obstacle, was to be preferred to a frontal assault. To preserve the soldiers from revolutionary infection, indeed, orders should be issued to simply shoot anyone who tried to approach them.[50]

Physical preparations for riots would start with the provision of adequate numbers of troops within a few hours' march of the likely trouble spots, without placing excessive reliance on either small detachments or on any questionable National Guard units within the disputed area. Especially in the June Days this meant calling in the more enthusiastic and vindictive National Guards from the countryside surrounding Paris, to reinforce the regulars who were at the spearhead of the fighting.[51]

Numbers were not everything in street battles, since the troops also needed a secure supply of ammunition and food. The lack of food in 1830 had caused serious difficulties, and in the June Days 'the arrival of a large convoy of munitions was decisive'.[52] From that time onwards it became standard practice to keep stockpiles in *mairies* and gendarmerie barracks. The idea was that a central 'military quarter' or dépôt (not without its own printing press for propaganda and proclamations) should support a network of such strongpoints scattered throughout the city. These outposts would dispute the insurgents' control of all but quite small areas, and if they were themselves cut off would hold out for several days until relieved by strong counter-attacking columns under central direction. Ideally the progress of the latter would be aided by widened streets and the absence of barricade material such as *pavés* or trees.[53]

There was also a lively debate about the degree to which small centres of resistance inside troublesome towns might be developed into major fortresses. Such *embastillement* was naturally anathema to the revolutionary left, who condemned the army for relying on firepower rather than on the political support of the population and its National Guard. Nor were large fortifications within cities particularly desired by the many officers who were more concerned to erect external defences against a foreign foe. In his eventual Paris plan of 1840 Thiers was careful to provide a continuous outward-looking *enceinte* which could be manned by the citizens – if necessary even against the garrisons of the suburban ring of closed forts.[54] In Lyon, however, the story was rather different. By 1834 the military authorities were successfully establishing several large forts within or dominating the insurgent quarter of La Croix-Rousse, which were welcomed by at least one local reactionary who said that 'Despotism is doubtless a detestable régime, but arbitrary power is a hundred times preferable to accepting the arbitrary rule of demagogy. It is better to live under an absolute government in Vienna or Berlin than in Lyon under the yoke of a Republic . . .'[55]

However, one does not have to look further than 1789 itself to realise that, even with *embastillement*, a city's garrison might still be overwhelmed by the mob. In February and March 1848 the army gave up its forts in Lyon without making a stand.[56] The choice was then between a compromise settlement which legitimated the revolution – as happened in both Lyon and Paris on this particular occasion – and a fighting retreat to an external stronghold from which retribution might later be launched. It was the latter policy that had been planned for Saint Cloud in 1830 – although in the event the king felt that the loss of Paris meant the loss of

everything, and abdicated instead. Yet in 1831 the Lyon army did retire
defiantly to the nearby camp de Rillieux to wait for something to turn up
– which it eventually did – while in 1871 it was Versailles that became the
refuge of the Paris garrison before it finally returned in vengeance to
suppress the Commune.[57]

In its rural counter-insurgency the army faced a rather different and
smaller-scale set of problems than it did in the towns, although the
underlying questions of loyalty, morale and low-level leadership remained the same. Because the rural National Guard had particularly
limited terms of reference, it could notoriously not be relied upon to hold
out against trouble on any large scale. The army or the urban National
Guard might therefore be called in to help at an early stage in any
disturbance, although there were usually long delays between the initial
crisis and the troops' eventual arrival on the scene. Once deployed,
furthermore, the army would face familiar problems of 'correctly reading
the political mood', of co-operating with civilian officials, and of
protecting the soldiers from attempted subversion. To these must be
added acute problems of accommodation and supply in remote areas
unprovided with barracks.[58]

The stresses and strains of rural counter-insurgency were often less
intensive but more continuous than in urban riots. The troops would also
be more widely dispersed in small units, which created some severe
problems of command and control. In his 1833 book on the Vendée,
Roguet *fils* well described the frustrations of the 40,000 soldiers deployed
to pin down an insurgent force of at most 6,000, in a landscape of dense
and impenetrable *bocage*. When they first arrived, the government's
conscripts would typically be active and enthusiastic, but after a few
weeks of fifteen-man patrols, futile ambushes and sweeps, unhygienic
billets, and hostile civil authorities, morale would inevitably slump.[59]
Only the Gendarmerie and the Customs service were consistently reliable
and effective, since they were more permanently deployed and had access
to excellent intelligence sources – but they were too few in number. For
the clumsier line infantry, by contrast, the Chouan guerrillas, the
smugglers and the bands of deserters who roamed the countryside
seemed to be totally unseizable. Direct military action was generally
ineffective, and attempts to organise gangs of 'counter-Chouans' or other
irregulars usually only made matters worse.[60]

There is something very modern[61] about Roguet's whole analysis of
the Vendée, in which he scrutinises the cycles of repression and political
action during the four crises that broke out between the 1790s and the

1830s. He concluded that the best policy was what we would perhaps today call '*Hearts and Minds* linked to *Police Primacy*' . . . or what Hoche in the 1790s had been moving towards when he said that 'Bayonets are almost powerless here where moral and political means supplement everything, provided there is bread.'[62]

Apart from moments of concerted uprising, such as Lamarque faced when he brutally suppressed the Vendée during the Hundred Days, Roguet believed that military action should be merely an auxiliary to a phased, long-term process of opening the countryside to modern economic progress. Inspired in part by Suchet's political methods of controlling eastern Spain, and in part also by the methods of social analysis implied by the works of Sir Walter Scott,[63] he envisaged a steady transformation of the hostile farmyard clergy and nobility of the Vendée into a more enlightened and loyal leadership class. He also believed that the government's existing 'Strategic Routes' should be extended into each village – and re-named to indicate a more politico-economic than military purpose. In keeping with the St Simonism of many 'African' commanders, moreover, he hoped that the army could earn its keep by doing much of the construction work itself.[64]

If the theoretical principles of limited European warfare and siegecraft had been well understood since at least the time of Vauban, those of Algerian conquest and colonisation had to be designed from scratch. They represented a new area of doctrinal development scarcely less significant, in its way, than that of the emerging science of strategy for *La Grande Guerre*. Much the same could also be said of internal security within Metropolitan France, where there was an equal sense of designing a new methodology by trial and error, in order to arrive at its essential principles. On 5th April 1850 the *Moniteur de l'Armée's* review of Dusaert's *Essai sur l'Art de la Guerre* could say that 'Even the taking of barricades now has rules' . . . although it might have added that Blanqui and his socialist friends were simultaneously starting to think of some new rules of their own for the *making* of barricades.[65]

Inseparable from any experimental process of trial and error, of course, is the possibility of error. In their limited European wars between 1823 and 1849 the French made relatively few mistakes because they – and they supremely above all others – already understood the principles that lay behind this type of action.[66] In Algeria, on the other hand, they were entering unknown territory. They suffered some disasters and many hesitations, taking more than ten years to define the terms of their colonisation and the shape of their African army.[67]

In counter-insurgency operations within France there were other disasters and other hesitations. In a multitude of different ways this was less unknown territory than campaigning in North Africa; but the scale and political dimensions of the problem were both relatively new. Finding the correct role for a 'national professional army' in an age of revolutions was a daunting task – but it was eventually achieved with considerable success. The army's internal turmoil had practically disappeared after the first few years of the July Monarchy, while that of the civilian population was to appear but rarely after 1851.

Part 2

The nature of military thought

3

The makers of military thought

What is military thought?

If we are to explain the richness and vitality of French military thought in the aftermath of the Napoleonic wars, we must understand not only the army from which it sprang, but also the nature of 'military thought' itself. This is not a concept which has received much useful definition in the past, and it has been taken to stand for many different things by many different writers. Anti-military wags have dismissed it as inherently a contradiction in terms, while post-Sedan witch-hunters have lovingly alleged its systematic decline in France from the vibrant 1780s through the experienced but unscientific 1820s, to the mentally inert 1860s.[1] Loyally patriotic apologists have been just as quick to attribute almost every action of the high command, in whatever era, to some deeply intellectual master-plan. Modern sociologists, on the other hand, have been less interested in the professional military debate than in officers' *mentalités* as expressed in voting patterns, class affiliations or religious beliefs.

We should perhaps be specific that for our present purposes we are looking at the type of military thought which is concerned primarily with the army's role in fighting wars, or preparing to fight them, rather than with the army's place in the wider society. We are also assuming that in the French service *La Grande Guerre* was generally seen as the most important type of war that might be fought, even if it remained a somewhat abstract and unlikely idea for much of the time. By the same token limited, colonial or counter-insurgency operations were ultimately considered to be secondary, even though they might be making deep and unremitting demands on the army – often worryingly close to home.

All this may seem to add up to a somewhat perverse set of priorities for the French army in those years, in view of the primacy attached by civilian politicians to both internal security and international harmony – or by military careerists to African adventuring. It is nevertheless a view of the world which was strong in this army, and which was often reflected in the professional literature of the times. It was fuelled by the extraordinarily powerful memory of 'Napoleonic' *servitude et grandeur*, and kept vibrantly alive by revanchist suspicions and Bonapartist celebrations alike. The Cossacks had visited Paris in 1814 and again in 1815, after all; so nobody could be unaware of the possibility that they might return.[2]

Since it is primarily through the written word that we can today glimpse the thought patterns of those distant times, we have little option but to approach 'military thought' by way of the phenomenon that we may perhaps call 'military literature' – or in other words, anything that happened to be written down on subjects related to war and armies. This only partially simplifies our problem, however, because several commentators have confused the idea of 'military literature' with any 'literature', in the grand literary sense, that happens to have been written by soldiers. The works of the ex-officers Chateaubriand, Lamartine, Stendhal, and de Vigny would therefore presumably qualify; and perhaps also those of Maupassant and Daudet, who both served as *Mobiles* in 1870.

This is already a highly significant slice of general French literature, and some of it even treats military subjects.[3] Unfortunately, alas, it sheds but little glory on the army, due to the near-indecent haste with which every one of these authors quite sensibly returned to civilian life. Victor Hugo himself had to take active steps to avoid enrolling for the École Polytechnique – which might have led to a military career – although both Laplace and Comte were later to accept the more 'civilian' option of teaching there for a time.

Apart from these 'noteworthy fringes', the professional officer corps managed to produce only a very few, and very minor, literary figures. There was apparently a certain cult of 'literature' in the African army,[4] and Baudelaire's friend Paul de Molènes did make a military career. The novelist commandant of St Cyr during the Second Empire, however, was perhaps more typical. He was unkindly hailed by a reviewer as a 'colonel in the cavalry but a corporal in literature'.[5]

That the army produced few literary giants may be regrettable, but it scarcely amounts to an indictment of military efficiency. We have no need to shake our heads, as do some recent commentators, when it transpires that many officers deplored the moral corruption of 'modern novels',[6] or that the army's writings were 'merely' on professional subjects. Nor, conversely, need we follow those military apologists who have attempted to show that the best generals were also inevitably the best exponents of prose style.[7] Although it has been persistent in France for at least a century, the bizarre idea that an army's quality may be judged by its literary standing is at root entirely sterile.

What, then, do we mean by 'military literature'? Some have taken it to be the whole body of writing about war and armies, including commentaries by civilians no less than by soldiers. Hence the record of parliamentary debates about recruiting or replacement would qualify, as would anti-military tracts and civilian novels. Hugo's version of Waterloo might thus be placed alongside Stendhal's, and Balzac's various 'military types' alongside de Vigny's.[8] It may be worth mentioning that one of the most influential pieces of writing in French military circles, Joseph de Maistre's *Soirées de St Pétersbourg*, came from the pen of an Italian diplomat accredited to Russia;[9] while surely the most effective of all nineteenth-century French battle-pieces, Zola's *Débâcle*, was written not only by a complete civilian but by the leading Dreyfusard himself.

Such an all-encompassing definition of 'military literature' runs the risk of being too broad and amorphous. For our present purposes, at least, we must narrow it down to the debate about military subjects that was conducted within the army. Yet here, again, we encounter 'literary' assumptions in a different form.

Many commentators, who should know better, have assumed that 'military literature' consists exclusively of 'great works' about war – the lasting masterpieces which electrify a generation at the same time as they lay bare the higher aspects of strategy, military organisation and 'the philosophy of war'. They look at the curriculum as defined by Clausewitz – those essential considerations which impart to senior commanders what de Gaulle called 'familiarity with general ideas, the notion of the mutual relationships between things . . . meditation applied to a wide sweep of observation'.[10]

This approach certainly has the advantage of limiting the books qualifying as 'military literature' to an easily-manageable number, since there surely cannot be many timeless texts of military philosophy written in each generation – let alone in each country in each generation. For 1815–51 it is generally assumed that we have only Clausewitz and Jomini, and even then the breadth of 'general ideas' possessed by the latter has often been called into question.[11] In any case, neither of these two great writers happens to have been French by birth – which has led some

commentators to despair entirely of the French army, and others to turn
to the many 'second league' figures such as Marmont, Morand and
Duhesme. It is ironic that the Prussia of Clausewitz is generally deemed to
have had a more active military debate than France, even though she
could boast rather fewer such 'second league' figures.[12]

Although Swiss, Jomini did at least write in French; he served for ten
years on Ney's staff in the *Grande Armée*, and based his analysis on a
number of characteristically French assumptions. Thus his classic *Précis de
l'Art de la Guerre* of 1838 is full of references to the current French debate,
not least in its emphasis upon the 'small but good' army that could
manoeuvre freely under the direction of a brilliant commander.[13]
Although he deserted Napoleon and took Russian service from 1813 until
his death in 1869, Jomini often resided in France and has been seen as the
French champion in a 'duel' against the Prussian Clausewitz.[14]

Jomini was nevertheless not particularly popular in France. It was easy
for Bonapartists to dismiss him as yet another deserter, like Berthier,
Bourmont or Victor; and it is clear that he was a personally difficult and
insecure character, who devoted much of his long life to self-advertise-
ment and the repetition of a few fundamental ideas. After his initial burst
of insight, around 1803, into the geometrical principles of strategy – in the
Traité des Grandes Opérations Militaires – his contribution lay mainly in
applying those principles to various campaigns drawn from recent
military history. His lucidity of style and apparently 'scientific' method
certainly won him many imitators and disciples; but these were mainly
Germans or Anglo-Saxons – such as Warner, the Archduke Charles or
Napier in the first generation, or Willisen, Halleck and Hamley in the
second – rather than French. Within France there was too much
competition from other articulate senior officers who had seen no less of
the great wars than had Jomini himself. There was thus a sense in which
the French were happy to pass on their own military perceptions to each
other, while leaving it to foreigners to provide commentaries for other
foreigners. The title of one piece which had appeared in Paris in 1808 did
nevertheless reflect a Jominian approach to strategy: it was an '*Essay on the
Mechanism of War, or application of the first principles of mechanics to the
movement and action of Army Corps*'; and a comparable idea would find its
way into a number of the subsequent textbooks.[15] Thiers would draw
upon Jominian historiographical techniques for his best-selling *History of
the Consulate and Empire*, and there was also a certain school of admirers in
the *Dépôt de la Guerre*. This school, however, was no more than one
among several active in France at the time.[16]

Jomini's work should not, therefore, be portrayed as a beacon standing alone on a dark night. It was inspired by important precursors, from Lloyd[17] and Tempelhof to Valentini and Bülow. It perhaps seemed to be startlingly new to the epic decade in which it first appeared – but it was soon to be joined by a flood of other works and alternative schools of thought, which Jomini in turn would absorb and elaborate.

We cannot properly understand Jomini and his impact unless we place him squarely in the context of the more general French military debate – taking minor literature together with major, and privately-circulated discussion papers together with published articles and books. We may also perhaps extend the list of subjects that have relevance to this 'military' world view, beyond the higher principles and strategies to the details of tactics, training and regimental life. In the following pages, therefore, our discussion of 'military literature', and by extension 'military thought', will attempt to look behind the tiny number of 'masterworks' to the multitude of opinions and ideas that were being exchanged all the time in the background – not necessarily well-rounded or elegantly expressed, but nevertheless revealing of the active mental climate that characterised this army.

Within the debate we may detect certain distinctive 'schools' or 'cohorts' to which military writers belonged. The membership of these groupings was more nuanced than in the case of political loyalties, however, since almost all participants in the military debate were united in a central loyalty to the army and its particular orthodoxies. There were certainly disagreements, as there are in every army – for example between traditionalists and reformers over questions of recruitment or regimental training – but for the most part those who thought deeply about the army tended to reach generally similar conclusions. If they were polarised at all, it was against civilians, bureaucrats and inarticulate fellow-officers who seemed to stand in the way of what the 'army' saw as progress.

From Napoleonic strategists to Fourierists and romantics

A few of the influential writers of this period had formed their ideas before 1789, just as a number of eighteenth century texts retained their popularity long into the new century. De Saxe's, Guibert's and the Prince de Ligne's spiritual analyses of morale; Gay de Vernon's textbook on fortification; Gassendi's on gunnery; Grimoard's on staffwork and Lacuée Cessac's handbook for officers on campaign – all of these enjoyed considerable longevity. The 1791 infantry drill manual itself, indeed, had been written under Guibert's influence and persisted with only minor alterations into the 1860s.[18]

In many fields of endeavour it is quite common for handbooks to evolve only very slowly. This is especially true when – as in this case – there is only fashion, as opposed to serious technological change, to be accommodated. The 1791 drill manual was actually a perfectly adequate basis for battlefield tactics, although individuals were free to graft their own variations upon it. Thus in 1804 Marshal Ney added some new movements for the use of his own Army Corps, albeit still envisaging attacks in line – and then in actual combat he invariably made his attacks in equally non-reglementary columnar formations.[19] None of this necessarily invalidated the original manual, since it remained the essential starting-point for whatever the commander might choose to do.

Much of the eighteenth century's grand tactical and strategic geometry, from which Jomini had developed his thinking, also continued to be published alongside that officer's slightly newer formulations and popularisations. The old art of war was not seen as incompatible with the new, because the 'new' armies of the Restoration, July Monarchy, Second Republic – and even Second Empire – were seen as essentially the same as those of the *Ancien Régime* and early First Empire. They were 'small but good', as opposed to those of the late First Empire which had been tainted by self-defeating corruptions of scale. Hence for example as late as 1832 General Koch, Jomini's own collaborator and former *aide de camp*, apparently saw no anomaly in publishing the ex-émigré Ternay's text which discussed 'march manoeuvres' in a distinctly old-fashioned manner, scarcely mentioning Napoleon's important innovations in this art.[20] Koch perhaps saw the book as a worthy classic from a past age rather than as a step beyond the work of his former patron – but it is equally possible that he saw it as 'a neat, contemporary, legitimist corrective to Bonapartist ideas', closely aligned with Jomini's own thinking on this sensitive matter. We should not forget that Jomini fully embraced the political as well as the tactical Restoration, and tended to look forwards only in hindsight.[21]

The men who had held active commands in the wars knew more about the frustrations and frictions of campaigning than they did about rarefied geometrical theories. Nearly all of them found it easy to transcend pedantry, and the best of them were able to combine this with an understanding of political and higher strategical combinations. The price most of them paid, however, was that they tended to be better at narrating direct personal impressions, prejudices or postures than in abstracting eternal principles. The Emperor himself was perhaps the infuriatingly supreme example of this, since his various attempts at generalising about war, mainly from his restless retreat in St Helena, were notoriously self-conscious, disconnected and Delphic.[22] He reminds us that – apart from the occasional Caesar, Vauban or Slim – the very highest commanders are almost invariably incapable of transmitting their most important inner perceptions to a later generation.

Among Napoleonic veterans there is a distinction to be drawn between relatively junior officers who saw mainly the excitements of the front line, and higher commanders who saw more of the inner circle of decision-making. In the first category were the likes of Marbot or Fézensac, who left stirring memoirs; while in the second were the Soults, Suchets and Gouvion St Cyrs, who left only a crisp narrative record of a selected few of their campaigns, without looking far into how they might be interpreted.[23] From around the time of the Second Empire it became fashionable to cull broad maxims and principles from the memoirs of such famous Napoleonic figures – and the more famous the better – but this process usually sacrificed whatever coherence and unity of thought there might originally have been.[24]

More useful for theory than either of these groups was that select band of critical writers who not only experienced command and understood its principles, but made the crucial next step towards analysis. The didactic works on the art of the Division commander, and related subjects, by Marmont, Morand or Duhesme must surely rank among the very best writings of their kind.[25] They contain the traditional eighteenth-century military canon, but blend it beautifully with the lessons of modern experience – no sterile formalism, but plenty of open-minded discussion and the earnest advice of practical men who know what they are talking about.

There was an equally constructive type of writing by officers who attempted to mould the Napoleonic experience into a new theory of war, even though they had not themselves exercised high command. The liberal Pelet took part in many campaigns, then wrote their histories and finally rose to command the Staff Corps. He was able to keep abreast of all new developments in an exemplary manner, even adhering to the unfashionable idea of a mass army. He might have become the French Clausewitz if only he had collected his writings in a single didactic work; or the French Scharnhorst if only the army had been differently structured and the Staff Corps more prestigious.[26]

The sceptical, half-pay General Vaudoncourt looked back to Bülow; but also made the significant addition of a citizen army. The engineer Rogniat put forward a plan for military reform which drew specific refutations from St Helena. The gunner Chambray and the staff officers Carrion Nisas and Mathieu Dumas equally staked out a certain fame as 'military philosophers'. Each of them contributed some structured speculations on what they had seen, all interspersed with nearly as much straight military history as Jomini himself had written.[27]

The appearance of a large number of Napoleonic memoirs, histories and analyses happened to coincide with the opening of many new controversies within the middle and late Restoration army, concerning such issues as the role of the Staff, the best way to fortify Paris, the need for a supply of horses independent of potential enemies like Britain or Germany, the revision of infantry and cavalry regulations, or the need for a reserve status for ageing generals. Behind everything, however, was a widespread dissatisfaction with pay and conditions, especially by officers on half pay. This led to several celebrated summaries of the army's deficiencies, both by extremist officers who had employment – such as the ultra-royalist Clouet – and by those who did not – notably Lamarque, Vaudoncourt, Allix, LeCouturier and, indeed, Morand himself.[28] There was thus already a distinct 'school' of liberal or Bonapartist half-pay military journalists who were doing in the 1820s precisely what Trochu was to do more famously in 1868. They were translating their personal dissatisfaction with their chosen career into a constructively wide-ranging, but nevertheless hostile analysis of that career – and all in the hope of winning promotion within it![29]

This burst of reforming zeal diffused into the various channels of moderately predictable official complacency, or of opposition journalism, which eventually settled down following the upheavals of 1830–34. There was not to be quite such a unanimous movement inside the army before the general enthusiasm for the coup d'état of 1851, although that is not to say that there were no longer any groups of creative theorists. These groups existed, with more or less cohesion, but were not really part of any single movement of the whole.

There was first of all a new type of vituperative opposition journalist, generally drawn from a lower level of rank than the more celebrated Bonapartist half-pay Restoration generals – and often legitimists who had come through the Bourbon Guards or Cavalry. From 1833 the *Journal de l'Armée*, for example, had Majors Puvis, Beauchamps, Bléton and Noblot, who soon became notorious as 'utopian innovators' putting forward many searing indictments of an army whose intellectual life they were at least stimulating, if not exactly representing.[30]

We have already discussed the 'African' generals; hard-fighting men of action who were to win all the plum commands in 1848, both in Paris and on the frontier. They were nevertheless sufficiently 'intellectual' to produce a considerable pamphlet literature dealing with questions of African government, operations or colonisation; and each of them attracted his own group of young acolytes. In metropolitan France there were other theorists gathered around a few crucial figures, such as General Pelet at the *Dépôt de la Guerre,* Préval[31] in the ministry of war, or the charismatic Duke of Orleans in the Palace. Especially around 1840 this last found himself at the centre of a range of military reforms, in collaboration with Thiers, which covered everything from the Chasseurs à Pied to the inauguration of 'strategic' manoeuvres for large units. At a slightly lower level there were certain generals whose approach to large-unit training was winning them a reputation for efficiency and intelligence, and around whom some of the best officers in the army were collecting. Aymard at Lyon was one such 'training general', while Castellane at Perpignan was even more celebrated for his preparatory courses for troops destined for Algeria.[32] Both of these men usually had at least a Brigade permanently at their disposal, so were well placed to overcome the problems of a dispersed 'regimental' army, and to practise the techniques of massed European warfare.

A particular centre of bright and athletic young officers could be found in the Chasseurs à Pied, founded in 1838 as an experimental battalion to teach and develop light infantry and musketry skills. The Chasseurs soon established themselves as an élite force, growing to twenty battalions by 1853, and even qualifying as a separate arm from the Infantry. Their officers conducted a lively discussion in the military press, defending themselves against the old and reactionary, at the same time as they successfully exploited the Chasseur mystique as a lever for promotion.[33] A similar process of using reform ideas as an aid for personal preferment could also be seen, albeit on a smaller scale, in the various training specialities – from gymnastics to primary education – that were starting to appear within the line regiments.

Many officers absorbed a form of liberalism from the currents of thought of society as a whole. The cavalry Captain Durand[34] wrote most uncompromisingly in this vein, and some of his tenets reached to very near the top of the hierarchy. Succeeding generations of Polytechnicians also propagated the social theories of St Simon and Fourier, and the military press was full of demands for some of their more practical ideas to be tried out. Of these, the most popular was the use of troops for public works – not only in Algeria, but also in France itself.[35] By the Second Empire, however, these had been discontinued and the military Fourierists themselves discredited. The army had always interpreted liberalism on its own terms, and easily relinquished it when it was no longer useful.

One other strand of the civilian consciousness was also picked up and exploited by the army at this time – namely the Romantic Movement. A Romantic military literature started to appear which maintained a certain continuity with the past, but introduced a new sentimentality of its own. De Vigny was certainly a major figure in the army's self-image, even though not personally a serving officer for long. Although his musings on a new, internalised form of discipline drew heavily upon the existing military thinking of the 1790s, he also added a distinctively modern, wistfully 'poetic' element.[36] This caught on rapidly, not only in the voluminous outpourings connected with the Napoleonic legend, but also in press discussions of the soldier's place. Ambert, writing in the *Sentinelle de l'Armée*, was especially celebrated for his work in this vein. He would typically evoke the suffering and greatness of the simple peasant conscript who withstands the heat and danger of Algeria, yet still finds time to rescue a baby from the village that he has just razed to the ground.[37]

War was even elevated into an artistic thing in itself. Several writers referred to the 'poetic'[38] nature of action, and the exhilaration of playing a violent part in a clearly defined quarrel. At an even more gruesome extreme there was de Molènes' description of a burning village in the Crimea, which he saw entirely in terms of the delicately attractive glow which it added to the quality of the light.[39] This was the great age of military art, no less than the gestation period of the idea that war was a wonderful purifyer of civilisations. As the more sobered generation which had seen the wars of Napoleon receded into the past, its successors could only give their imaginations free play over the great question of what war was really like.

Military writers and the military press

The military press in the early 1820s consisted only of the *Journal Militaire Officiel*, containing notices of new regulations and promotions, and occasional technical compilations such as the *Mémorials* of the Dépôt, the Engineers or the Artillery.[40] In 1824 these were joined by a *Bulletin des Sciences Militaires,* which formed part of a broader enterprise of bibliography intended to cover all academic disciplines, under the direction of the Baron de Férussac – a Staff officer who had become a leading scientist. The military part of it was edited by Koch, and then by Jacquinot de Presle, both of which officers were teaching at military schools.[41] The content, however, consisted almost exclusively of book reviews, and it was not until the next year that Vaudoncourt was able to launch a genuinely discursive magazine, the *Journal des Sciences Militaires*. This included contributions from many liberal officers on half pay and some, such as Vaudoncourt himself, who were quite capable of discussing such matters as the place of war in society with intelligence and knowledge. Direct political comment, on the other hand, was strenuously avoided. There were no editorials as such, and the frustrations of its contributors were hidden by the dry technicality of most of the articles.[42]

With this precedent before them, an 'association of general officers' took the plunge, braved official suspicion of any liberal or critical military journalism, and started an even wider periodical – the ultimately spectacularly prestigious *Spectateur Militaire*.[43] By 1827 this appears to have transcended professional jealousies, and to have won the approval of the minister of war. Contributors included some of the cleverest men in the army, such as Lamarque, Valazé, Marbot, Fririon and Pelet – although by this time none of them had yet risen to positions of real power.[44] They continued to represent something of a fringe group, although certainly less so than had been the case with the original *Journal des Sciences Militaires*. As time went on the *Spectateur* was to gather articles both from well-entrenched generals at the top, and from articulate subalterns at the bottom, of the promotion ladder. Within five years both it and the *Journal des Sciences Militaires* had forgotten their opposition pasts and had become entirely respectable centres of informed military debate.

After the July Revolution there were several new military journals consciously modelled on their Restoration predecessors. The conservative *Revue Militaire*, which experimented with including uniform prints in each copy, lasted less than a year between 1833 and 1834; however the reformist *Journal de l'Armée,* started in 1833, was more successful. In 1836 it was claiming a circulation of 5,659 – although few collective subscriptions – with readers apparently interested in a 'more active defence of military interests'.[45] Since the journal cost twelve francs per annum, it was beyond the pockets of the rank and file. In 1837 it was forced to close. The demand for a combative paper, however, had been made clear. A *Journal de l'Infanterie* failed to take this hint in 1834, and had to close the next year. It was also largely a subalterns' production, including articles by Captain de Tourreau, among others.[46]

These efforts to create a popular military paper were all failures, but there was another in 1835 which succeeded spectacularly. This was the *Sentinelle de l'Armée*, edited by the ultra-royalist Captain Hippolyte de Maudit.[47] It had larger pages than its octavo forerunners, and quickly gained a reputation for liveliness. It picked quarrels with rival papers and successive ministers of war. It revealed alleged abuses in army adminis-tration, and kept a particularly close watch on promotions. It was exactly what many subalterns were looking for, and by 1841 it claimed a circulation of 5,000. Apart from a brief prosecution in 1846 it flourished until the press laws of the Second Republic forced it to close. Many subalterns made their debuts as writers in the pages of the *Sentinelle*, among whom it is particularly worth mentioning Itier, Mussot, Delvigne, Beurmann, Merson, Calais, and Ambert.[48] Most of these were articulate men who nevertheless each had some dispute with authority. It is tempting to think of their readership as not dissimilar, and it was certainly true that official circles frowned on the *Sentinelle*. In 1840 Soult, as minister of war, went as far as to have a rival paper, the *Moniteur de l'Armée*, founded specifically to combat it. The *Sentinelle's* claim to be a non-political paper put it in a category outside the full rigour of the ever-changing press laws, although senior generals were still horrified by its subversive potential. They associated it with the anti-military salvoes of the civilian press – although it was far from that – and tried several times to prevent publication of the names of its contributors.[49]

The *Moniteur de l'Armée* adopted the more popular format of the *Sentinelle*, but devoted every issue to refuting its theses. It gave more sober news of court and ministerial activities, and lost no opportunity of stressing the virtues of the French national character, of obedience and of 'chivalry'. Even the commercial ethos of the July Monarchy was extolled, as containing the risks and calculations of war but without the battles.[50] As a military paper, however, the *Moniteur* felt obliged to agree that literacy was a good thing, although at the same time warning of its abuse. Its dilemma was almost as acute as that of the *Sentinelle* which, while forced by its 'non political' and right-wing attitude to approve of the hierarchy, could not restrain itself from pointing out the peccadilloes of senior officers in practice.

A few other military papers were started before 1848, but being foreign to the contest between the *Sentinelle* and the *Moniteur*, they failed to enter this market, and were rapidly wound up. They attempted to be truly 'non political', but found that this restricted them to a sorry pabulum of 'those old barrack tales which are so charming, and often so naïvely patriotic'.[51] Inferior Bonapartist poetry, turgid memoirs of forgotten skirmishes, and the occasional gaudy uniform plate were all they felt justified in printing, apart from the call for increased literacy that was something of a hallmark of the press in this period. Among papers of this type were *Le Veteran – Journal des Temps Passés* in 1839; *Le Musée Militaire – Journal de la Litterature Militaire* in 1845; and *La France Militaire* in the same year. The last is of interest in that it succeeded in persuading members of the 49th Infantry, at Lyon, to open a co-operative subscription; but its production was so amateurish that it was unable to expand this precedent.[52] Sergeant Boichot's scorn for the military papers written with official approval thus seems to have been generally well deserved.[53]

As for the writers themselves, they were as varied and individual as creative people anywhere. However, we can venture a few generalisations about them by applying a simple statistical analysis to a sample of 352 military writers active between 1815 and 1851.[54]

In 1835 the Infantry provided 61% of the officer corps, but only 54% of the writers began their careers in that arm. The figures for the Cavalry were comparable, with 20% and 17% respectively. The Staff Corps, by contrast, had 5% of the officers but 6% of the writers; the Artillery had 10% of the officers but 13% of the writers; while the Engineers, with only 4% of the officers, provided 10% of the writers.[55] There was thus an important sense in which these last three 'scientific arms', and most notably the Engineers, could claim a disproportionate share of this army's military expertise, over and above the special knowledge essential for their own branches of the service. This was an assumption that had actually been common in the Engineers for many years, but the question now was whether the newly-formed Staff Corps would be able to steal their laurels.

The social class of the writers can be established only for the generals in the sample, where the picture seems to reflect Chalmin's assumptions for the army as a whole.[56] About a third are from property owning families, a third from the '*bourgeoisie d'affaires*', and a third from the '*bourgeoisie des capacités*'. When we look at military origins, however, a clearer indication of the writers' distinction emerges. Whereas in the army as a whole about a quarter of the officers attended a military school, the figure for the writers is 54%. This even excludes some 26% of the writers who had been earmarked to rise rapidly through the ranks during the Revolutionary and Napoleonic era, when attendance at a school was especially rare.[57]

The pattern for the place of birth of military writers was very similar to that for the officer corps as a whole, with disproportionate numbers coming from the North-Eastern frontier and from Paris, and relatively few originating in the centre and West. This pattern further reflects the distribution of literacy in France, which may be the more significant correlation. Possibly surprising is the finding that some 13% of the sample were born outside metropolitan France, of which only a quarter were from French overseas possessions. With the international upheavals of the Napoleonic Empire, however, a considerable influx of foreigners is understandable enough.[58]

One indication of the motives for writing may be found in the rank at which a writer first took up the pen. Table 1 shows the distribution.

Table 1   Rank at which military writers first wrote

| Rank | Military writers | | Officer corps as |
	Number	As % of 352	a whole (as %)
Other ranks	2	0·5	—
Lieutenant/Sous-Lieut.	47	13	55
Captain	90	26	32
Commandant/Lieut-Col.	47	13	7
Colonel	31	9	2
General	128	36	2
Professor or intendant	5	2	2
Unknown	2	0·5	—
Total	352	100	100

There are peaks of writers at the ranks of Captain and General, with a distinct tendency for writers to take up the pen more readily as rank increases. There were doubtless pressures on more senior officers to publicise and explain their views, just as there were even stronger pressures on more junior ranks not to. Representing the extreme case of this, only two 'other ranks' have been included: the famous Boichot and Commissaire, who were elected to the assembly of 1849. A few others could perhaps have been found, and there are several tantalising articles in the military press signed anonymously by *'un sergent'*. On the whole, however, the men did not write.

There does seem to have been a distinct group which wrote from the hope of obtaining recognition and promotion, or in frustration at having been denied it.[19] This was especially true of long-service Captains, although some of them did in fact succeed in winning the promotion they desired. Fifteen per cent of our sample also experienced long periods on half pay during the Restoration, and they too may be classed as 'frustrated' writers. Twenty-eight writers, or 7% of the sample, may be classed as holding 'extreme' political views.

Another group were those who wrote retrospectively, from retirement. Eleven per cent of our sample were already retired when they first wrote, while many of those who wrote from retirement were not writing for the first time. We repeatedly find that they had already been the most prolific theorists before they ever thought of turning to autobiography.

As far as the subject matter of the first writings is concerned, roughly a third dealt with general questions of military policy, of the type that might be discussed in Parliament. A third of the writing consisted of history, memoirs or moral exhortations designed to help in training or regimental cohesion. Finally, a third dealt with technical aspects, of which about half were scientific and half related to strategy and tactics. If we are looking for abstract theories of war, therefore, it is only within that final sixth of the total production that we should search – although of course underlying theories would often inspire the other forms of writing. and , indeed, action. In the next chapter we will turn to examine this aspect, and consider just how theory was supposed to be translated into practice.

4

The impact of military thought

An art or a science of war?

Despite his later failures, the great example of Napoleon was present in everyone's mind after 1815 as a reminder simultaneously of the importance of generalship in modern war, and of the high qualities – even genius – which a general needed to possess. High command in war was for the French still essentially a personal, intuitive matter, with headquarter staffs still no more than consultative and secretarial. More modern or 'scientific' staff institutions had not yet been developed as far as in Prussia, although the Staff Corps, under Guilleminot and later Pelet, was constantly pressing for reforms in this direction.[1]

It was only too easy for opponents of 'the staff idea' to point out that the Prussians had usually been worsted in their encounters with Napoleon, and that a small manoeuvre army of the modern French type was naturally more responsive to inspired personal leadership than a shambling mass army of *Landwehr*.[2] If national mobilisations were starting to require rather more advance planning than they had in the past, that could still be handled by the officials and temporary committees in the Ministry: it did not require a permanent General Staff to make elaborate, pedantic and rigid contingency plans in peacetime. By the same token, when it came to manoeuvres before the enemy the French could dispense with the unwieldy Army Corps and return to the earlier, and lighter, Division as the essential self-contained all arms formation.[3]

The general's personal qualities were still felt to be of paramount importance, and this perception was by no means dimmed by the highly individualistic campaigns in Algeria. However there was also a feeling that modern battles were spreading over a wider area of country than in the past, so the general would need to increase his means of supervision and control.[4] He had to be able to direct every part of his machine, looking both upwards to the higher political context and downwards to his men's morale and welfare. He had to possess an expert understanding of the terrain, the enemy, the logistics and the tactics. As each of these skills began to accumulate a growing body of 'scientific' analysis, furthermore, there was a correspondingly growing feeling that the art of generalship itself might constitute a 'higher science', or even a 'philosophy',[5] superior to any other. A good general was therefore believed to be *ex officio* something of an intellectual giant.

This was the starting point for any debate in France about generalship. The point was normally missed that any system which depended upon the individual quality of its leaders was by that very fact inevitably more chancy than the collective and collaborative Prussian system. Hence the French placed perhaps excessive reliance on the personal qualities of the *Grand Chef*, and the way he happened to turn out on the day of battle, while the Prussians seemed to be less insistent that each individual commander should necessarily be a paragon of genius. Although 'The German Schoolmaster' of 1870 may or may not have been superior to the French *Instituteur*, he ultimately enjoyed the enormous advantage that he was being asked to provide a less exceptional or original product. His aim was competence and teamwork rather than unorthodoxy and personal *flair*.[6]

However this may be, in France the question tended to be focused less upon the techniques of staffwork than on those by which generals might be taught their job. The educational system was certainly highly élitist, although doubtless less unorthodox than it was ideally intended to be. We will return to it in due course. To supplement it, however, there was also a considerable production of handbooks for the senior commander. For example a number of books analysed the battle speeches of great men – especially those as recounted by Thucydides – with a view to assisting the 'electrification' of French soldiers by means of similar rhetorical devices.[7] In an age before technological change became rapid, a large part of successful leadership was held to depend on such things.

The problem with more analytical works on the art of war, however, was the question of how far they were really useful. Officers inevitably suffered from a gut feeling, common among men of action and of 'honour', that it was better to fall back on common sense, the lessons of experience and the traditions of the service than upon some abstract and paradoxical intellectual construct.[8] Nor need we necessarily disagree with them. All too many military theorists through the ages, from Caesar through Jomini to Liddell Hart, have shown undue haste in claiming the credit for victories that were actually won by other officers. Conversely there are all too many writers, from the itinerant Chinese strategists in the age of Sun Tzu,[9] through de Grandmaison's believers in *l'attaque à outrance*, to the MacNamara school of graduated deterrence, who have been cited as convenient scapegoats for generals defeated in the field. One may be forgiven for suspecting that the relationship between written theory and combat practice is often more complex than this, and even tenuous – existing more in the minds of self-serving polemicists than it does in operational practice.[10]

The 'key texts' that commanders take with them into battle often turn out to be maps and intelligence reports rather than volumes of doctrinal analysis, just as the writers with most influence often turn out to be playwrights, novelists and journalists rather than scientists specialising in the art of war. There is indeed a certain sense in which 'military theories' are naturally doomed to irrelevance in any army – and perhaps this is doubly true of the French, where discussion is both so free and so frequent that every proposition is no sooner uttered than it is immediately contradicted.

Many French soldiers maintained that war was an art to be learned only by experience, and reacted strongly against the eighteenth century's penchant for geometrical 'rules'.[11] Even some of the notoriously mathematical writers on the science of fortification were involved in this salutary reaction, and the Chevalier Allent, for example, was at pains to stress such things as the unpredictability of accidents in the terrain.[12] At this time there was also some doubt about exactly what constituted a 'science' even among the leading civilian scientists themselves so, since these were often the same men as taught at the École Polytechnique, the army may not have been entirely oblivious to their doubts.[13]

The École Polytechnique itself was nevertheless firmly rooted in scientific method and the physics of Laplace. It was anxious to find 'laws' where a layman might see only chaos. Because its products were destined to become the leaders of the 'technical arms', and hence of all 'military science', this ethos was a matter of considerable importance to the way that the army as a whole would look at its strategy and tactics.

Polytechnicians could agree that in combat it should be a general's 'scientific' aim to achieve a numerical superiority over the enemy at the key point. This very obvious idea was popularised by Jomini and his school, and was hailed in many quarters as a brilliant insight, equivalent in its way to Frederick's equally straightforward concept of the 'oblique attack' half a century earlier.[14] A number of writers therefore set out to codify the ways and means by which a decisive concentration might be made, and from there it was but a short step to regarding strategy and tactics as sciences in the full sense.

It was an approach that could easily be abused. Favé's *Histoire de la Tactique des Trois Armes*, for example, entered into an exceptionally pedantic discussion of all the possible results of combats between various combinations of horse, foot and gun. It succeeded in creating a lifeless taxonomy of possible battles, but scarcely gave generals the useful guide to judgment that they needed. Paradoxically it was more this type of over-scientific approach, if anything, rather than any lack of science, that helped to prevent the French from agreeing upon a theory of war.[15]

Rather more useful, perhaps, was the concept of probability that had been present in Pascal's work, but which was now given a new lease of life by Laplace.[16] Several soldiers took this as a cue to look at the theory of risk in warfare, and how it might help a general to make decisions.[17] There was a widespread assumption that probabilities could be estimated with reasonable accuracy, although in default of a real science of operational research no one could cite such mathematically precise examples as we have seen since 1939. As the Engineer Captain Lenglet put it in 1826, in relation to the selection of candidates for promotion,

However much care one may put into appreciating the knowledge and moral qualities of each man, the very nature of these aspects means that we cannot hope for a rigorous exactitude; but we should at least try to avoid the avoidable errors, by submitting to calculation as much of these things as it is possible to obtain. What the geometer LAPLACE has to say about the enormity of the errors that are habitually commited in the estimation of probabilities applies equally to every other un-calculated evaluation, where errors in the initial data are complicated by those committed in the deduction of their consequences.[18]

Somewhat less scientific were the combat veterans who preferred practical 'rules of thumb' to logical systems of strategy and tactics. They pointed out, for example, that a doctrine which required subordinate commanders to 'march to the sound of the guns' had proved to be invaluable in war – and there were a hundred other contingencies which might be similarly covered.[19] If only it could have been compiled systematically, a code of such rules might have ensured uniformity of action throughout the army, and might have given commanders a solid framework upon which to base their individual manoeuvres. The attempt to create such a code, however, was a failure. The higher war school or 'military university' which was needed to mould it was widely discussed but never established. Generals continued to lay down their own personal guidelines at the start of each campaign – implicitly refusing to recognise any unified doctrine of action for the army as a whole. All they saw in the art of war was merely an 'infinite number of notions'.[20]

A few psychological principles could be agreed, such as the moral value of surprise; but in general it was recognised that the truly scientific parts of war were no more than subordinate details. The general would still need personal *coup d'oeil* and experience to combine them felicitously. Each situation would be in some way unique, so it was futile to try to legislate for all of them. This philosophy of generalship lay behind the oft-repeated but only marginally helpful slogan that 'everything depends on the nature of the ground and the state of the weather'.[21]

Towards 1850 a somewhat greater urgency in isolating 'principles of war' became apparent, including somewhat less positive aspects than had been detailed before. Morale was being increasingly emphasised, under the influence of the Romantic Movement, although it had not yet attained anything approaching the prominence it was to be given later in the century. Military history was also enjoying a greater popularity than ever, partly because its study had been recommended by many of the great captains including Napoleon himself.[22] The would-be general was expected to unravel his own principles of war from a thoughtful familiarity with the classic campaigns. It was felt that guidelines derived from internalised study of this type would be more valuable than lists of maxims designed to be learned by rote. There were several schemes to make systematic anthologies of Napoleonic memoirs as aids to analysis, but in the event it was never done. The organisation best placed to do it, the Dépôt de la Guerre, preferred to apply its historiographical resources to regimental histories for building morale, and legal research for administrative purposes.[23]

The regimental libraries intended for officers were certainly intended to contain 'classics', especially those which were relevant to the art of war. They were to cover a fairly standard course of military history and theory, from Caesar, Polybius and Vegetius up to the present, and several schemes to extend their scope into more general realms were not pursued. Doisy's rather academic discussion of the science of bibliography, for example, does not seem to have been followed up, while Durand's total rejection of military science could easily be dismissed.[24] Bossuet was widely read, and Pagezy de Bourdéliac's stress on the moral and analytical advantages of studying general history came nearer to official thinking;

but even his proposal was annotated 'impractical' by someone in the ministry of war.[25] History continued, on the whole, to be seen in terms of military history.

Those subalterns who had attended a military school had supposedly received two or more years' training in the basic sciences of modern warfare, but when they joined their regiments they found little formal provision for any expansion of their studies. The great majority of officers who rose directly from the ranks had to make do with a much narrower professional background. Once an officer joined his regiment, the demands on his brain were essentially a matter of mastering the regulations for drill and service. If he wished to study higher strategy he would have to do it in his own time. Inspectors certainly encouraged this, but it was only in 1845 that regiments were formally told to hold regular officer discussion groups on military subjects, and even these failed to become widespread until well into the Second Empire. They frequently took a form barely distinguishable from routine tests on the minutiae of the regulations, and embraced wider horizons only if the colonel was especially interested.[26]

To make good this deficiency inspectors would repeat vague injunctions to 'look at the tactical possibilities of the ground' on route marches, or just to 'make good use of spare time'. The best men were certainly moved to interview veterans of Napoleon's campaigns, or to follow that master's delphic advice to 'extract the general principles' out of military history.[27] Promotion, however, was known to be related less to one's grasp of Jomini than to Préval's interior service, with many officers gaining their ideas about higher theory only from the garish pages of Ambert, or partworks like Liskenne and Sauvan, or the 'Victories and Conquests of the French'.[28]

The type of subaltern who hoped to rise through his intellectualism would tend to be prominent in the pages of military journals and active in regimental schools, but less well endowed with leadership qualities and correspondingly less well viewed by inspectors. Frustrated in their hopes for advancement, such intellectual subalterns would only redouble their appeals for promotion to be linked to education and professional knowledge.[29] For colonels and inspectors, however, promotion by examination seemed to promise results which would be too risky because too 'unsupervised' – or in other words no longer within their own personal control.[30] Nor could it take account of precisely those qualities of honour, courage and personal 'presence' through which the army was held together.

Exercises

If there was widespread agreement that would-be generals could learn much from books, there was also an awareness that military theories could be tested and practised through large unit exercises. Such exercises took place on a huge scale in Germany and Russia, which gave added ammunition to those who wanted the French to do the same. A series of camps was eventually started in the late Restoration,[31] although their general value in cementing 'military virtue' was often esteemed more highly than their use as a training ground for generals.[32] They also inevitably placed more emphasis on drilling within the regiment, which was a basic precondition for higher manoeuvres, than they did on the higher manoeuvres themselves.[33]

There were classically two possible points of view on large unit exercises. On one hand there were earnest young critics in the military press who deplored the fact that manoeuvres were agreed in advance or, when two generals did come to manoeuvre freely against each other, that there was a certain lack of realistic battlefield conditions. Such critics were sensitive to defects in the French system, and often fell into the class of 'frustrated subalterns' that was eternally critical of the high command and yet so avidly heeded in the post-mortem after Sedan.[34]

Other commentators went further still, and claimed that true realism could be attained only in real wars, notably in the Algerian campaigns with which the French were so familiar. This critique would also dismiss the German and Russian training camps as no more than 'monster serenades' and 'painted wars',[35] or in other words giving no particular advantage over the French.

Probably the truth lay somewhere between these two opposed points of view, and the French drew more value from their training camps than their critics would allow. There was certainly a growing use of large units during the period with which we are concerned, of which perhaps the most interesting was the Marne camp of 1842. This was planned by the Duke of Orleans, with the rather reluctant co-operation of Soult, as a full blown exercise in *'la belle et bonne stratégie de guerre'*.[36] The idea was for three large formations to assemble at Troyes after marching under war conditions from muster points at St Omer and Lunéville. Two weeks would then be spent in 'free' strategic manoeuvering over a much wider area than had previously been used for such camps, with two regiments acting as markers for the supposed 'enemy'. Alas, the Duke was killed at the moment these ambitious plans were about to be executed, and the troops were diverted to his state funeral in Paris instead. Nevertheless he had laid the blueprint, and exercises along similar lines – albeit on a smaller scale – were actually held in 1844 and 1847.[37]

There were also large-unit tactical camps almost every year, each at around Divisional strength. They might be used to test some new system of drill, to bring troops to a high standard of campaigning proficiency, or to familiarise them with the specific techniques of siegework. At St Omer a complete face of a fortress was specially constructed for this last purpose, while Castellane at Perpignan and Aymard at Lyon used the actual fortresses for their mock sieges. Still bigger sieges had been held at Metz since the previous century, and were seen by resident engineers and gunners as the high point of their training year. The use of umpires in exercises of this sort was also introduced from Germany during the July Monarchy, and must have done much to rid the operations of their earlier formalism and predictability. It is certainly false to suppose that in the matter of training exercises for generals the French were particularly backward.

In map exercises the Germans do appear to have been more advanced than the French, and sponsored several war games for subalterns which failed to make an impact in France either in direct translation or through local variants.[38] This was perhaps due partly to the differing demands of a peaceful and untroubled North German plain on one side, where the lack of real battles made imaginary ones a training necessity; and a troubled, combative Mediterranean land on the other, where there was more than enough real combat to go round. It was also partly due to the excessively stylised nature of the early war games, which were centrally based on Chess, combined with the tactical – as opposed to strategic – focus of the more realistic later games. In an age when would-be generals were being told that strategy was a new and exciting science, while tactics were routine and unchanging, this may have deterred all but the obsessively determined.

Inspectors did at least insist that subalterns should know something about field fortifications and topography, holding annual tests in each regiment for basic skills, and an army competition for sketch maps and 'reconnaissances'. There were far more entrants for these competitions than there were published authors in the military press, so it must have been quite a widespread activity. The body of the entries, in fact, forms the only large-scale, standardised piece of military work coming down to us from that level in the hierarchy, and the views of the Infantry Committee upon it afford us an interesting view of the professional capacity of French cadres at that time.[39]

It would seem that very few of the writers of reconnaissances took account of the higher problems of strategy, or of the co-ordination of 'little war' into a greater whole. To this extent the criticism that the army was too 'regimental' would seem to be justified, although it was also credibly argued that subalterns had little need of the higher knowledge more appropriate to colonels.[40]

Another criticism made by the Infantry Committee was that the reconnaissances showed more imagination than solid topography and statistics, and one report even gave a detailed casualty list from an imagined battle on the terrain surveyed.[41] If this reveals a background of fantasy in officer training it is perhaps a serious criticism; but if it is considered merely as a zealous desire to explain the probabilities of the case under study, it can surely be seen as laudable. More important, perhaps, was the general feeling that the standard of topography was low. Out of 1,846 entrants in 1841 only 39 gave 'satisfaction' while 174 'merited encouragement'. By 1850 there were only 702 entrants but a higher standard, with 46 giving satisfaction and 178 meriting encouragement.[42] The motives behind this type of work, however, were not as pure as they might have been. The hope of catching the inspector's eye was never far away, and in 1841 the Twenty-First Line seems to have received a rumour that immediate promotion would come automatically to anyone who submitted a reconnaissance. No less than fifty were executed in the regiment, and when the expected promotion failed to materialise there was considerable discontent.[43]

Ultimately the would-be general tended to be left very much to his own private reading and reflection. He was still seen as an individual possessing high personal qualities, rather than a standardised product of the – still very controversial – Staff Corps. On the other hand the general was undoubtedly considered to be an extremely important figure, and it would be misleading to suppose that only scant attention was paid to his duties.[44] It was repeatedly stressed that his willpower was of paramount importance to a campaign, just as it was stressed that he was supposed to be a master of an increasing bulk of literature. In this atmosphere the lack of a rigid science of war – a science which was in any event impossible to formulate – cannot have affected the army's efficiency nearly as much as has sometimes been assumed. Indeed, one might speculate that the constant political and military upsets suffered by the French high command in this period must surely have made it less complacent than that of any other nation.

Sources of invention

If there were some doubts about the existence of a science *of* war, there
was at least a widespread enthusiasm for the use of science *in* war, and this
included pseudo-sciences like gymnastics or fieldcraft alongside genuine
sciences such as metallurgy or ballistics. This was an age in which the twin
ideas of Science and Progress were high in everyone's mind – an age in
which the foundations were laid for stupendous achievements in military
technology during the second half of the century.

From whence did this scientific movement spring? It certainly owed
much to international civilian advances in physics, chemistry and
engineering; but in its specifically military guise it at first relied heavily
upon a few semi-amateur enthusiasts who were either members of the
army or closely allied to it. These men belonged to a wider class of what
we may call the 'military inventors' of their age – a diverse and varied
group which saw few successes but many failures: few technological
breakthoughs but many quixotic or impractical schemes.

The 'small but good' French army perhaps felt itself especially
dependent upon the type of 'combat multiplier' that inventors could
provide, just as the French navy – faced by an overwhelming British
superiority in traditional capital ships – was forever on the lookout for
new ways round. There was thus a significant demand for the many new
ideas being thrown up by the Industrial Revolution, although at the same
time a major opening was also created for some rather wilder ideas that
had little truly scientific content. A rocket army, a steam gun army and a
heavy artillery army were all recommended at different times by the
technically-minded, as panacea solutions to France's military problem.
They took their place beside other schemes for irregular light infantry
armies, light cavalry or 'Cossack' armies, civilian assassin armies and even
balloon armies.[45] Each of these ideas had some sort of Napoleonic
precedent to which their authors could appeal, and each of them was
symptomatic of an advanced country with a small army that felt itself
surrounded by larger but less civilised neighbours.

In the crisis of 1830–33 the Bureau of Military Operations put together
a collection of all the inventions and related proposals that were
submitted to it during that time.[46] An analysis of these can give us a
revealing cross-section of the pattern of invention during these years (See
Table 2). Predictably it is the soldiers who were most likely to propose
a light infantry or other type of unit, while artisans were more interested
in machinery. At least one aeroplane was proposed, and several tanks,

although such ideas often received scant appreciation from the bureaucrats who had to assess them. For example one project was annotated as
follows: 'Monsieur Guillin's memoir is the work of an uneducated man: it
contains many ideas which are either bizarre or impossible to execute; in a
word this former officer is clearly anxious for employment . . . '[47]

Table 2 Authorship of projects, 1830–33

Subject of project	Author's origins:					Total
	Active army	Non-active army	Other military	'Grande bourgeoisie'	Artisan	
Machines/ arms:	5	3	1	0	9	18
Manoeuvres/ tactics:	6	8	1	1	3	19
Organisation/ Free Corps:	12	9	3	4	3	31
Various:	4	8	2	3	5	22
Total	27	28	7	8	20	90

With inventors as with strategists, it proved impossible to call upon
innovative, world-beating quality without simultaneously summoning
forth a whole undergrowth of peripheral yet colourful figures. As in most
countries and in most eras, there could be no 'great names' without a
widespread background debate between smaller men. The French were
by no means short of world-beating names, however, ranging from Haxo
the influential engineer to Lamoricière the inventor and populariser of
the Zouaves. Major Itier reformed cavalry drill and based his promotion
upon it, while La Motte Rouge was one of the influential group of
designers of new systems for bayonet fencing.[48]

Lieutenant Delvigne of the Restoration Foot Guards, who had risen
from the ranks but who had to resign in the July Revolution, led the way
in rifled small arms and wrote extensively about them after 1830.[49]
Colonel Combes then took up his mantle and demonstrated an advanced
rampart rifle in the Antwerp siege, and later in Algeria. Especially after a
reproof from Bugeaud on the Sikkak in 1836, he went on to become a
champion of the many suggestions then current about light infantry and

the gymnastic pace, and was recognised as an important forerunner of the *Chasseurs à Pied.* [50]

From 1838 onwards the Chasseurs became one of the vital centres of military invention. Because they were able to detach many aspects of musketry science from the heavy gun Artillery, and many aspects of light infantry training from the heavy Infantry,[51] the Chasseurs were able to perfect and blend both skills together in a way that had not previously been seen. They established shooting schools and a rifle workshop, together with an innovative drill manual and a *cadre* of resourceful young officers. Among the latter were the noted rifle designers Captain Tamisier and – once his grievance against the plagiarist General Garraube had been recognised in 1840 – Lieutenant Delvigne once more. Most important of all, perhaps, was Chef de Bataillon C. E. Minié – the inventor of the revolutionary hollow-base bullet which was finally to place an accurate long range rifle in the hands of every soldier in every nation.[52]

The Chasseurs were also centrally interested in the nascent science of gymnastics, following the spectacular lead given by the Spanish martinet, Colonel-Professor Amoros. Beyond this, also, the Chasseurs drew upon a long tradition by which half-pay officers or frustrated subalterns would devise ingenious schemes for light infantry, guerrilla or counter-guerrilla units – units which their authors would then promptly volunteer to lead. At least one such proposal even went as far as to recommend the entire list of officers whom the author would eventually wish to employ.[53] No less a figure than Bugeaud himself tried to attract the minister's attention in a very similar way around 1830.

Schemes for this type of unit were particularly popular because they seemed to offer the maximum number of promotion posts for the minimum outlay in capital or technology. They were seen as somewhat 'anti-establishment', looking back to late eighteenth-century speculations which called for internalised discipline, local knowledge, physical training and advanced fieldcraft.[54] Green coats and double-barrelled 'buck and ball' muskets were also popular, as symbols of a deliberate rejection of formal or gentlemanly tactics – and indeed the Chasseurs prided themselves on their unorthodoxy to almost the same extent as many of the other inventors were notorious for it. This movement was to reach its highest peak of fame and achievement in the work of the former Chasseur Ardant du Picq, during the Second Empire.

Outside the Chasseurs, more strictly technological inventions were widely encouraged in the Artillery. Captain Montgéry was a keen student of rockets and steamships, while the prolific and liberal General Paixhans made a name for himself as a champion of giant mortars. Like many another military intellectual, however, Paixhans seems to have surprised his superiors by his unusual hobby, and was noted in his dossier for being far happier when immersed in it than when he was actually commanding troops.[55]

Perhaps inevitably, the Committee of the Artillery found itself too closely tied to the status quo to develop these ideas fruitfully. Quite apart from the moral issues which some soldiers still felt were raised by new weapons,[56] the Committee felt bound by its mandate to undertake routine administration, and obvious technical improvements of details, before it made any leaps into the dark. Thus in the Restoration there was a heated controversy over the relatively unimportant question of redesigning the standard gun carriages and caissons. The Artillery Committee found itself holding the ring between the normally reserved General Valée,[57] who wanted a design modelled closely on British patterns, and the prolific liberal half pay officer Allix, who was testing a different type. In 1827 the decision finally went in favour of Valée, who was politically 'safer' than Allix, but not before the work of the Committee and the Artillery factories had been disrupted for several years.

The start of the war in Algeria then concentrated attention on mule-portable mountain guns, after which the manufacturing effort was diverted to converting the army's muskets to percussion priming.[58] Finally in 1840 the fortifications of Paris required a large number of new iron cannon – which in turn demanded a research programme to find a suitable alloy.[59] All this left little spare capacity for more radical innovation, and the dreamers were usually placated by being given the use of test ranges and perhaps the occasional Commission to judge the results.

There was at least little reluctance to give leave of absence to would-be researchers, although the ex-gunner Ducastel did believe his experiments were inadequately supported. Against this we have Paixhans' repeated leaves, while the engineer officer Victor Considérant was actually given a grant to pursue his subversive socialist researches for four years.[60] The artillery officer LeChevalier was released to conduct experiments on the best stick length for rockets at the navy's 'rocket workshop' at Toulon, and the Marquis d'Espinay, another amateur rocketeer, was accommodated at the St Etienne artillery range in 1823 – although in the event he failed to turn up.[61] Gunnery manuals started to include extra chapters on rocketry, but little more was done than that.

In the field of small arms, Marmont was already testing a fine breech loading rifle in 1815, but it failed due to financial stringency and the opposition of the Artillery.[62] A similar Belgian pattern was rejected in 1830 as too fragile, as were some subsequent commercial patterns. Equally a metal cartridge, which might have done much to assist breech loading, was rejected in 1842. Far more positive in their effects were the innovations in projectile and chamber design that were developed by artillery officers who almost seemed to believe themselves in competition with the Chasseurs. Thiéry, Thouvenin, Thiroux and Piobert each made valuable contributions in this field, the last two as professors at St Cyr and Metz respectively.[63]

Research into traditional ballistics was continued under the Artillery Committee on the Metz ranges, sometimes in co-operation with the professors of the Metz artillery school. The various artillery regimental schools also conducted research, while some of the experimental devices were manufactured at the precision workshop which had been attached to the central 'Artillery Dépôt' in Paris since 1794. In addition, a School of Military Pyrotechnology was opened in 1824 inside the regimental school at Metz.[64] Nor were creative imaginations in short supply elsewhere. The technical journals were full of ideas such as Michaloz's successively fused grapeshot, Favé and Louis Napoleon's compact howitzers, or Thuillier's camouflaged countermines.[65]

One other centre for research was the *Dépôt de la Guerre*, where the Staff Corps was centred and where the army kept its maps, intelligence reports and historical records. The *Dépôt* was directed by the head of the Geographical Engineers, and annually sent out cartographers to work on the great 1:50,000 map of France that took forty years to complete.[66] From 1828 onwards the *Dépôt* also established a 'statistical' section for the systematic collection of information on foreign armies; and it intermittently published a *Mémorial* with articles on scientific and topographical subjects. These included, for example, experiments with such essential staff equipment as telegraph systems or field duplicating machines.[67] Equally after 1846 it was a Staff Corps officer, Captain Coynart, who made several perceptive studies of the use of railways in war, including troop-carrying capacity and loading times. Despite some excessively dire warnings against boiler explosions, this was a most necessary piece of work, which was supported by some practical tests.[68]

If the Staff Corps brought a different perspective to its researches from the Artillery, it seemed to suffer from a somewhat similar failure to develop them. In part this was caused by a contemporary attitude to 'the method of making inventions' which placed the categorisation of information ahead of its practical exploitation.[69] In part, however, it sprang from the *Dépôt's* traditional role as just a centre for Topography; a role which was reinforced when the Geographical Engineers were formally incorporated into the Staff Corps in 1831. The increasingly broad sweep of modern campaigns further reinforced the need for maps, as did the progress currently being made in civilian cartography.[70] To take one example, the standard method of portraying relief underwent a major change at this time, with several different systems being put forward. General Dode's commission of 1826 eventually decided in favour of the hachuring advocated by Haxo and the engineers of the Metz school, over the 'magical effect' of the shading advocated by the geographical engineer Colonel Puissant.[71]

Its mastery of the new sciences associated with this field at least lent the *Dépôt* a technical prestige which it felt was equivalent to the metallurgical and ballistic skills of the gunners. Such a narrow concentration on one particular aspect was unfortunate, however, since it was one more pressure which helped to leave the French Staff with a less general role than that of the Prussians.[72]

Part 3

Military thought within the regiment

5

Regimental life

The essential military world-view

After their own chances of promotion and the rigours of the occasional campaign, the military issues of greatest importance to most officers were those raised by daily life and training inside the regiment. Questions of man management, health, education, discipline and minor tactics seemed to cover much of the army's activity, and profoundly shaped both its language and its very identity. These questions permeated every part of the military debate, and led to a distinctive view of the world which marked out French officers not merely from civilians, but also from the officers of the other major armies. A characteristic set of values was forged in these years which was to remain essentially unchanged for much of the following century.[1]

The way the French approached these matters was moulded by the paradox inherent in their 'national professional' army itself – with its curious amalgam of liberalism with reaction, and social vision with rigid hierarchy. The army of the restored Bourbons could not return to the 'dehumanising' form it had known in the *Ancien Régime* ; but neither could it fully embrace the progressive and democratic achievements of the new age. Instead, it had to display that particular 'spirit of regularity and order'[2] which was embodied in the idea of constitutional monarchy and expressed in the Charters of 1814 and 1815. In Morand's phrase the army had to be 'in conformity with the Charter'.[3] It was therefore no accident that one of the first names to be mentioned after Waterloo was that of Guibert, the pedantic late eighteenth-century drill master who nevertheless looked forward to revolutionary progress. [4] In its search for a new formula for man management, the army felt it could draw inspiration from Guibert's special mixture of patriotic liberalism with technical precision, or what in Britain was to become known as 'Sir John Moore's System of Training'.[5]

The problem was defined as a matter of fostering 'Military Spirit' while removing 'Discouragement': of suppressing subversion and disease while overcoming 'the idleness of garrison life'.[6] All this amounted to a very wide-ranging requirement which could not be solved by purely administrative measures. Instead, there was a need for a new ideology – and even a new vocabulary – whereby liveliness, personal initiative and fun could be delicately mixed in with some strict rules of obedience, personal efficiency and loyalty.

According to the formula that finally emerged, a deadening attention to the minutiae of the regulations would be eschewed as 'Petty Corporalism', just as a system of 'Passive Obedience' would make men into 'Mere Automata'[7] on the 'German' model. Much more 'French' was the sort of 'Civilising' and 'Humane' approach which tried to 'Understand the Passions'[8] of the soldier and instil in him an internalised form of discipline. The soldier would thus ideally be an 'Intelligent Bayonet' who inhabited a 'Regimental Family' policed by a 'Firm but Paternal' discipline from above, and by mutual 'Surveillance' from below. He would act out of patriotism and personal enlightenment rather than fear or brutality, but would restrain his individualism short of slovenliness or 'Slackness' (*laisser aller*).[9] He was a friend to all his 'Comrades' and fellow citizens – apart from a minority of subversives or public women who frequented the towns, and especially the cafés. He was particularly fond of children and dogs,[10] and would bear any hardship with 'Resignation', 'Gaiety' and even 'Gracefulness'. Honour and 'Emulation' were essential motors to his behaviour at all times.

One noticeable feature of this new French military ethic, as perhaps of every other through the ages, was its readiness to link together every conceivable type of threat, no matter how diverse, as part of a single identified 'enemy'. In rather the same way as a Nazi might have viewed Jews, Freemasons, Gypsies, Communists and Bankers as all somehow mystically the same, so the French army of the Constitutional Monarchies often seemed ready to regard Wine, Women, Socialists, Arab Snipers, Prussian Shell Fire and Cultural Anomie as essentially indistinguishable phenomena. Each of them threatened to undermine the army's cohesion, health and morale. Each of them increased the perceived dangers to a profession which knew it always had to live with danger, and which often felt itself to be embattled and besieged.[11]

In fields as dissimilar as hygiene, politics, mental health, discipline, and minor tactics, officers fused the conventional wisdom of the day with specifically military considerations to create their own moral code for the preservation of the army.[12] Reinforced by this code, they would find ready answers for almost any problem that might arise, because everything seemed to be connected. It was, for example, surely no coincidence that the words for 'morals' and 'morale' were the same, to the extent that 'The soldier's morality is linked so closely to his discipline . . . that it is impossible to neglect the one without compromising the other.'[13]

Oilskin capes would be recommended as much to forestall grumbling as to repel the diseases attendant upon dampness.[14] Alcoholic soldiers were condemned as much for the political ideas of their companions as for their physiological symptoms,[15] and it is noteworthy that while much has been made of the men sent to Algeria for their political extremism, their numbers were more than matched by those sent abroad for their drinking. Even the use of light infantry skirmishers in battle would be recommended in moral-patriotic terms – as 'The formation most suited to French intelligence and agility', or some such – rather than as simply a device to minimise casualties. It was in this sort of way that the many connected ideas of the officer corps merged into each other, and the various aspects of the army's health and welfare became simultaneously illuminated and confused within a single ideology. 'Every religion', as the *Moniteur de l' Armée* remarked on 3rd October 1841, 'was similarly created with both a useful and social objective.'

The welfare, hygiene and education of conscripts – as opposed to volunteers – was seen as a particular duty that was now incumbent upon the state.[16] Young men whom the law had dragged from their families had a right to expect the advantages and moral guidance of family life when they arrived at their regiments. As the inspector Meynadier put it,

If our duty is to instruct our soldiers in peacetime and to guide them in war, we should also look after them constantly, prevent them from being corrupted, so that when they return to their families – which have entrusted them to us – they do not dishonour the army by pernicious habits that they may have been allowed to contract in it.[17]

Officers met this need by casting their net far wider than previously into the social and educational theories of their age, adopting many ideas that had been considered revolutionary thirty years earlier. Primary schools were opened in all regiments; gymnastics, swimming, skirmishing, fencing and even dancing were taught for the first time, while increased attention was paid to hygiene. There was a penal reform movement, an officers' cartography movement and a community singing movement. The Infantry was given courses in engineering and gunnery, and its dress was radically modernised.

Each of these innovations generated its own miniature debate, but a recurrent theme common to all of them was the debilitating effect of idleness – with which the peacetime army was plentifully endowed – upon soldiers. It was argued that unless the men were kept fully occupied, they would find some activity which undermined either their health or their combat-preparedness. At the end of his recommendations to the 18th Line in 1833, for example, General Jamin concluded that 'One cannot apply oneself too much to preventing the soldier from being left in inactivity',[18] just as Canrobert said that 'The fire of the most terrible battles, the hardest fatigues under the most murderous climates, destroy an army less quickly than idleness and indiscipline.'[19]

It almost seemed that in an army which prided itself on its professionalism, the fact of doing something was more important than what was actually done – and certainly in the crisis of 1830 the first reaction of many colonels was to intensify the Sisyphian round of drills and parades, even though the troops were perfectly trained already.[20] Activity was therefore seen as an antidote not only to mental, venereal and alcoholic diseases, but also to political ones.

Activity was certainly the best cure for the homesickness and apathy, known as 'Nostalgia', to which many young conscripts were vulnerable. The shock of army life could lead the innocent soldier into '. . . sad reflections; the moral and the physical react on each other; the result is a discouragement, a boredom, a morosity which makes him forget the advantages of the military state and see only its annoyances; he becomes malcontent, argumentative, mutinous; punishments only harden his already altered character. . . .'[21]

In its still more dangerous second stage, Nostalgia could become a physical disease: '. . . a slow fever soon invades the afflicted unit. Apathy and langour penetrate every rank. Soldiers who fall into this state of inertia become indifferent to the approach of danger and the insults of the enemy; sometimes they even hail him as a liberator.'[22]

Alcoholism or the rather curious form of indiscipline known as 'musket smashing' might also follow, and these contributed the greatest proportion of serious offences in the army.[23] The average regiment also had around two hundred venereal cases per year, so it was scarcely an accident that inspection reports would habitually assess each garrison for its availability of girls and drink before descending to more military considerations.[24]

Officers were agreed that humane discipline, physical welfare and the creation of leisure activities were the solution to the problems of garrison life, although the degree of importance attached to each of these aspects varied widely. General Trézel believed that they were all absolutely fundamental, rather than merely auxiliary;[25] but others were suspicious that 'Reasoned Obedience', and even 'Education' itself, might be alternative names for licensed insubordination.[26]

Infantry inspectors and regimental cadres

Every regiment was visited annually by an inspector for up to a fortnight, during which time he would make an assessment of its military qualities and recommend certain changes that accorded with general policy. The resulting inspection reports – for which a complete series exists between 1831 and 1845 – can therefore give us a unique window into both what was actually going on within regiments, and what the most closely concerned generals believed *ought* to be going on. For this purpose the Infantry can perhaps offer us the most useful example, since it was the numerically biggest arm, and also the least encumbered by technicalities. It is upon the Infantry, therefore, that we will concentrate our attention.[27]

Inspections usually took place in the autumn at the end of the year's training cycle, and in some cases after a summer manoeuvre camp. They were conducted by either an itinerant inspector attached to one or more military areas, or by the regular commander of each area. Thus Harispe, who commanded the Army of the Pyrenees for most of the July Monarchy, was responsible for inspecting his own troops, whereas in areas of greater dispersion, such as central France, a prominent Divisional general might be sent round specially from Paris. In addition there were sometimes smaller spring inspections by the Brigade generals attached to each of the twenty-two military areas, and in times of crisis such as 1831 these might be made even more frequently.[28]

After their inspections, the generals would foregather in Paris to draw up the year's seniority lists and make recommendations for promotion to the minister. After that, a 'rump' of the meeting continued to sit as the 'Infantry Committee' to discuss all the other issues and lessons arising from the inspection, and to suggest improvements in dress, administration, discipline and training methods. The minutes of these meetings form as valuable an indication of the thinking of generals as the inspection reports themselves.[29]

This period saw a tightening of centralised control by the inspectors, which was supported by a sustained effort to revise and codify the regulations for the various parts of the service. There were new editions of the drill books in 1831 for the Infantry, 1829 for the Cavalry; a unified interior service in 1833, and an ultimately abortive attempt to codify military justice.[30] The inspection reports themselves became twice as long by 1851 as they had been in 1815, taking in many aspects of health, education and administration that had previously been left to colonels. A vocabulary of words such as 'Fantasy' or 'Innovation' was developed to damn any colonel's attempt to rationalise official regulations on his own account.[31]

Inspectors were criticised mainly for their alleged interference between the minister and the colonels, and the minister was particularly careful not to allow the body of inspectors to become too powerful. The Infantry Committee's recommendations often had to be repeated year after year because the minister had not taken them up.[32] As far as colonels were concerned, on the other hand, the inspectors were annual irritants who appropriated many powers that they would have liked to keep for themselves. Especially in the Bourbon army there was a feeling that the colonel was almost the proprietor of his regiment, and there was a strong reaction against centralisation and the legal restraints – not to mention extra paperwork – that went with it.[33] Among the lower ranks, however, centralisation was generally welcomed as a guarantee against the arbitrary authority of the colonels, although there were still complaints that it didn't go far enough or that the inspections were too short.[34] They were also always scheduled in advance, which ensured that the colonel could whitewash many things during the week before the general arrived.[35]

Between 1832 and 1845 some twenty-two Divisional generals passed through the Infantry Committee, at different times, normally sharing a relatively high level of social cohesion and education, and perhaps also a somewhat reactionary political tone.[36] Although it could sometimes show itself capable of suggesting imaginative reforms, the committee was more often conservative and cautious. When reviewing innovative pamphlets submitted by subalterns it was notoriously reluctant to recommend them to a wider public,[37] while on questions of unit discipline it was almost always pessimistic. All this, however, should not be allowed to obscure the fact that these men, no less than other officers, were open to the new military vocabulary, new 'Military Spirit' and new ideas for lightening the rigidities of garrison life.

An essential requirement for the conscript soldier was that he should 'Resign' himself to his many hardships in the interest of the group – a skill that was usually reckoned to need at least a year to learn.[38] For officers, however, the idea implied rather that one should sense one's precise status in a complicated hierarchy, and live up to it neither too little nor too much. Ambition and the 'individualism of the French character' were considered to be prime military assets, but they often had to be constrained in the interests of social harmony among the officers of each regiment.[39]

There had to be a healthy 'Division of Labour' between the cadres – and indeed this vocabulary of economic theory sometimes crept into the debate.[40] It was accepted that in peacetime it was hard to provide enough responsible jobs for all the officers,[41] but that this only made all the more reason to develop the various new leisure activities and courses that were being proposed. Certainly a 'Corporalist' régime was to be eschewed, in which each rank took an undue interest in the duties of its subordinates.[42] It was more important to spend one's time studying the rank immediately above, so that promotion would present no embarrassment when and if it finally came.[43]

Regimental solidarity often depended mainly on the character of the colonel and lieutenant colonel, combined with the level of personal tensions or problems between the officers. Many of the same moral exhortations that applied to the soldiers were therefore entirely appropriate for their officers as well, and private study was recommended as a means of keeping them out of mischief.[44] It was never good to have a reputation for 'talking politics', and as bad to be in debt. One should not be nervous, one should not give orders too softly or inaccurately, and should be neither jealous nor brutal towards one's subordinates.[45] Excessive intellectualism might be as much a qualification for premature retirement as illness, madness or sloth. It was only after all these tests had been passed that an officer was fully accepted by his colleagues and by the superiors on whom his promotion depended. The 'twin aspects of loyalty and ability'[46] could apparently cover many things.

Apart from the personal inadequacies of some officers, there was a problem with regimental command structure which arose from the place of administrative officers. Under Napoleon each regiment had a central administrative dépôt with a 'council of administration' composed of officers risen from the ranks as quartermasters or supply experts. Such men could attain position and prestige without having to compete with their social superiors in the mainstream of the officer corps. As majors commanding the dépôt, they would be effectively second in command of their regiment. They would also have a private fiefdom in the shape of the 'supernumerary company' of craftsmen, who made all the uniforms and shoes for the unit. These companies had existed in the *Ancien Régime* but were standardised in 1831 as part of a drive to increase the decentralisation of logistics. However there were complaints that as quasi-civilians their members would be especially open to subversive influences.[47]

It was a great disappointment to the administrative officers when the rank of lieutenant colonel was created in 1815 to take over the executive responsibilities of the majors, who thereby sank into something of a bureaucratic backwater.[48] By the same token the colonel found himself saddled with a 'double' who might form coteries against him, not to mention the extra time that candidates would have to spend as lieutenant colonels before they could finally be promoted to command their regiment.[49] In 1828 the *Conseil Supérieur de la Guerre* hoped to avoid these problems by recommending a return to the earlier system, although in the event nothing was done.[50]

Food had always been purchased by individual corporals for their squads, or at most at the level of the company, so a regiment needed to draw only money, munitions and tailors' patterns from above.[51] In Napoleon's time this system had been seen as a great aid to mobile operations, and especially in Algeria it was extended by a variety of novel expedients. The disadvantages were nevertheless soon apparent, since 'improvisation' on campaign could easily degenerate into uncontrolled pillaging – and 'decentralisation' in administration could allow a proliferation of middlemen with all too many opportunities for corruption. It could be argued that Napoleon had won his victories despite, rather than because of his administrative system,[52] although in fairness it must be admitted that his particular style of operations was probably the worst that could possibly have been designed from a logistic point of view.

Be that as it may, malversation was suspected at every level of the administration, and stories abounded of quartermasters who retired as millionaires. Several schemes were therefore put forward to control them, or even to remove their power of purchasing stores altogether.[53] Ideas for creating large central dépôts on industrial lines nevertheless seemed to be merely substituting one chance of corruption for another, and the Ouvrard scandal of 1823 came as spectacular confirmation.

The Corps of Military Intendants, formed in 1817 for higher logistics and administration, was a further focus of controversy. Its creation had involved the fusion and partial demilitarisation of the *Inspecteurs aux Revues* and *Commissaires des Guerres* who had conducted administration for Napoleon.[54] These two bodies had divided the work, respectively, between inspections of unit accounts and supervision of transport, dépôts, hospitals and other establishments. This had allowed each corps to specialise in one area, and especially the *Inspecteurs aux Revues* to liaise closely with regimental commanders. The new combined corps, on the other hand, could only too easily lose this link and do all its jobs superficially.[55] Since it was now given greater authority to inspect regimental accounts than its predecessors, furthermore, it undermined the position of the majors once again.[56] Non-administrative officers were also irritated by the Intendants' pretensions in claiming some of the privileges and ceremonial recognition normally accorded to colonels and generals. The gulf widened when it was realised that several of the new Intendants were civilians who had won overnight promotion through their education and recommendations, but who knew nothing of military practice or discipline. The final insult was added in 1822 when units whose accounts were being inspected were supposed to march past the Intendant and pay him full military honours – a regulation which was modified only in 1839.[57] A residue of this resentment continued to simmer until it burst forth again after the defeat of 1870, which the Intendance was widely believed to have created.[58]

Below the commissioned ranks came the ncos, and in the French army they were considered especially important because of the 'Surveillance' and example they could give to young soldiers, to instil 'Military Spirit'.[59] The French army boasted the highest proportion of officers and ncos to private soldiers of any European army, and many commentators attributed its success in war largely to that fact.[60] The use of ncos as an intermediate screen in the chain of command was also appreciated, since unfortunate consequences were thought to result from excessively close surveillance of the commissioned ranks by the soldiers.

The French army could never get enough good senior ncos for its needs, both because of 'the career open to talent' and because conscription returned most of the best candidates to civilian life just as they attained the necessary level of experience. Throughout the Restoration, and to a lesser extent afterwards, generals were constantly talking of the 'nco crisis', and suggesting that it could be resolved only if the lot of the senior ncos could be made more attractive. Not only would this

encourage the re-engagement of conscripts, but it might also make more
ncos think twice before they sought a commission.[61] Some overdue
measures were taken in 1849 to improve ncos' pay, pensions and security
of rank, and more public service posts were opened to them upon
retirement; but these measures were still generally though to be
inadequate.[62]

The skills required of ncos were also increasing at this time, with more
regulations to be observed, and more paperwork to go with it.[63] It was
essential that ncos should be able to read, and it was this more than
anything that prompted Gouvion St Cyr to set up the primary schools
within regiments in 1818, which were to become standard during the July
Monarchy. There was also a need for ncos to maintain a strong moral
ascendancy over their men by maturity, ability and a length of service that
would ideally be some eight years or more.[64]

Problems of everyday life

Whereas the officer corps, especially its commissioned members, had
access to the military debate through either the written word or the
inspections, the same could not be said of the private soldiers. They did
not write memoirs and rarely articles. Whenever an organised protest was
made, or a programme drawn up, it would be at once repressed.[65] We can
see them only through the eyes of their superiors, who were naturally
most concerned with management, control and the preservation of
military spirit.

The inspection reports show that most regiments which had survived
the first shock of acclimatisation in Algeria showed high general morale
but relatively little of the regularity and grasp of 'theory' that was so much
prized in metropolitan France. Those stationed in Metropolitan garrison
towns, on the other hand, enjoyed plentiful time to master the intricacies
of drill, outpost duty and education, but also too great an opportunity to
succumb to the temptations of civil life. No one, however, seemed to find
enough time to apply absolutely all of the innovative new schemes and
courses that the reforming commanders were trying to introduce. The
daily timetable was usually very crowded, and when something had to be
left out it was often the novelties that were chosen, rather than those more
traditional activities that made for smart drill and turnout.[66]

The army's pay was also poor, and for the rank and file it remained
unchanged between 1800 and 1840. Even after that it was kept very
much less than the average artisan's, on the theory that the army served

for honour rather than for money, and that higher wages would make just another temptation to drink.[67] There were schemes for savings banks, however, starting with one created officially in 1820, and followed eventually by the ambitious replacement bounty system of the Second Empire. Unfortunately several of the other schemes were tainted by republicanism,[68] or designed for the officers rather than the men, so none became the truly popular generators of thrift that had been hoped.

The widespread use of closed barracks in unfortified towns was something of a novelty in the nineteenth century, and many of the buildings were unsuitable conversions from religious houses closed during the Revolution.[69] They were often overcrowded and allowed little segregation between ncos and soldiers.[70] Beds were shared by two men until at least the late Restoration, with bedclothes distributed randomly to different beds from one day to the next. Middens were sited unscientific- ally, and mess tins were common to a whole squad.[71] Unsurprisingly, these conditions created serious problems of moral and physical welfare, with the death rate running at nearly double the national average for that age group.[72]

Medical officers had a generally low status; notably lower than that of the chaplains whose pastoral duties they often seemed to be assuming, or at least replacing by 'scientific' – and notoriously 'liberal' – methods. There was therefore a movement to improve the situation, which bore fruit in 1834 when training hospitals were established and medical officers were formally assimilated into the officer hierarchy. The Intendance, however, was maintained in its position of total control over medical supply, allowing it to interfere in daily medical practice to an unaccept- able degree.[73] In 1848 this control was removed, but only to be reimposed a year later, along with the closure of the training hospitals on the grounds that their students were too rowdy.[74] The medical corps thus remained underprivileged into the Second Empire, although it was at least starting to attract some sympathetic attention.

There was doubtless a certain prejudice against medical officers as a result of their liberalism, with both Larrey and Broussais falling victim to the Restoration purges. Their methods could not be ignored, however, and Broussais' somewhat inappropriately-named 'Romantic Medicine' enjoyed a notable vogue. More practical than psychological in his approach, he placed particular emphasis on the temperature and the quality of the air.[75] This appealed to line officers concerned with preventive medicine or the siting of camps, and it was also cited in support of the woollen 'cholera belts' adapted from the Arabs to prevent over-rapid cooling after rigorous marches in the blazing heat.

The July Monarchy's new uniforms, which became a model for the rest of the world, were deliberately based upon Broussais' medical theories. They were thoroughly tested for their ease of circulation and made less tight and impractical than the showy Napoleonic patterns which they replaced.[76] Vaccination was also introduced at about this time, and can be seen as another sign that the army was taking increased precautions for its health over a very wide range of its activities.[77] It particularly stressed both of those two great nineteenth-century inventions – cleanliness and temperance. The evils of drink were perhaps the most common theme of all, but the evils of dirt came not very far behind. Turkish baths for barracks were rejected on the grounds that they could cure only those skin diseases that were found exclusively among civilians; but some shower baths were introduced and swimming was widely recommended by inspectors.[78]

When it came to mental health, it was certainly not the case that psychiatric casualties occurred only in the age of high explosives. Officers knew far more about symptoms and prevention, however, than they did about cure – and would typically dismiss a soldier who shot some of his comrades merely as suffering from 'assassination mania', without further explanation.[79] Nostalgia posed a much greater military problem and demanded a more elaborate explanation. It was found to grow alarmingly whenever a strange new environment was encountered, as it did in both the Greek expedition of 1828 and in Algeria,[80] but also when new conscripts first arrived in the army. Hence the disease was diagnosed as stemming from an absence of the 'soft emotions' that a man might find in his family, his village or in marriage. In its second stage a rest cure at a local health spa, or even a total return home, were all that could be recommended; but in its initial stages 'soft' treatment within the regiment could win results.[81]

'Softer' treatment was also being recommended at this time even for those who were not under mental threat. The idea of internalised discipline was growing, whereby the military ethic would be absorbed like a religion, especially by the long-service soldier: 'One is a soldier only when one no longer misses the parental home, when one is inspired by *la gloire*, when one is attached to the flag – worshipping one's flag; one is a soldier only when there are these aggregations of sentiment which form true regiments.'[82] When this was the case, the officer could rely on the 'military' thing being done by subordinates without their needing to be told, let alone coerced.

Subtle persuasion and 'Surveillance' were the watchwords,[83] with firm but paternal ncos exerting their influence by their omnipresence and example. Punishments could be 'soft' provided that detection was almost inevitable, or as one inspector put it; 'The surest means of establishing discipline is to anticipate faults by an exact and sustained supervision.'[84] After this a more positive military spirit could then be instilled by 'Emulation', 'Self-Esteem' or 'The Needle of Honour'. These techniques consisted essentially of harnessing natural competitiveness and personal pride to the regimental value system, so that one could make a game of seeing who could be the most military. Officers were aware of the crucial importance of peer group pressures, and hoped to harness the 'Fraternal Correction'[85] of other soldiers instead of a more formal discipline.

One may speculate that these high ideals were present far more in exhortation than in actual practice – and the Algerian army, in particular, was notorious for precisely the disciplinary brutalities that were so widely condemned as archaic and illiberal. Equally the fraternal correction within military schools often degenerated into lethal *brimades* or bullying.[86] Nevertheless the lip service paid to liberal discipline was certainly prolific. Among others, the Second Line Infantry was described in these terms in their inspection of 1836: 'The police and the discipline are soft and firm at the same time, there are no serious offenders; the officers have been invited to lend a kinder ear to the complaints which their subordinates might make to them.'[87]

Most other writers also stressed that obedience could be obtained only from men who were understood and 'managed'. It was necessary to 'lead men by their true interests and by their sentiments',[88] to avoid swearing at them and to establish an amicability between all ranks. Instructions to this effect were incorporated in Préval's internal service regulations of 1833, and were thus accepted as official policy.[89]

As in all such liberalising movements, a reaction was mounted by traditionalists who painted the new orthodoxy in more radical colours than it deserved, and who portrayed its more extreme champions as typical. A series of articles appeared praising 'Passive Obedience' over 'Reasoning', although the advocates of the new ideas were really asking for no more than for traditional discipline to be based on realistic psychology. Because of their vision of the power of psychological persuasion, indeed, they could if anything see a greater disaster in store if propaganda was run from the wrong side. Lieutenant Taverne, for example, wanted to 'understand' the troops, but was especially anxious for a discipline which would be '. . . strong and indispensable, alone capable of restraining the torrent of so many passions whose release would be all the more terrible for being more compressed'.[90]

Equally the inspectors, who used the new vocabulary quite freely, were quite capable of keeping the punishment of officers secret, or of supporting an unjust subordinate in the interests of the hierarchy.[91] There were some of them, too, who like Castellane mounted a personal crusade in favour of a strict observance of regulations, and against the *laisser aller* of the African army.

Some officers, however, did want to take the new ideas to an extreme, and to institutionalise them. Perhaps the true hallmark of the subaltern 'innovator' was that he was forever seeking guarantees against arbitrary treatment of subordinates by superiors. The officers' promotion laws of 1818 and 1834 were great advances in this respect, but similar principles were supported by only a few enthusiasts when it came to guarantees for ncos and soldiers against their officers. The power of a colonel to break an nco without reference to the latter's captain became a particular bone of contention, especially as it was formulated in the 1818 regulations.[92] There was a call for a return to the regimental tribunals for such cases that had existed before 1790. These were not reinstated in the 1833 internal service regulations, although at least the captain's views were required to be known. Only in 1848 was the involvement of a tribunal made automatic, despite a fierce opposition from the upper echelons of the hierarchy.[93]

A somewhat similar issue was the idea of providing officers or civilian lawyers to defend soldiers in courts martial. Again there was a considerable groundswell of opposition, but again the 'parliamentary' view prevailed.[94] More disappointing for the reformers was the failure to codify and modernise military law. Ministers seemed to hold office for periods that were too short to allow the necessary effort to be sustained.[95]

One area which saw a marked expansion in this period was 'social arithmetic', or the collection and analysis of administrative statistics. Thus an attack on the replacement system around 1840 precipitated a scrutiny of the higher crime figures among replacements than among conscripts, while the growing interest in penal reform brought a generally more sophisticated approach to the study of military criminality. Full figures started to be published regularly after 1832, and can give some indication of the scale of the problem.[96] Offences fell into two categories – 'faults' which were punished immediately at company level, and 'Crimes' which went to court martial at Division level.[97] Faithful to the nineteenth century's love of a multiplicity of distinctions, these were then further broken down, with the more serious 'Faults' coming before a regimental 'Council of Discipline', from which convicted soldiers could be sent to a special discipline company, or up to a month in prison. The full courts martial could impose more severe sentences, but these were divided between 'Correction' – usually simple prison or public works – and the savage 'Afflictive and Defamatory' punishments including execution, forced labour and confinement in irons.

The discipline companies took approximately a thousand men a year, but were felt to be too corrupting and discouraging for anyone but known recidivists and 'Bad Subjects'.[98] After 1842 the Infantry Committee started to ask for some intermediate type of unit for convicts who were still capable of rehabilitation, with the discipline companies being reduced to their own notoriously uncomfortable punishment sections.[99] The intake of the companies was in fact reduced as a result of these demands, but not sufficiently to make the reform truly effective.

Military offenders would normally be imprisoned indiscriminately in the regimental guardroom, but some efforts were made around 1840 to provide individual cells for recidivists who might corrupt the others.[100] Colonels tended to resist this movement, however, seeing it as one more increase in bureaucracy and outside meddling with their authority. As one member of the 1844 Infantry Committee summed it up, this view saw 'paternal' discipline as more, and not less, arbitrary:

He rejected the assimilation that was being attempted between the army and the whole of society. The army is and ought to be regulated by entirely paternal obligations. Faults should be repressed as much as possible within the family, and since the number of them that Councils of Discipline are obliged to hit hard is extremely tiny, it would be bad administration to drift into a system which would need more personnel and cells, out of proportion to the dimensions of current barrack space. [101]

When it came to the design of central prisons, on the other hand, the army showed itself fully open to the new ideas coming from America and elsewhere, and built its own modern prisons at Montaigu and St Germain en Laye.[102] These, or at least the latter, were designed to moralise inmates as well as deprive them of liberty, although this 'moralisation' was often merely a synonym for 'hard work'. The various stages of a prisoner's reform were once again made the basis of a rigid classification, and hence the degree to which he was permitted to mix with his fellows. The ultimate sanction was the 'Dark Cell' beloved of the Romantic imagination, although once again its efficacy was very debatable.

6

Regimental education

'Mutual' education and moral instruction

Education in all its forms was a central theme in the 'new military ethos' that the French were forming at this time, since it symbolised not merely the need for a 'thinking' or 'moral' army, but also the nation's obligation to improve the personal qualities of the conscripts entrusted to its care. The army was to be the 'school of the nation',[1] in both the narrow sense of teaching useful skills to the nation's manhood and in the wider sense of acting as a model for other institutions. The army was to be an élite which would spread moral values and a moralising example throughout society.

The need for literate ncos and the demands of a career open to talent were powerful motives for educating the soldier; but so was the need to keep pace with the remorseless intellectual advances of the civilian world: '... from the débris of our glorious army will be born a new army; enlightened, moral, in harmony with the institutions by which we are governed, the wise liberties which we must not lose, and the advances of reason that nothing can halt . . .'[2]

Demands to tie promotion too narrowly to education, on the other hand, were usually resisted. Even in peacetime there was notoriously all too little of it to go round, whereas inspectors were usually suspicious of bright young officers who had more brains than military bearing or 'nobility'.[3] Education was therefore often welcomed in moderation, as part of general culture, rather than as an end in itself.

Some officers held a distinctly cynical view of the value of education for soldiers. For example the inspector of the Sixteenth Line in 1834 doubtless spoke for many when he let slip the revealing statement that 'The instruction is good and the soldier has not an instant of idleness.'[4] In other quarters, equally, any form of science was associated with the liberal opposition, just as reading was supposed to go with 'Reasoning' and intellectualism with 'Innovation'.[5]

Most officers nevertheless agreed that basic skills in reading and writing were important, so there was at first little serious resistance to the very ambitious new efforts being made to organise regimental schools. There were some precedents from the Napoleonic period and earlier – and some limited modern experiments in foreign armies[6] – but the idea of establishing a primary school within every regiment was strikingly novel when it was incorporated in Gouvion St Cyr's liberal promotion law of 1818. A central 'Normal' school was set up in the Royal Guard as a model for the line regiments, using a 'Mutual Education' (or 'Lancaster') method borrowed from contemporary English experiments. This method allowed a single educated officer to run a school for perhaps two hundred men, using the more advanced pupils to coach the beginners through their lessons. Each class would shout out its texts in turn and in unison, creating a disciplined cacophony that must have been music to the ears of any drill sergeant worthy of his salt.[7]

In the Restoration, however, mutual education was widely associated with suspect groups such as liberals, Bonapartists and the utopian St Simonians. The latter's programme was particularly appropriate, since it called for the application of reason to human affairs in order to harness the power of 'association'. This would then produce a rational multiplication of returns on outlay that would be quite disproportionate to the original effort – or in other words a result almost identical to that expected from mutual education.[8] One of the leading champions of the latter method was the near-subversive liberal half pay colonel Laborde, while his collaborator Appert – who organised the Normal course in 1818 – was personally involved in the La Rochelle plot and later stated that education was itself a revolutionary act.[9] In the liberal atmosphere of Gouvion St Cyr's ministry such men could be tolerated, and the more so since they had such prestigious Napoleonic names as Suchet and Macdonald behind them. In the reaction of the following years, however, it was precisely these associations which condemned them. Appert was arrested for his part in a prison plot and funds for regimental education were cut off, with colonels being encouraged to send their men to local Jesuit schools instead. In almost every regiment except the Guard, which was thought to be above suspicion, mutual education fell into disuse until the very end of the Restoration.

When the liberal-Bonapartist generals returned to power in 1830, on the other hand, there was a marked revival of interest. The reforming colonels of 1818 had now risen to be the inspectors, and it was no coincidence that many new programmes were put forward during the early years of the July Monarchy. Some were too rarefied for the inspectors to stomach, with such subjects as cosmography or contemporary politics;[10] but eventually a standard textbook for reading was agreed. It was by a village schoolmaster named Roland, who came from the area near Soult's chateau in the Tarn. His method was simple, strictly military, and remained in use until the end of the Second Empire.[11]

At about this time a study of conscript literacy had shown that only half of the men called up could read, and this had led civilians to agitate for the reforms in national primary education that were embodied in Guizot's law of 1833.[12] By 1843 it was the army's boast that all its illiterates could read by the time they left their units,[13] although the accuracy of this assertion is very questionable. Returns from colonels during the intervening period certainly indicated that some 70,000 men would be attending regimental schools at any one time, of which 80% would be in the primary courses;[14] but the unreliability of these returns was itself well known. The schools were among the most vulnerable features of regimental training, and would be quickly abandoned if there was no classroom, or if the unit was on active service. Conversely, 'education' could be quickly improvised just before an inspector arrived, or a class of star pupils put through an impressive demonstration.[15]

Three levels of regimental school came to be recognised, and were gradually standardised. There was the simple mutual education in reading, writing and arithmetic, which could qualify a soldier to become an nco. The 'Second Degree' was more advanced, and designed for ncos who wished to become officers. In theory one could use this course to qualify for entry to a military school, although in practice this was very rare. Normally all that was taught was elementary history, geography, military accounting, fieldworks or topography, and perhaps one or two ambitious courses such as literature or the all-pervasive cosmography.[16] Finally, courses were usually provided for the officers themselves, who were constantly urged to extend the scope of their ideas, especially those connected with the art of war. Several suggestions were made that all this should be taught in special schools attached to the territorial military areas, or that there should be a separate college for ncos similar to the Austrian one established in 1810.[17] These ideas were eventually rejected, however, since such schools would create a new privileged élite, would detach ncos from their units, would encourage 'excessive intellectualism', and would in any case cost money. One of the greatest advantages of mutual education was that it was extremely cheap to run, and was much easier to organise than, for example, the permanent garrison schools of the Artillery and Engineers.

Mutual education within the regiments did not fulfil all that was promised for it, and there were many complaints of apathetic teachers who were poorly rewarded for their pains, or who could not get the books, paper and equipment that they required. Classes were often disrupted by the military timetable, or the constant changes in teaching methods which preceded Roland's system. Schools rarely continued when the regiment was stationed in small detachments, although some were organised at company level.[18] In the absence of promotion strictly by examination, also, there were complaints of inadequate motivation of the pupils, and inadequate depth in the method, despite the existence of a limited system of ministerial prizes. Roland had hoped that his students would be carried along by the 'Impulsion' of the stronger pupils upon the weaker, with inner understanding replacing excessive verbatim repetition; but in practice this does not often seem to have happened.[19]

Another charge laid against mutual education was its tendency to reverse normal hierarchies and to make a sergeant, for example, the temporary pupil of a literate private from his platoon. Several writers welcomed the flexibility which they thought this practice produced, and linked it to the reformist attitude to discipline:

The monitors are generally young, and it is truly singular to see an old sergeant obeying his subordinate, and even expressing his gratitude for the trouble he is taking to instruct him.

When the time to end school arrives and they are recalled to military exercises, then the monitors become pupils in turn, and our old instructors redouble their zeal and activity to make the work less onerous, and to repay their young masters. This arrangement is very suitable for establishing unity of spirit between all the soldiers of a regiment . . .[20]

All this was anathema to some officers, however, and the educationalists were condemned for undermining the hierarchy. Troops were sometimes forbidden to attend schools of this type, and it was many years before they were universally accepted.[21]

One of the means employed in mutual education was to practise reading from wall charts or books that were considered to be morally beneficial, while at more advanced levels there were full courses of history designed to give the soldier a proper love of his country. These things seem to have arisen less from a deliberate propaganda programme than as a natural unplanned response to the needs of the schools, and even to the existence of left-wing educationalists themselves. Thus the more pressure there was for education, the more the authorities were asked to define just what the soldiers should be given to read, and it was natural that they should opt for 'right thinking' texts rather than any other. There was never any formal institution designed to mould the literature available in schools, however, although this did not prevent the left wing from condemning simultaneously – and contradictorily – both intellectual repression and poor official planning of it.[22]

Regimental libraries were of two sorts: those attached to the primary school, and those reserved for private study by officers. Especially the latter were widely advocated in the military press, and their opponents condemned as 'anti-scientific';[23] but in practice the difficulties were great. There was a considerable transport problem as the unit moved from garrison to garrison, and a new room to house the books would have to be found in each place. Enthusiasm often waned after a few years, and four out of the thirty-four regimental libraries mentioned in the inspection reports are specifically described as languishing in crates for protracted intervals.[24] It was eventually recognised that static libraries at each Divisional headquarters would be a better use of resources, but little was done except – surprisingly – in Algeria.[25] The reading material provided by a beneficent government for its lonely outposts on the Atlas became a standard feature of official propaganda, although in France such things were left to the enterprise of individuals.

Apart from a few standard texts supplied by the minister, including sets of military regulations, approved reading charts and mutual education methods, both types of library were dependent upon private sub-scriptions, usually from the officers of the regiment.[26] As a result, it was rare to find libraries of any great size, and during the July Monarchy less than a third of the regiments had an officers' library at all.[27] It was still less common for a regimental school to have sufficient books for all its pupils, and it might have little more than a few elementary manuals.[28]

The school reading charts[29] are among the few pieces of direct evidence surviving for the way in which this army talked to its private soldiers. The qualities they sought to instil are more 'military' than 'chauvinist', for as always it was its own cohesion that concerned the army most. Comradeship, honesty, sobriety and love of the regimental family were stressed, as was the avoidance of 'passion' – including left-wing ideas – either in garrison or war. The intricacies of the regulations and of tactics were touched upon, but they took second place behind stirring anecdotes of heroic and patriotic deeds from the French army's past. The only political controversy which emerged, in fact, was the question of whether these shining examples should be drawn from the wars of Napoleon or of the *Ancien Régime*.[30]

This was the time when the modern discipline of history was being born, and the army was only too ready to take the cue and expound upon its own past. Throughout the nineteenth century there was a movement to collect the unit histories of every regiment in the army, including those which were defunct but which might be revived in a war mobilisation. The effort was redoubled around 1840 under the inspiration of the Duke of Orleans, and was backed by a systematic search for archives in the *Dépôt de la Guerre*.[31] The problem, however, was to draw useful lessons from the past while avoiding the twin dangers of political controversy and mere chronology. Generals agreed that history could be a powerful technique for moral instruction, but preferred it to be limited to simple respect for the traditions of the service.[32] Courageous deeds could be allowed to speak for themselves, and writers should not discuss the causes of the wars in which they took place: 'In events where politics played a principal role the writer should extract the exclusively military part from the mass of facts relating to the general history of the country.'[33]

Many history books that came to the notice of the inspectors were criticised for 'commenting' too much, and hence failing to provide 'pure' history. More acceptable, apparently, was to rely upon anecdotes which, although true, could be 'poetised' without involving controversial issues.[34] Troops would be given an example to follow, in the form of the ideal soldier who emerged out of a series of vignettes and caricatures.

Officers would presumably reinforce the teachings of the wall charts and history books in their everyday dealings with their men. There was, however, another source of moral guidance that was somewhat difficult to reconcile with the army's aims, and that was the church. During the Restoration there were chaplains attached to each regiment under the direction of the minister of war and his 'Grand Chaplain', but outside the direct authority of the colonel.[35] Friction could arise when they assembled the regiment without giving adequate notice, or when they organised 'spies' to report on the beliefs of officers and men alike. This in turn could undermine the church's role as a builder of morale, and lead to many recriminations.[36] The atmosphere within the Restoration church was already highly evangelistic in itself, and it created still more military complaints when a strong element of pacifism started to be associated with it.[37] It was scarcely surprising that the July Revolution saw the abolition of military chaplains in all but a few native battalions in Algeria, although demands for their reintroduction were not slow to follow. Especially the French officers facing fanatical Moslems on the battlefield found they needed to redefine their own ideology, although there were also a growing number of writers within France who were inspired by a religious ethic. The romantic writer Ambert, for example, waxed lyrical on the resemblance between soldiers and monks, or how the military spirit of self-sacrifice resembled the Christian ideal.[38] By the time of the Second Empire there was a strong religious influence in the army, but without the formal reintroduction of chaplains.

Physical education and physical labour

Just as a number of enthusiastic or ambitious young officers had latched on to primary education and libraries in their thrust for recognition and distinction, so there was a comparable movement in the less strictly academic field of physical exercise. A rash of private methods appeared: for gymnastics, bayonet fencing, digging and a number of other pursuits besides. Almost all of them drew their strength from the hope that 'light infantry' skills might grow in stature until they were recognised as a specialist technicality to rival those of the 'scientific' arms;[39] and correspondingly exaggerated claims to scientific status were made for many of them, not to mention claims to moralising virtue or to tactical utility:

By this new physical education, which develops strength and address, men learn – both as individuals and in groups – to surmount difficulties which were until now considered insurmountable. It is particularly appropriate to soldiers, in that it gives them a sense of their power, when they act in unison, with intelligence and submission, to overcome certain obstacles that are often encountered in war.[40]

The idea was to create something like a military version of the circus acrobats then in vogue; giving units the ability to cross rivers or scale walls which had until then halted armies.

Unfortunately, many of the claimed military justifications for gymnastics proved to be somewhat shallow under close scrutiny, and were often more suitable for small groups of hand-picked storm troops than for the whole of a conscript army. One branch of gymnastics, for example, was purportedly designed to allow troops to escalade fortresses without ladders – an undertaking declared suicidal by all the canons of engineering science. Swimming was justified on the tenuous basis of a few desperate aquatic assaults during the Revolutionary wars, while the teaching of artillery drills to infantrymen was based on the unlikely hypothesis that all the key gunners in a battery would be swept away at once. A more pertinent explanation for these activities surely lay more in the institutional need to keep the men occupied, the army professional and the officers interested.

One common argument came from a certain idea of the French national character, since fencing, dancing and gymnastics were alleged to develop not just the soldier's endurance, but also his agility, grace and personal *air dégagé*.[41] These were prized as national military qualities in the same way as the English might value their 'solidity'. Indeed, fencing and gymnastics could almost be seen as the French equivalent to football, and have held a comparable position in the Gallic educational system ever since the early nineteenth century. Fencing had the added military appeal of utility in duelling, although inspectors were increasingly turning to wrestling or stick fighting as means of meeting the same need without the same social dangers.[42]

Perhaps rather more symptomatic of the spirit of the times was the idea that some of these exercises would allow soldiers to make a game out of their training. Serious benefits would be obtained from sports which were fun to play, and even officers might be encouraged to forget their dignity and take part. 'Emulation' – that all-purpose stimulant of group cohesion – would make the troops vie with each other for small prizes, or simply for the glory of winning.[43] Indeed, in almost all of these exercises it was usually a sign that official approval had been given to an idea when some small prize had been instituted – presumably in the hope that it would help reconcile soldiers to the rigours of military service as a whole.

Gymnastics established itself as the most successful of the new exercises, and as early as 1821 a 'Military Gymnasium' had been set up under the Spanish Bonapartist colonel Amoros, an early exponent of Pestalozzi's educational system.[44] He was anxious to link the mental and moral development of the individual to his physical training, and the plans he had presented to the minister for a central gymnastic course were more like an ideal university for officers than a simple introduction to regimental gymnastics. They contained lectures in such subjects as physiology and psychology, quite apart from an extremely thorough training in every conceivable regimental exercise. Officers were sent to this school from each regiment to learn how to run courses upon their return – but it was common for them still to be with Amoros three years later.[45] When they finally did rejoin their regiments they would often wish to apply exercises that were impractical, or dangerous, or both. The complaints against Amoros grew steadily in number and there was a series of mutinies at his school which he found it convenient to blame upon the liberal atmosphere of Paris.[46]

In the late Restoration a chain of gymnastic schools was set up in the provinces in an attempt to avoid the Amoros bottleneck. These usually each trained around the equivalent of a company of picked men from the regiments stationed in their area, but they still specialised in very advanced gymnastics, and suffered many accidents. Inspectors took to making a clear distinction between exercises that could be applied usefully to the great mass of conscripts, and those that were considered to be extreme *tours de force*. The dessicated Castellane had some lengthy differences with his subordinates over this issue, while D'Alton in 1833 found that the colonel of the Thirty Fifth Line was ' . . . totally convinced that gymnastic exercises will never produce the results that are apparently expected of them. I cannot but share his opinion.'[47] Towards the end of the July Monarchy the situation had been somewhat clarified. Most regiments did a few simple exercises to fit the men for long marches and rapid drill, while the more spectacular displays were confined to enthusiasts from a few élite units such as the *Chasseurs à Pied*.[48]

Fencing shared a reputation with gymnastics for helping the soldier develop confidence in his own prowess – although adherents fell into two distinct schools. On one side were those who saw it as an elegant exercise which conferred 'nobility': on the other were those who wanted it to be a realistic training for battle, if not for duelling. As with other forms of gymnastics, the 'realistic' school had originated in Germany, although many French officers were quick to follow. The Cavalry followed Müller's exercise for sword and lance, while the Infantry – despite prolific evidence that it was scarcely ever used in battle – started to train in fencing with the bayonet.[49] Especially in the Infantry, this led to yet another plethora of private methods. Despite official efforts to standardise on that of Pinette in 1836, there was really little uniformity even in 1849. The method used by the *Chasseurs à Pied* was perhaps the least complicated, and with the *cachet* of that corps behind it, it was found to be growing steadily in popularity.[50]

Finally, regimental singing schools were set up in 1845 as an auxiliary branch of gymnastics, although it seems that colonels often neglected them. They were scarcely justified by any of the needs of warfare, apart from a vague notion that community singing was moral, bellicose and democratic.[51] It could ease the rigours of a march and intensify the effect of a charge. The singing school was also supposed to cement regimental cohesion, and forge 'a link of good and agreeable comradeship added to the noble fraternity of arms'.[52] As a source of 'soft' emotions, furthermore, it could even be used as a specific against Nostalgia.

In common with most of the other branches of gymnastics, however, singing was ultimately seen as a 'sport' or leisure activity. As a moralising influence it lacked something of the hard cutting edge that went with more serious labours involving hard physical work. By contrast 'Practice in constructing field fortifications' – or in layman's terms, 'Digging' – could be portrayed as a splendidly productive and socially useful undertaking. It would improve the men's physique at the same time as it produced an artefact that did not actually have to be a field fortification! Roads, fortresses and even railways could be made by the soldiers at little extra expense, it was hoped, to the public purse.

On one side of this debate there was a question-mark hanging over the propriety of using conscripts as cheap labour in this way, but on the other were the apparently much greater arguments in favour of showing that the peacetime army could be genuinely productive.[53] Anti-military critics and economists could be confounded at the same time as the soldier and the worker were drawn closer together in a common task. As with education and gymnastics, in fact, a large number of ambitious projects were generated by this idea, including both self-interested schemes by subalterns[54] and industrialists, and more idealistic visions by dreamers.

Some of the idealists who examined the relationship between the army and production came to the conclusion that all workers required military organisation: that the army was a grandiose model for the ideal factory, complete with guaranteed rights of work, food, accommodation, medical care, fair leadership and pension. Others stressed the army's need for the moral uplift of hard work, and even the idea that a massive labouring militia would make the regular army superfluous altogether.[55] Regimental education could even be harnessed to this, in order to give an industrial apprenticeship to the soldier-workers, although quite what fully military training was envisaged was rarely made clear.

From the army's point of view, digging public works had several disadvantages, not least of which was its supposed affront to military 'nobility'. Officers often said that if they had to supervise digging, they would prefer it to be for some strategic purpose higher than building houses for Maltese immigrants to Algeria. It was with this consideration in mind that three of the four major projects of the period were mounted:

the 'Strategic Routes' of 1833 to open the Vendée,[56] the various roads and colonies built in Algeria to further the conquest, and the fortification of Paris. The fourth scheme was a matter of pure industrial speculation, when the St Germain railway company employed troops for some time in 1835, in the hope of saving money on civil labour.

The legal difficulty associated with public works was that they were associated with the forced labour given to convicts as a punishment.[57] Projects within Metropolitan France therefore required special enabling legislation before the army could be used, although this scarcely prevented grumbling in the ranks. The instinctive reaction of generals was to try to make digging exciting and honourable by instituting small prizes for the best workers, although it was found that when supplementary wages of any size were awarded, the troops would only land themselves in new problems by spending it on drink.[58] Discipline was also supposed to suffer when soldiers were commanded by civil engineers, as they were in the Vendée and on the St Germain railway. When military engineers were used, on the other hand, the complaint was that they interfered in strictly military matters between the officer and his men. The close supervision required by digging work also forced officers to live closer to the men than usual, and produced innumerable complaints that this weakened the officer's authority. Considerations of this type led several commentators to conclude that only properly trained engineer battalions should be used for public works, since they regarded it as their normal form of service.[59]

The army did recognise some advantages, however, apart from the increased health of the troops who had been digging. Especially towards the end of the Paris fortifications, when the system had been properly organised, there was a noticeable rise in the morale of the large army camped around the city. The fortifications came to be seen as an equivalent to the large manoeuvre camps for which the generals were constantly pressing. They concentrated the men's minds upon the military ethic and the task in hand, and and although public works were not the ideal way for such a camp to be employed, they were a long way better than nothing.

In the case of the Paris fortifications – and to some extent with the St Germain railway – there was also a deliberate policy to use the army in order to bypass labour disputes with civilian workers. In the former case there was a perceived urgency in the completion of the linchpin of national strategy, while in the latter the motive was purely profit. Because troops were paid less than civilian labourers, were available immediately in any required quantity, and were unable to take industrial action, they appeared to be an economically perfect tool.[60]

In practice, however, the desired economies did not materialise. It was reckoned that for simple digging the soldiers would do a half of the work expected from civilian labourers for a third of the wages;[61] but the difference was soon lost in additional overheads such as accommodation, and in the general inflexibility of military organisation. The public works undertaken by the army actually cost more than they would otherwise have done, and the Paris fortifications were the last major experiment undertaken outside Algeria.

The idea of military colonies was, if anything, older than the use of troops for public works; but it stemmed from very much the same fundamental ideas. In the period with which we are concerned, there were also several contemporary examples in Russia, Sweden and the Austrian frontier regions,[62] which suggested that land grants to veterans could be an effective way of bringing wild areas under military control. The idea had first been aired in France in relation to the reclamation of *Les Landes* – but its potential application to Algeria quickly became obvious after 1830.[63] The Cavalry, in particular, were interested in ways of encouraging native horse production, and felt that it would not be too unmilitary to set up cavalry horse farms staffed by their soldiers.[64] In the case of the Infantry, however, soldiers would be involved in considerably more hard work if they had to grow crops. It was found by experience that the system could work only if the colonists were given their land and then released from all but the most tenuous links with the army.[65] Since it was always at the back of Bugeaud's mind that that a military colonisation of Algeria would obviate the need for civilian authorities, the discovery that his colonies were reverting to 'civilians' in this way came as something of a disappointment, and the idea was not widely developed apart from the settlement of some native troops.[66] French soldiers in Algeria continued to be used to build roads, barracks and fortifications – but this was often only because local labour was unobtainable.[67] When disease-ridden swamps had to be drained, it was the penal companies that were used, although to many of the Line Infantry the distinction may perhaps have appeared to be somewhat academic.

Apart from Algeria and the three large schemes in Metropolitan France, officers would increasingly encourage digging on practice fieldworks, and sometimes on small civil works.[68] If the large projects had been found to be fraught with pitfalls, the original need to improve relations with civilians still remained. Any suitable natural disaster could thus be turned into an occasion for favourable army publicity, and could be linked with the educationalists' concern to 'improve' the conscripts before they were demobilised:

One day History, after having described the fabulous exploits of our forbears, will halt with satisfaction before the works of our young army. She will depict her as submissive and devoted, rushing to help humanity in fires and floods, releasing among the population each year 50,000 men who are accustomed to Order and to every virtue by an education, free from errors, which will become the support and the pride of their families; which will protect the throne and the law with its impenetrable shield, so that, finally, everyone will truthfully say that the army is the noblest and most useful part of the French people.[69]

The army in peacetime was intended to be – and indeed even formally incorporated, in the form of the *sapeurs pompiers* – a sort of fire service against natural disasters, just as in war its role was to limit the damage to the nation which came from outside.

7

Tactical training

The tactical debate

In common with most soldiers, the inspectors saw the general moral health of the army more in terms of the way it was to fight than of its political purity. Politics could serve as an excuse for interference with the promotion tables, and it was central to days of riot or subversion; but to most of the army it remained peripheral. As with the Paris fortification and the large manoeuvre camps, the civilian opposition read sinister political meaning into the army's preparations for war on the frontier. However these preparations were seriously intended within their own terms of reference. They formed a very great part of the time spent in training, and were a leading preoccupation for inspectors.

The shape of the battlefield had altered radically during the fifty years that ended at Waterloo, and it was to alter again during the subsequent generation. Skirmishers and massed artillery were forcing the two opposing lines further apart than before, leaving an apparently 'empty' no-man's land between them. The firefight might splutter on for as long as three or four days, with each side keeping deep echelons of reserves behind a relatively thin screen in contact with the enemy. Armies had also become larger, extending into less accessible terrain and with longer frontages. Commanders found it increasingly difficult to supervise every part of their line, and individual soldiers found that their personal initiative was starting to become correspondingly more important.[1]

It is true that there were still some tightly compressed stand-up fights at close range in the old style, such as Borodino or Waterloo; but these were starting to become exceptions. More typical, perhaps, was a battle like Leipzig – with four times the frontage of Waterloo – or Bautzen – fought as a dispersed series of brawls in a wood, of which Stendhal reported he could clearly see 'everything that one can see of a battle, that is to say nothing'.[2]

Generals felt they should revise their tactical theories not only in response to changes in the shape of the battlefield itself, but also to suit the 'national professional' shape of the new French army. Neither as small and professional as the British, nor as large and national as the Prussian,[3] this was seen as posing some original problems of leadership and doctrine. The French therefore felt they enjoyed a valuable opportunity to draw a compromise between British firepower and Prussian flexibility, in order to create an original fighting technique of their own.

Another institutional pressure which helped to create new visions of the battlefield was the fierce inter-arm competition for funds and for the minister's ear. Just as individual inventors would hope to win personal advancement by their projects, so it was with arms of the service. Any arm which could show some technical development likely to increase its own importance in a future war, would often win propoprtionately greater prestige and influence. Thus the various new sciences and pseudo-sciences that were constantly coming forward were each carefully scrutinised, to see if they might be harnessed to this game of cap badge oneupmanship.

The traditional 'technical arms' – the Artillery and Engineers – were secure in their scientific expertise; and although the Cavalry and Staff Corps might have to struggle to keep up, they too had reserves of specialised expertise that could scarcely be questioned. The Infantry, however, was the largest arm numerically but the least favoured technically: it was often dismissed as merely a centre of static and unscientific drudgery. In an attempt to break free from this problem, therefore, it now threw itself with fervour into the search for a 'truly light' infantry that would combine a number of new specialities, and help promote its general interests among the other arms. By running faster, shooting straighter and accepting a greater decentralisation of command, it was hoped that this type of unit would combine – to perfection – the enthusiasm of free citizens with as much professional expertise as any young subaltern could possibly desire. The *Chasseurs à Pied* were created only in 1838,[4] however, nor was their promise ever fully realised. They may be seen as the logical outcome of a long and wide-ranging debate, and their tactics were unquestionably enormously influential; but they had to take their place beside some still more influential counter-currents which stressed the heavy infantry above all, and regarded light troops as merely auxiliary.

Many officers saw the movement towards a 'loosening of rigidity' not in terms of light infantry at all, but still within the terms of traditional close order drill. There were therefore efforts to modernise the drill manual; to make it easier for a young conscript to learn; to base it on common sense rather than geometry, and generally to reduce its complexity – but all without sacrificing the 'shoulder to shoulder' unison that was felt to be so essential. These efforts were at least a move forward from the late eighteenth century's *grandes querelles* which – contrary to the arcadian vision of certain modern writers[5] – had often been somewhat sterile and pedantic. In the Restoration there was a widespread reaction against 'Makers of Systems'[6] and a reliance, instead, upon the wide fund of practical experience that had emerged from the Napoleonic Wars.

From this experience there emerged a new awareness of the fragility of battalions in combat, and the importance of 'friction' or chance as solvents of cohesion. This in turn led to redoubled analysis of the relationship between formations, training and morale. The unit's actions were carefully studied; for example the precise moment when it should open fire, when it should charge, when it needed drill movements and when it should send out skirmishers. A literature appeared which covered these subjects in more detail than in the past,[7] at just the same time as 'tacticography', or the art of marking maps with detailed tactical information, took a great stride forward.[8]

Perhaps the most influential tactician of these times was Bugeaud himself, who had formed his ideas in the Peninsular War and then in the Alps in 1815.[9] He was a believer in keeping his troops well in hand, firing only at short range, and making a carefully-judged counter-charge if necessary. His battalions would be self-sufficient, providing their own firepower and shock action independent of other agencies. These were essentially eighteenth-century tactics, and had been used to great effect by Wellington's Infantry. They were handed down in turn to the army in Algeria and to St Arnaud, who commanded in the Crimea.

By the 1850s the debate had thus matured to the point at which it had produced what amounted almost to three separate tactical doctrines. Firstly there was a 'battle of killing' designed around the skills of the agile, sharp-shooting Chasseurs. Then there were the 'Tactics of Common Sense' based on a simplification of the drill manual for a mass army.[10] Finally there were Bugeaud's tightly-controlled Line battalions trained to follow a version of the eighteenth-century drill, but reinforced by a number of precautions against the ill effects of physical and psychological 'friction'.

The two figures who have become best known as interpreters of Bugeaud's school of tactics were Trochu and Ardant du Picq, who were both believers in small long-service 'professional' forces. Both were the sons of crown servants, were graduates of St Cyr, and rose through those two classic mid-century highways to promotion – Algeria and the *Chasseurs à Pied* respectively.[11] They saw battle as a logical interplay of moral and material factors that could usually be won if one remained master of one's own troops. It was like a chess game that could be lost in two ways: either by being outmanoeuvred by the opposition or – much more damaging – by having the chessboard itself overturned. In other words one could lose a battle either by neglecting the basic rules of manoeuvre – for example by letting oneself be ambushed or enfiladed – or by losing control of one's own men: by allowing them to open fire before the order, by allowing them to drift away to the rear, or by allowing them to charge forward with unrestrained *élan*. Every available technique of leadership, supervision and psychological persuasion had to be exploited in order to keep the soldiers in line. The methods of moral teaching for peacetime thus merged easily into those of tactical training for war, since in each case the enemy was the same anarchy, lack of military spirit or loss of central control.

The experience of 1870 led many commentators to see all this as criticism of *laisser-aller* in the African army, and hence of the African influence on Bazaine's Army of the Rhine. On the contrary, however, it was precisely out of the African army that these tactics had grown. They were designed to maintain the integrity and resilience of small units beleaguered by larger swarms of enemy. High-spirited bayonet chases might sometimes be required; but ultimately it was its cohesion that formed the army's main weapon. It is instructive to note that both the 'Africans' and their best critics were at one in insisting upon this, leaving room for speculation that the narrow opposition of men like Castellane was motivated primarily by his own failure to shine in Algeria.[12]

The Algerian war did help to crystallise the army's tactical doctrine, but it did so only as part of a wider whole. The war envisaged for Europe was equally to be one of a small professional force against a horde of poorly trained reservists, and indeed Bugeaud had written his *Aperçus* with this in mind before he ever set foot in Algeria. Whereas Wellington had transported colonial tactics from India into Spain, Bugeaud reversed the process by creating his personal school of colonial warfare on the basis of experience in Europe. The function of Africa was therefore less a matter of inventing new errors than of closing the door to a particular set of old ones – notably the the idea of large but untutored armies of French conscripts. Napoleon had already discredited this during his last few campaigns, but the initial Algerian experience had served to confirm the finding. In all but direst of national emergencies, therefore, it was the golden days of Austerlitz and the Boulogne camp which became the new ideal, with formations drilling perfectly in close order and at the quickstep; maintaining cohesion in the face of all dangers and despising all comers.[13]

The problem of fear

The chief problem attached to the 'Boulogne' training camp ideal was increasingly realised to be the absence from it of the emotion and chaos of real battle. The drills which had been modern in 1805 were steadily being overtaken by events, and additional precautions were starting to be required to prevent combats from degenerating into 'soldiers' battles' where higher direction was lost.[14] The more urgently the debate highlighting this problem was accelerated, furthermore, the more easily new battles – such as Inkerman, 1854, or Melegnano, 1859 – would be identified as falling into the same general mould.

It was the risk that a panic might 'overturn the chessboard' which first attracted the attention of tactical theorists, because it was that which was most likely to upset the fine calculations of the Prussian drill. There was a flood of writing after 1815 which pointed out that 'The (*technical*) art of command is a small thing in front of the enemy; the essential is the art of winning the obedience of a multitude agitated by fear . . .'[15] Men were not automata to be kicked into their places, but were timid and complicated animals who needed to be coaxed and inspired before they would stand steadily in such a dangerous and unnatural environment.[16] More than anything else, it was a sound grasp of this fact which formed the strength of French military analysis in the nineteenth century, and which lay at the root of the prevalent view of battle as an interplay of moral forces. It was perhaps a blindingly obvious thing to say, and it had been said often enough in the eighteenth century; but it had been given additional force by the Revolutionary and Napoleonic Wars. The moral effect of massed artillery and the problems of controlling massed skirmishers were both relatively new; while in counter-guerrilla operations small outposts had found themselves uniquely isolated.[17] The call for morale was thus starting to be separated from the necessities of the Prussian drill, and often seemed to be invoked as an argument against it.

The problem of morale generated a great interest in 'encadrement', or the qualities of the ncos. Partly, of course, this stemmed from political and disciplinary necessities in an age of mutinies and nco insurrections; but in the minds of many generals, at least, it also had a technical military rationale. If one could be sure that the ncos were sound, one could leave detached units much more to their own devices. The ncos, after all, were much nearer to the daily lives of the rank and file than the commissioned officers, and in battle the same was true to almost the same extent. When he reviewed the Thirty-Fifth Line in 1845 General Fabvier character-istically argued from tactical to moral considerations in this context, rather than the other way round:

The Infantry fights mainly by its fire. The aim is to bring it up and deploy it rapidly on the ground; to weld together every young soldier's willpower and effort under the direction of leaders who are more skilled and experienced than they are. Thus in a platoon the three ranks are supported by a fourth line of 'file-closers'. Each of these can and should regard himself as the chief of a platoon of ten to a dozen men over whom he has total authority . . .
. . . A boundless confidence will bind the soldier to his leaders, once he has been the object of their care and solicitude for several years. His obedience will anticipate their desires, and woe be to an enemy who receives the fire of a platoon directed by file-closers and a captain who are loved by their soldiers. It is certainly good that the soldier should know how to aim his shot – but one should never break this bundle of wills united by a single man.[18]

It was not the ncos alone who were involved in the surveillance of men in battle, for the private soldiers were also expected to watch one another. Veterans would set an example to the less experienced, who in turn would benefit from the low level surveillance of small groups of mutually-supporting comrades:

It is not at all the love of pillage which motivates the soldier on the battlefield, which draws him on to cross entrenchments and to break the enemy's battalions. A more noble sentiment inflames his courage. National honour, particularly the honour of his regiment, and especially the example of the brave men who fight at his sides – *voilà* the true causes which turn an uncouth peasant into an intrepid soldier, a hero . . .[19]

The need to service the morale of the troops was also implied by another characteristically French idea of this time: the use of the offensive. In the eighteenth century it had been noticed that bayonets were very rarely crossed, and that what was usually referred to as a 'bayonet charge' was only a menacing gesture which would either drive off the enemy before serious contact had been made, or was itself outfaced and came to a standstill outside the range of cold steel. After the Napoleonic Wars this perception was refined and expanded as a result of direct observations until it could be specified, for example, that the few occasions on which genuine bayonet fighting took place almost always occurred in villages or woods, where flight was difficult.[20] The way seemed to be opened for a rather 'impressionistic' view of the battle, removing it at a stroke from the hard physical facts of numerical superiority and regulated firings that were so beloved by the Germans:

. . . Formed masses are destined to defeat the enemy through his eyes, rather than to spread death in his ranks; and for myself I am so far persuaded of this truth that I believe it would be entirely irrelevant whether these masses were composed of men or of tailors' dummies, so long as the enemy was kept in ignorance.[21]

The battle was thus something that took place essentially in the minds of its participants, and a bold show could make good many material deficiencies. Rogniat argued that the tendency of modern battles to degenerate into long range firefights was entirely due to the timidity of troops faced by unfamiliar improved projectiles. Decisive results – and what general did not have those as his aim? – could be achieved relatively easily if only one side or the other could be persuaded simply to move forward. The very fact of this movement having commenced would usually be enough to convince the enemy that he was opposed by an exceptionally determined unit. Once this belief was instilled into him, he would turn and almost irreversibly run.[22] From here it was but a short step to the idea that nervous soldiers might be unable to stand still under fire, but that if they could be persuaded to sublimate their nervousness by running forwards rather than backwards, the enemy might mistake it for a determined assault, and so the overall effect would be effectively the same.[23] In this connection, however, the point was always made that if the enemy should chance to stand, the disaster would be greater than ever, so the use of this mechanism was largely discouraged. Generals preferred to use professional troops, whose morale they felt they could trust, to make controlled attacks only at the moment when the enemy was thought to be wavering. The soldier should '. . . never let himself be carried away by a blind or imprudent ardour which might occasion disorder in the ranks and sacrifice an advantage which the unit might perhaps have been about to secure. Calmness, attention, discipline, mutual understanding and *sang froid* can double the strength of a unit and assure its glory.'[24]

Beside this professional school of thought, which wanted infantry to make deliberate attacks at a calculated moment, there was another view which held that the attack itself could raise morale. Where Prussians – and many French liberals – might see morale as emanating mainly from the soldier's identification with his national government's policy, there would be those who thought that morale depended on the more immediate stimuli of the battle itself. Standing in the open under fire would obviously not raise morale, whereas the act of making an attack might well do so. If everyone shouted and lowered their bayonets menacingly at the last moment, they would overcome their fears of the final assault and be carried away on a wave of crowd hysteria.[25] The elation that could be created by this method was a commonplace in nineteenth-century military writing, from De Maistre's *Soirées de St Petersbourg* onwards to Tolstoy's *War and Peace*, and beyond. Inside the French army it was strikingly expressed by Ambert – himself a student of De Maistre – in the following terms: 'One goes into battle as if to one's mistress: the same palpitations, same embraces, same hopes and same uncertainties ... Oh, War! It is the sensuous tremor of courage, the poetry of action, the realisation of the most beautiful of dreams.'[26]

At a rather less ethereal level, it was certainly recognised by most generals that nothing prepared troops for war as well as war itself, and that experience in small wars was the equivalent to what we would today call 'battle indoctrination' – training with live ammunition and many days' marching and sleeping rough.[27]

Behind all these subtle and psychological arguments there lay a feling that the attack was the natural way for Frenchmen to fight. British beef and German sausage might create specialists in the art of standing still under fire, but the mercurial Frenchman could not be so inhibited. If he was not advancing he was running away – so it would be as well for his generals to give him attacking tactics. In the 1841 Chamber of Deputies Lamartine put it, archetypically, as follows:

Oui, the French soldier is everywhere acknowledged to be the first for *élan*, for movement, for improvisation in hand to hand combat. It is action itself; ease of movement, rapid, instantaneous and communicative, which is multiplied by the *élan* of individuals and of units; and which, thanks to the sudden personal or collective sentiment, thanks to the electrical intelligence spread equally through each and every member, makes for two things – two immense things – two things acknowledged in terms which have become proverbial by the two greatest generals that France has had to fight, namely Suvarov and Lord Wellington. (*These are that*) The French army is the army that marches best, and the French soldier is the first soldier in the universe on a battlefield, provided that he is marching forward.[28]

The Frenchman was also considered to be particularly well suited to the arts associated with the skirmisher, since these too rested on the flexibility of the offensive: 'Skirmish tactics, by isolating the French soldier, by abandoning him, as it were, to his own powers, to his very self esteem, should give him a sure advantage over troops accustomed to act in masses against masses, to fire by consolidated platoons, battalions &c &c.'[29] It was an integral part of the French belief in a small professional army that its members should be endowed with the flexibility and intelligence which was genuinely considered to be a national characteristic. By the nineteenth century this feeling was starting to exert a far more dramatic influence on the shape of the army than it had ever done during the eighteenth.

Drill

An army with a strong sense of the importance of morale and national characteristics could not be expected to show much interest in the minutiae of the Prussian drill as it had been standardised in all armies during the late eighteenth century. In France it was encapsulated in the Ordonnance of 1791, which purported to be a 'reformed' adaptation of Frederick's methods but which in practice remained almost as rigid as its prototype. A few short cuts such as Guibert's 'Column of Attack' were included, but only as an afterthought in a document which fundamentally relied upon professional standards and a preference for manuvre in line. Opposed to this, many veterans of the Napoleonic Wars pointed out that in their experience few of the complex drills of the Ordonnance were ever executed in war, and that all of them could be profitably simplified.[30] It was a maxim that 'any troop which manoeuvres (*i.e. conducts drill movements*) before the enemy is in a state of crisis', while Morand wanted 'The Ordonnance reduced to a few pages', and Gouvion St Cyr wanted to see a set of 'tactics of common sense'. Provided the troops could change between line, column and square in a crisis, what use were all the markers, pacings and spacings which so cluttered the Ordonnance? As Buchet repeatedly told his officers, 'Unless one forms oneself to the practical application (*i.e. of the Ordonnance*) one will remain in a very restricted routine.'[31] The average intelligence of the soldiers was not high, and especially in an emergency call-up for war their training could not be elaborate. It seemed only reasonable to use a less pedantic drillboook, and to train the men for what they would really be called upon to do in battle.

The 'tactics of common sense' had not only a simpler content than the Ordonnance, but also a different approach to battle. Fire support was to be left to skirmishers and artillery rather than to the deployed lines of infantry themselves.[32] Attacks were to be made in columns rather than lines, and defences to rest on rapid counter-attacks rather than the dubious tenacity of a firing line. The whole system was inspired by the practical psychological insights gained in the wars, and took full account of the human frailties which war evoked.[33] It was a robust tactical system for use with mediocre troops, requiring merely good regimental and staff officers who could keep their men enthusiastic, and who understood the complexities of modern combat. In these circumstances, therefore, the argument reverted to questions of command and control rather than to the details of the drill itself.

The Ordonnance was also criticised on other grounds apart from its complexity. The scale of modern operations made the available drill grounds seem far too small for realistic training,[34] just as larger units necessitated simpler formations, faster paces and devolution of executive orders away from the higher commander.[35] It became standard to manoeuvre almost entirely in battalion columns, and to deploy into line only for giving defensive fire. The top-heavy regimental and brigade columns which had sometimes been seen in action were universally condemned. Finally, it was amazing to realise that the tactical manual with which the Napoleonic Wars had been fought made no mention of skirmishers at all. There was an urgent need for a standardised manual for this particular branch of the service.[36]

In 1826 it was decided to bring the Ordonnance of 1791 into line with some of the new ideas, while retaining its acknowledged place as the inspiration of all war manoeuvres. This suggestion, however, immediately exposed some of the fundamental defects in the army's view of its tactics. There was found to be a strong conservative feeling that would tolerate no changes in the Ordonnance whatsoever, and as late as 1844 members of the Infantry Committee could still be found who thought of it as a 'religious cult'.[37] The regulations were a vital tool of the centralisation to which the inspectors were committed, and supposedly provided so thorough a precision in basic manoeuvres that they would release one's concentration from the very pettiness of which the drill sergeants were accused: 'It is not a sophism to say that in our profession one must first learn a lot and then unlearn it a little.'[38]

Besides, Napoleon himself could be quoted as saying that if the movements necessary for war could not be found in the Ordonnance, at least they could be tacked together using elements from it.[39] Inspectors might unanimously welcome simplified methods of teaching drill,[40] but they were reluctant to alter its content. They normally resolved to err on the side of pedantry rather than of the looser moral supervision that the reformers were seeking.[41]

The 'Tactics of Common Sense' could be parodied as a set of 'Tactics of Anarchy', in which formed battalions were thrown away whole to form skirmish lines; where the precise columns of the Ordonnance degenerated into amorphous mobs, and where the line opened fire without orders and without order.[42] It was true that various young officers could be found who had suggested each of these things, and that practical examples of their success could be adduced from the wars; but they were nevertheless an extreme extrapolation of what most reformers really wanted. They were enough, however, to induce a considerable body of opinion to hold out against change, and to muddy the waters by accusing the reformers of sordid self-interest:

After so many glorious examples of the excellence of the old order, it would be unfortunate for the army if the worrisome and exclusive spirit of innovation should prevail in this important question, which is dividing the opinions of many military writers. Since there are usually disguised questions of sensitive self esteem at the heart of every public polemic, which are too easily affronted by contrary views, ... the good faith of the debate suffers and – far from advancing towards a solution – the question becomes pinned down on diametrically opposed opinions.[43]

The proposed reforms in the Ordonnance were tested in manoeuvre camps, at Bordeaux and then St Omer, by a commission which included some of the foremost infantry generals to emerge from the wars; Pelleport, D'Alton, Curial and Schneider.[44] They cast their net wide for suggestions, and commissioned the retired General Brenier to draft a reformed Ordonnance as a basis for discussion.[45] The divisions which were evident in the debate as a whole, however, soon came to the surface inside the revision commission, with Pelleport standing out for the 'classic', or conservative, view and D'Alton championing the 'Romantics' or reformers.[46] The issue was ultimately decided in favour of the former, however, when Clermont Tonnerre, the reactionary minister of war, expressed his impatience at the speculative approach which the Commission was bringing to its work:

I think on this occasion that I should recall to your excellence that the object of this undertaking is not at all to rewrite the Ordonnance of 1791, of which the merit is so generally recognised, but merely to add certain dispositions to it, and to correct a few light imperfections that a long experience of war has revealed.[47]

When the new Ordonnance finally appeared in 1831 it was no less pedantic than its predecessor, and made only slight concessions to the reformers. The use of a two-deep line on the English pattern was made no more than a possible option, while the loading routine for the musket was only slightly rationalised, and the men were permitted to slope arms on either shoulder on the march. The fastest pace allowed was 130 steps per minute instead of 120, and a few useless complexities of battalion drill were abandoned.[48] Of perhaps greatest importance was the inclusion of skirmish drill for use by the *voltigeur* companies of each battalion, although this fell far short of the total overhaul and simplification which the reformers had hoped to see. The reforms contained in the Ordonnance of 1831 were thus retrospective rather than innovative. The debate about them opened a number of new avenues, but the final published document did not in itself seem to change very much.

Light infantry and the *Chasseurs à Pied*

The most serious threat to close order tactics came from the growing role of aimed fire at long range. Apart from a few expert sharpshooter units, infantry had traditionally been expected to point their muskets only very roughly towards the enemy before firing, and to depend on sheer numbers to achieve a sort of 'claymore mine' effect at close range. It was a commonplace that beyond about seventy-five metres formed bodies would inflict only negligible casualties per minute by volleying at each other in this way. They might disrupt their own steadiness and cohesion, and might become involved in a protracted firefight at long range – but these were precisely the things that Bugeaud's tactics were designed to avoid.[49] Target practice was also encouraged more to improve steadiness during the complex loading sequence than to enhance accuracy. The fundamental principle of infantry fire remained the employment of troops in large masses where they could be kept well under control.

This assumption was challenged first by the advent of the skirmisher, whose fire might at last be individually aimed, and then by improvements in the technology of the small arms themselves. If flintlock muskets gave far more accuracy when aimed than when unaimed, then the use of aimed percussion rifles promised to be much more deadly again. The military cosmos even seemed to be in danger of turning to a very un-French idea: namely that a battle could be won simply by the side that killed the most enemy.[50] However very few officers were really ready for this change in outlook, and some of the believers in tightly-drilled masses were unwilling even to allow the individual to take aim on his own. In the 1844 Infantry Committee, 'Several members protested against the proposition that the soldier should be the absolute master of his musket. They considered him as only a rack upon which the musket was destined to rest.'[51] In these circumstances a considerable effort of compromise was called for before the place of the new armament came to be generally accepted around 1850.

One of the difficulties with the trend towards a battle of firepower – or 'a battle of killing' – was that its advocates were often ambitious young subalterns who wanted to look into the technological future in a way that their seniors, who had seen skirmishers only as an unskilled auxiliary or diversionary arm during Napoleonic times, could not.[52] The rising generation was therefore opening a very novel debate, when it started to discuss sharpshooters in terms of a saving in manpower as against the number of hits scored. To them it seemed a matter of simple political economy to show that one hundred riflemen could kill more men than a battery of artillery at the same range but at a quarter of the cost,[53] whereas this type of reasoning appeared shockingly alien to the older generation. It seemed to miss the crucial questions of moral interaction or steadiness in holding ground, leaving plenty of scope for scepticism.

Senior officers, furthermore, were often heartily sick of young subalterns who styled themselves as innovators – particularly those who pressed for 'light infantry' skills such as shooting, fieldcraft, gymnastics, or bayonet drills for four-man rallying squares against cavalry. The light infantry was especially believed to be a springboard for advancement, so it tended to be officered disproportionately heavily by men who lacked other levers of promotion.[54] They were often attracted by its anti-establishment image; its technical aura as a closed speciality, and its disarmingly simple and cheap physical requirements.

As this movement gathered pace, the authorities steadily conceded an increasing value to target practice. Inspectors began to take note of practice scores,[55] and complained when there was no firing range available to garrisons. As in other types of education, they tried to ensure that the great mass of the troops were given a basic grounding, rather than that a few high-flyers should monopolise the available resources to perfect their own skills. As with other types of training, too, the authorities had to choose between a plethora of different teaching methods submitted by enthusiastic individuals.[56] Their eventual solution was to entrust the whole business to the *Chasseurs à Pied,* thereby removing a notorious source of agitation within the Line and supposedly 'Light'[57] Infantry Regiments.

The Chasseurs established a musketry school at Vincennes, which was soon training instructors from throughout the Infantry. Three additional schools were subsequently added for a time, and despite closure in 1848 they were reopened in the Second Empire – by which time most regiments had their own instructor, and musketry methods were starting to become standardised.[58]

By 1850 the cause of aimed fire and the new weapons had made considerable headway, and almost all serious tactical discussions were forced to give them a central place.[59] This was partly because of improvements in the weapons themselves; partly because of the new institutions devoted to them, and partly because a doctrinal formula had finally been reached which made a compromise between the believers in firepower and in morale.

It was now recognised that psychology had an important part to play in the process of aiming and flinching, and the nearer one approached the enemy, the more training was needed to guarantee accurate fire.[60] This came as something of a disappointment to those who wanted the whole mass of the army to be trained as sharpshooters, just as it was to those who assumed that a firing line could be trusted to open and cease fire without close supervision.[61] On the other hand it was argued that the more target practice was made available to the troops, and the more modern were their weapons, the more self-confidence they would have in action – an argument which incidentally made a perfect match to that of the believers in overdrilling during peacetime in order to reassure the soldiers in wartime.

Finally, it was often deemed expedient to sugar the pill of the 'battle of killing' by saying that only a little of the newly-efficient firepower would be needed before the enemy's morale collapsed and the action reverted to the old style of bayonet chase.[62] This realisation, however, was less than wholehearted, and it became twisted into a discussion of the best ways to demoralise an enemy so that he would not aim so accurately, or of how to cross a beaten zone fast enough to engage with the bayonet before losing unacceptable casualties. St Arnaud's Crimean instructions followed Bugeaud in their emphasis on crippling close range fire followed by a sudden bayonet onset – but they were more interested than he had been in the need to avoid protracted 'tireries' at long range with the new small arms.[63] New weapons made it more important than ever to hold fire until the last moment, since their increased range would normally tend to increase the temptation to return fire prematurely. By 1859 Louis Napoleon was advocating even less preliminary skirmish fire even than St Arnaud, and said that 'New weapons are dangerous only at a distance; they do not prevent the bayonet from being, as in the past, the terrible instrument of the French infantry.'[64] A new role for small arms had certainly been recognised in the army, but it had been ingeniously blended with elements of the old thinking.

The Chasseurs à Pied had at least been created, and could stand as a landmark to everyone who was looking for a revolutionary tactical theory, and who felt that it was time for the views of a new generation of officers to be heard. The Chasseurs also represented the first sustained, centralised attempt by the French to build an infantry that was 'light' in more than name, thereby harnessing the natural intelligence, agility and individual initiative of French soldiers in a more systematic way than hitherto.[65]

Some had argued that all the Infantry should have been given Chasseur training – and many of the Chasseurs themselves continued to see their methods as a model for the whole army. More popular, however, was the feeling that a professional army could win advantages by its specialised élites; that the Light Infantry speciality should be hived off and left to experts, and that even Napoleon had been culpable for failing to do this in the past.[66] The majority of commentators therefore called for a division of function within the Infantry between the skirmishers – originally just the Voltigeur companies within each battalion, but later the independent battalions of Chasseurs – and the remainder who were destined to fight in close order.[67] The Departmental Legions of 1815–20 had admittedly already included one 'Chasseur' battalion for every two of Line Infantry, which together with their organic Cavalry and Artillery had promised to provide a genuinely self-contained and 'balanced' fighting unit.[68] The political and administrative difficulties of this arrangement, however, had caused it to be suppressed before being put to the test. Greater separation between arms was accepted as the norm, although this did not stop Soult trying to create 'Departmental Tirailleur' battalions in 1833 as part of his attempt to establish a trained reserve.[69] When it came to the beginnings of the new Chasseurs in 1838, furthermore, this experiment preconditioned Soult to give his consent.

The disbandment of the Royal Guard in 1830 had represented the formal abolition of the 'élite' principle in the French service, but it served only to create a widespread hunger for new fields in which élitism might flourish. The Zouaves, the Tirailleurs d'Afrique and even the Foreign

Legion helped to meet this demand, but the Chasseurs à Pied did so even more.[70] Soult, and his aide General Hulot, showed themselves particularly enthusiastic, and were supported by Generals Houdetot and Rostolan. Of special importance was the support of the Duke of Orleans, whose association with the scheme enabled the original trial battalion to be expanded to ten battalions during the general army expansion of 1840.[71] These ten battalions gathered together many of the most distinguished officers in the army, and were given distinctive new uniforms. They were even referred to as a completely separate arm of the service – although in practice they tended to be lumped together indiscriminately with the rest of the Infantry.[72] After a winter training at St Omer in 1840 this 'new arm' at least made a triumphal entry into Paris at its novel 'gymnastic pace', winning the admiration of the press. The *Sentinelle*, of course, claimed that it was all a response to a campaign that it had mounted some years earlier, but was impressed by the deadly seriousness of the new drills, for all that.[73]

The exciting thing about the Chasseurs was that they were supposed to be experts at everything. Not only were they expected to shoot more accurately and with better weapons than any comparable unit in Europe, but they were also expected to run faster. Since the early Restoration the perfect drill style for this, known as the 'gymnastic pace', had been emerging. It called for the unit to keep step at over 150 paces per minute, with the type of high knee-raising that is still seen today in the Italian Bersaglieri. By using this pace it was found that formed bodies could cover ground almost as fast as cavalry, and with properly trained units as many as twelve kilometres could be covered in an hour and a half.[74] The idea was chiefly to manoeuvre for operational surprise by this means – for example in the *razzia* or other types of *coup de main* – but a tactical application was also envisaged. With new infantry weapons the beaten zone would be wider, and would therefore have to be crossed faster by a unit which did not lose its cohesion in the process. This was deemed all the more desirable since the slower pace of earlier days had itself provided too many opportunities for hesitation and demoralisation during the approach march to the enemy line.[75] The *Pas Gymnastique* was intended to overcome this problem by sweeping its participants along on a tide of moral elation:

The character of an attack by an infantry column is thus totally changed. Instead of the muffled tramp of the ordinary pace, the ground trembles under the strongly rhythmic beat of ten thousand men. No more vagueness in the march, because the masses advance rapidly with a menacing noise; and the meaningful movements of the long bayonets, gleaming like flashes of lightning, make every step count in their redoubtable approach. The novel appearance of this column advance was magnificent and imposing. It was the regularisation of the FURIA FRANCESE, institutionalised in the manual with the immense power of action that unity can bring.[76]

The new Chasseur drill regulations were urged as the answer to the whole tactical dilemma, since they combined many of the new special skills and moral qualities that were starting to be demanded in the age of the Byronic hero.[77]

Two difficulties prevented the realisation of this dream. In the first place, when units of Chasseurs were sent on active service in Africa – and later in Italy and the Crimea – they were not used for the tasks for which they had been designed. There were usually too few of them in any one place for their Gymnastic Pace to yield any real advantages, but their sharpshooting support was also left unexploited by the Line Infantry.[78] Generals tended to regard them as compact and highly trained assault battalions, and their losses mounted accordingly. Secondly, the promises attached to their name in the military press became excessive, and many generals in Paris came to suspect their value, or the motives of their proponents: 'It is especially in the battalions of Chasseurs, where ardent, impatient young officers are numerous, that ideas for change and improvement ferment: ideas which are presented in a form which is all the more lively and trenchant because the institution of the Chasseurs does not seem to be definitively fixed.'[79]

In the Infantry Committee many of these novel ideas were set alongside some of the less satisfactory Chasseur inspection reports,[80] and a halt was called on the expansion of the arm. This meant that any hope of standardising Line Infantry training on Chasseur methods had to be abandoned, and another reprieve was accorded to the idea of 'heavy' close order drill. Despite this setback, however, the Chasseur ideal continued to encapsulate many of the reformers' central ideas, and it was to leave an indelible mark upon the whole French military self-image for at least a half-century thereafter.

Part 4

Higher military thought

8

The military schools

The school system

Outside the regiment there were centres of military thought in the military schools and in the bureaux and committees of the ministry of war. We will discuss each of these in turn, beginning here with the schools.

The influence exerted by an officer's military school upon his thinking is a highly debatable matter. On one hand the school might be his first experience of the army and hence very formative, if not searing. On the other hand it might be able to give him only vague, general or 'background' ideas, lacking the practical realities associated with commanding troops in the field. Whichever was actually the case, however, there was at least a widespread belief that the curricula of military schools were a matter of great importance to the nation. There was an oddly emotive aura attached to such schools which focused undue attention upon them, just as the general increase in educational discussion at this time helped to spur demands for reform. There was a feeling that educated men performed even subordinate tasks more efficiently, and as the pinnacle of an officer's education the military schools therefore had an especially significant role to play.[1]

One of the first things that inspectors looked for was 'education',[2] or in other words a middle class background. Beyond this was a general feeling that higher educational standards were required in the officer corps because the art of war was itself becoming more scientific,[3] because more of the ordinary soldiers were now educated, and also because civilian society itself was expecting higher standards of its public figures.[4] All of these factors led to many demands for the schools to be reformed and opened to men rising from the ranks,[5] although this last demand was not well viewed by the authorities.[6]

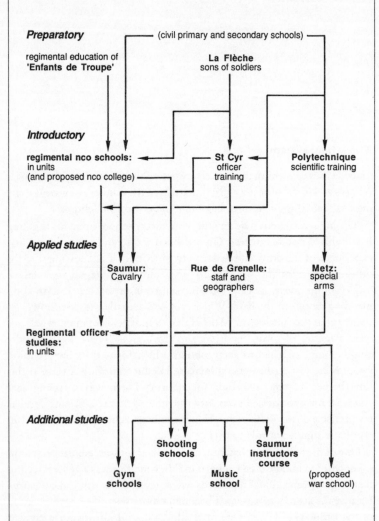

Principal education establishments in the French army 1815-51

Preparatory

regimental education of **'Enfants de Troupe'**

(civil primary and secondary schools)

La Flèche
sons of soldiers

Introductory

regimental nco schools:
in units
(and proposed nco college)

St Cyr
officer training

Polytechnique
scientific training

Applied studies

Saumur:
Cavalry

Rue de Grenelle:
staff and geographers

Metz:
special arms

Regimental officer studies:
in units

Additional studies

Shooting schools

Saumur instructors course

Gym schools

Music school

(proposed war school)

Note:
Arrows indicate possible progressions of a career.

Figure 1

M Fugmann Nicklinson

The *Loi St Cyr* of 1818 reserved two-thirds of subaltern commissions for graduates of fee-paying military schools, but this proportion was met in practice only in the technical arms. In the Infantry and Cavalry only a minority of officers passed through the schools, although a clear majority of the higher ranks were always filled by their graduates. This did not, however, imply that all the graduates shared similar attitudes. St Cyr was the starting point for those who wished to join the Infantry, the Cavalry or the Staff, and its entrants would often be well connected and confident. Those who lacked these advantages might attempt the rigorous entrance examination for the École Polytechnique. This was the first step into the Artillery or Engineers, where promotion depended more on merit. Failing that, they might slip into the lower social circles at St Cyr or even try to work their passage through the ranks – where they would have a distinct advantage over the normal run of ncos. Here, however, they would again find themselves in competition with their social superiors, since there were several 'back doors' for the well connected, such as the Restoration court Pages, the Saumur 'Volunteers' or the irregular African cavalry.[7]

After completing the two-year course at his initial military school, the young officer would choose his future arm and proceed to its *École d'Application* or 'Special to Arm' course. That for the Cavalry was at Saumur; that of the Staff in Paris, and those of the scientific arms at Metz. During this period there was a shift in the relative importance of each of these schools, as the Staff grew in stature and the Cavalry invoked pseudo-sciences in order to maintain its status. As for the Infantry, it had no *École d'Application* at all, but merely exhorted its officers to pursue private study within the regiment.

Each military school seemed to have its own distinctive idea of what constituted 'education' or a 'general grounding', and each would reflect the ethos of a particular arm or professional group. Thus at Polytechnique the best preparation for life was deemed to be an exhaustive course in speculative mathematics, while St Cyr relied much more upon a military and external brand of discipline.

This arrangement to some extent mirrored a social difference in the general French system of secondary education. The law of 1832 made a sharp distinction between the popular *Écoles Primaires Supérieures,* at which the emphasis was largely scientific, and the *Collèges* and other Bourgeois schools where the Latin Baccalauréat was taught.[8] In this atmosphere it became easy to accept the slogans of the Revolution that had seen 'all scientific advance coming from the people'.[9] Scientists often held opinions that were left of centre, and freethinking was still their stock in trade.

Perhaps the institutionalisation of class differences in this way helped to disarm opposition. Because Polytechnique was largely open to merit, and notoriously radical in its politics, it could be seen as offering an 'alternative' mental framework to the rigidities and social snobberies found elsewhere. Only the officers rising from the ranks were neglected, despite their demands for more education, although the special arms did at least have some advanced colleges for promising ncos.[10] Most regimental schools were pitched at a considerably lower level, while the fee-paying military preparatory school of La Flèche, designed for the sons of soldiers, was seen as a centre of wealth and privilege. It was attacked for perpetuating a military caste remote from society, and its abolition was demanded.[11]

Speculations and demands for reform were particularly common in the late Restoration, so when Gérard became minister at the July Revolution he attempted to put several of them into practice. Before his projects could be implemented, however, the bourgeois reaction had brought Soult to replace him. All that eventually passed was the expansion of regimental education and a handful of new scholarships to St Cyr, which were rarely taken up by deserving cases. Similarly the attempt to abolish La Flèche was commuted to the creation of a large number of scholarships to it.[12] In 1848 there was a new impetus to broaden the scope of officer training available to ncos, and to introduce free entry to Polytechnique and St Cyr.[13] As in 1832, however, these schemes were short-lived. In the reaction of 1850 they were quashed by Hautpoul, along with other reforms envisaged in the 'Public Force' bill of that year.

If viewed in terms of military writing, the schools form a particularly interesting case. Not only did their professors have the duty of summarising the current state of the art, but they also had a more direct and widespread access to young officers than was usual for military writers. Very few of them were civilians,[14] but most of the rest were noted by inspectors as being soldiers who felt happier wielding the pen than the sword. It was for this reason that Napoleon had refused to allow Gay de Vernon to return to the active army after teaching at Polytechnique, and Favé was noted in the same sense in 1849.[15]

A statistical analysis of 122 of the influential staff at military schools, including the commanders as well as the professors,[16] shows that a disproportionately low proportion of them came from the Infantry and disproprtionately many from the technical arms. The Cavalry was only slightly under-represented, and the Staff only slightly over-represented.[17] Well over a half of the sample had attended a military school themselves, and this was especially true of the professors of academic subjects. As for their geographical origins, the school staff came largely from Paris and the North-East, although rather more of them came from the Loire basin than was true of the sample of 'military writers' already cited.[18]

The liberal reputation of the school staff is based mainly on that of the students at Polytechnique, Metz and Saumur before 1823; although there were certainly some notoriously liberal professors such as Koch, Lecamus and Pailhès. Against these there were many others on the political right, and relatively few at those subaltern ranks that were most often centres of career frustration.

École de St Cyr

St Cyr, and even Polytechnique, remained largely centres of privilege. If their syllabi presented education in totally different guises, they were both ultimately intended to take adolescents from comfortable backgrounds and break them into the service of the state. This process was especially brutal at St Cyr, where the students were generally less academically gifted and, unlike at Polytechnique, there was no opportunity for the brighter graduates to enter a civilian department rather than the army. The régime had been softer during the few years following 1814, when the intake was entirely royalist and almost the senior section of La Flèche.[19] At this time the school's commander, Richemont, had said that 'the pupils should no longer be considered as soldiers'. By 1828, however, there had been a full return to the old cycle of bullying, rioting and stricter discipline. Successive commanders were chosen for their strong policies, especially when many landed families deserted the military career in 1830, at just the moment when international student rioting was growing to be as serious as at any other time in history.[20]

St Cyr certainly taught a wider range of subjects than Polytechnique, but apart from drill and the military regulations, none of them very seriously.[21] Being designed above all to instil group loyalty and military bearing, especially for Infantry officers with no *École d'Application* to pass out to, the school had quite low academic standards. Despite plentiful public lip service to such things, and some high quality civilian lecturers, St Cyr was mainly about long hours under a taxing and petty discipline, with institutionalised bullying of the first year by the second.[22] As in all French colleges, there was a great emphasis on examinations and tests –

especially in mathematics – but at St Cyr they were pitched at a far lesser level than at Polytechnique, and paid much more attention to rote learning. As in all French colleges through the ages, also, there were lamentably few team games, and too many 'bright eyes and pale faces' among the pupils.

Four sorts of mathematics were taught, including the emerging practical sciences of Trignometry and Descriptive Geometry. There were also Physics, Chemistry and the inevitable Cosmography. On the arts side there was a course in *Belles Lettres,* a great deal of German, History, Geography and Drawing. The last was closely linked with Field Sketching and Applied Topography. As specifically military studies, second year students took Military Art and History, Fortification, Artillery and Military Law. All pupils had target practice and the progressive stages of the drill manual. Thus although Latin was surprisingly absent, pupils were exposed to a wide range of the liberal arts subjects so favoured by the Bourgeoisie.[23]

Many criticisms were levelled against this method of officer training at the time and were as quickly countered; but like many such criticisms they were enthusiastically repeated after 1870 without the benefit of the other side of the argument. The charge that lessons were badly taught is perhaps the most telling, and much was made of it both in the reformist flurry of 1830, and in Tholosé's commission of 1842.[24] Too many classroom lessons were given in too short a time, and interspersed with too many other activities, for any but the most superficial coverage or assimilation. Private study could scarcely be fitted into the timetable, even though this was precisely the skill that inspectors would expect officers to have mastered as soon as they arrived in their regiments. The academic professors had no true tutorial responsibilities, and all too little say in their students' communal life or military prospects; yet they were criticised for appearing only for lessons. The real life of the school was in the hands of the military officers who maintained discipline, and of the second-year students themselves. The academic subjects were not supposed to be speculative 'as at the Sorbonne', and several of them were regarded as a joke: for example the practical topography work was welcomed as a chance to escape from close supervision within the school.

Radical change, however, was difficult to implement – and we have already noted the opposition to Gérard's proposed reforms of 1830. In 1842 Tholosé saw the teaching as superficial, but wanted to replace it by greater concentration on rote learning of the regulations rather than by any deep methodological training of the mind. If the reformers brought such a positivist mentality to the problem – and Tholosé was an eminent product of Polytechnique – it is perhaps rather to the credit of St Cyr that they were resisted. Less creditable were the riot provoked in 1843 by a suggestion to raise the pass mark in the periodic tests, and the successive simplifications of the syllabus which followed.[25]

It could be argued that a school of this type had no need of academic depth in any case, especially in view of the relatively lowly intellectual level of its students.[26] The industrious subaltern was at least pointed in the direction of further reading in each of a wide range of subjects, and the lazy were given briefings which prevented them from displaying total ignorance in front of their men. It was more important that they should absorb general military culture – for example by listening to the tales of veteran ncos on the staff. The drill instructor Viénot particularly impressed the young La Motte Rouge in this way, for all his fearsome reputation as 'the human incarnation of the drill manual'.[27]

The formal syllabus also included a number of purely military subjects. They have been criticised for being pitched much more at the level of the subaltern rather than of the general – although this was surely scarcely a defect in a school for subalterns. Pupils did nevertheless receive an introduction to 'strategy' in the Military Art and History course, and a brief survey of its content may offer us some clues to the way that general ideas on these matters were moving.

Under Napoleon the text had been Chantreau's *Eléments d'Histoire Militaire,*[28] which followed French practice by including a lengthy prolegomenon on comparative institutions from various ages and countries. While he realised that theory could do no more than educate the judgement, Chantreau included this plethora of examples as an aid to private study. He was writing before analytical techniques had been defined for either strategy or military institutions, so he hoped that assiduous students would memorise his 'infinite number of notions' on their way to formulating their own personal set of maxims. The one general principle he felt able to recommend was the need for soldiers to develop a pure morality and strict obedience to orders. However diffuse his view of the principles of war, he was certain that war was a matter for highly drilled regulars.

In 1826 Chantreau was superseded by Rocquancourt's *Cours Elémentaire d'Art et d'Histoire Militaires.*[29] Although even longer than its predecessor, it was designed more specifically for St Cyr and represented a clear improvement. It drew on the standard principles of Jomini's school, but still followed the Encyclopaedists' habit of covering the whole of history, albeit now influenced by the Restoration's interest in things Gothic. Discipline was recommended for its practical utility rather than its moral content, and science was invoked whenever possible.

Rocquancourt's book was designed to be a reference work for the whole of an officer's career. It had a splendid annotated bibliography, which gives guidelines on every important military debate. Rocquancourt was perhaps a trifle dogmatic, but he saw the limitations of Jomini and of Clausewitz alike. The latter's metaphysics, self-contradictions and untranslatable adaptations from natural science were deplored, but we are told that 'For all that his treatise is not by a man without talent.'[30]

This reasoned rejection of Clausewitz by an eventual Director of Studies at St Cyr is both well informed and deliberate. It is a far cry from the mockery by Jomini which has often been seen as a cause of a disastrous delay in the 'French discovery of Clausewitz',[31] and consequently of some revolution in officer education. The fact was that Clausewitz did not offer answers to the problems facing the French at this time, since he preferred large conscript armies, ignored colonial warfare and mocked the topographical obsessions such as were to be found in the French Committees of Defence. He was no less correct than the best French theorists of the day, but he was writing about a different army.

Rocquancourt was superseded only in 1858, by Labarre Duparcq's *Eléments d'Art et d'Histoire Militaires*.[32] At last the St Cyr textbook was reduced to a more practical size, although this was at the expense of much of Rocquancourt's subtlety, and perhaps also his high standards. The new book was more dogmatic and, in tune with the spirit of the age, laid an increased stress on moral elements which sometimes seemed to clash with the Jominian geometry that was still included.[33]

The teachers of Fortification, Topography and Artillery would have had almost as much influence on their pupils' military ideas as those of Military Art and History. These professors were changed only infrequently, and must have created a considerable continuity of ideas in the way their subjects were taught, although Military Art and History was an exception, with five different professors during the July Monarchy.[34] Such a high turnover must have led each new incumbent to rely heavily on the textbook which he inherited from his predecessors.

École Polytechnique

If St Cyrians were exposed to a bewildering variety of influences, Polytechnicians were directed along a much narrower path. They were destined to become military or civil engineers, and given advanced and intensive training by some of the finest scientists in Europe. The quality of the best students, however, often led them out of science and into distinguished careers in business or politics.[35]

Many freethinking Polytechnicians saw the army's role as the employer of such talents as a model for general industrial organisation, and were much impressed by the St Simonian brand of political theory.[36] The school became involved in many of the political disturbances of the capital, although in scale its rioting was probably little more serious than at St Cyr. The military discipline at the two schools was certainly tightened up along a very similar timetable, and both shared a notorious record of misconduct.

In 1814 the Restoration was faced with a situation at Polytechnique that was a microcosm of its general dilemma – how to combine monarchy with a constitution, or in this case loyalty with science. Whereas the St Cyrians at that moment were hand picked and politically trustworthy, the Polytechnicians were selected by an impartial examination which took little account of attitudes to authority. The minister told the king that what was needed was therefore 'A sufficient guarantee of the principles of delicacy and honourable sentiments . . . without wounding the political principles which permit all citizens to aspire to every post.'[37]

The failure to provide such guarantees was demonstrated by the riots of 1816. For a short time thereafter the experiment of demilitarisation was tried, combined with a strong dose of morality and religion; but as at St Cyr the experiment failed, and in 1822 the school was handed back to the minister of war. Successively in 1832 and 1844 the discipline had to be tightened in response to further riots, although the scientific reputation of the school was apparently entirely unaffected.

The syllabus always laid overwhelming emphasis on mathematics: Descriptive Geometry, Geometrical Analysis, Physics, Chemistry, Architecture, Drawing, and a composite package of Grammar, *Belles Lettres,* History and *Morale*.[38] In the Empire Gay de Vernon had run a course of Military Art and Fortification,[39] but this was discontinued in the Restoration. It attempted to draw an uneasy compromise between an emphasis on science and mathematics on one hand, with on the other the more modern idea of framing a unified system of the military art which should include all the parts. Thus he believed in the all-important *coup d'oeil* of a genius; but thought it was most likely to emerge from the technical education of the special arms. He appreciated the mobility and surprise which had been taught by Napoleon; but still believed in the power of fortresses to limit wars to the frontier region. In common with the 1818 Committee of Defence he was ready to accept the need for fortified camps and 'active' resistance; but he betrayed his specialised perspective by recommending fortresses simply because they provided 'the most direct application for Descriptive Geometry'.[40]

In this way the particular attitudes of the Engineers were transmitted to the Polytechnique, although it was to be 1851 before Military Art was taught there again, by Louis Napoleon's friend Favé. To judge by his published works, this officer probably brought to his subject all the magisterial and pedantic stickling for detail which has been the hallmark of a certain type of French professor throughout history. His method was a laborious multiplication of classifications which explained little while describing all. The mathematical positivism of Polytechnique, indeed, made it especially vulnerable to this vice.[41]

Military Art was at best a fringe occupation at Polytechnique, where the principal controversies were centred on technical differences within the scientific subjects themselves. Should the mind be trained in a general way to apply science to any question as it arose, or should this training be more closely tied to 'drills' designed to meet the most likely problems? In the Restoration Clermont Tonnerre[42] and Laplace seemed to be revising the syllabus towards the latter method, but in the event were only narrowing the speculative nature of the mathematics that were taught, in order to substitute their own brand of positivism. They did not introduce any applied studies, and even reduced whatever 'liberal studies' still remained.

In 1836 Chambray challenged this method of teaching, and argued for a more 'useful' syllabus.[43] As with Tholosé at St Cyr, however, his argument was largely an attempt to exclude more general subjects such as Physics, Chemistry and Figure Drawing, and to simplify the teaching of what was left. Both these 'reformers' are open to the charge that they wanted to kill the good along with the bad in the schools they were discussing. St Cyr was designed for the mediocre, but Tholosé took this as a cue to try to reduce its scope still further. Polytechnique had a genuine function in catering for *esprits d'élite,* and although it sometimes did this at the expense of the mediocre, Chambray seemed to want to destroy the function altogether. There was a clear choice[44] between a very theoretical or intellectual syllabus, and a lowering of standards; and it is certainly to the school's credit that it stuck with the former, enabling it to continue to stimulate its best products to their highest levels of attainment.

As with St Cyr, however, Polytechnique can certainly be criticised for defects in practice. The ideal pupil must have been very rare, and he would in any case almost always opt for a civilian rather than a military career. Military graduates tended to be the less gifted members of their intake, often somewhat baffled by the rigorous course and mentally unprepared to make the dramatic leap to Metz, their *École d'Application*, where they would finally come up against the real world of practical gunnery or of trench-building.[45] Despite all this, however, there were many graduates of Polytechnique who made brilliant military careers, just as there were many elements in the army that were deeply envious of the school's superlative theoretical grounding.[46]

École de Metz, and Regimental Artillery Schools

The Metz school for Artillery and Engineers was intended to do for these arms what St Cyr did for the Infantry, if not for the Cavalry – to create the *feu sacré* of military group loyalty,[47] and to some extent teach the daily tasks of life in those arms. Its syllabus consequently included a very full course of military studies originating in the work of Gassendi and Allent's commission of 1807.[48] This course was to include considerable applied work and a simulated siege. Military service regulations were taught, as well as Riding, Ballistics and Pyrotechnics, Military Construction, Field Sketching, Military Communications, Machines, Factories, Hydraulic Works, as well as the speciality of the arm to which the individual was destined. In addition there were courses in Applied Mathematics and Physics, and in 'Applied Tactics and the Art of War'. This last actually included very little strategy and was mainly concerned with administrative arrangements in armies since the Romans, as well as the 'Influence of fortifications on frontiers'. As such, it institutionalised the strategic conceptions which the Engineers brought to the Defence Commissions in the Ministry.

Pupils fresh from Polytechnique found, perhaps predictably, that the Metz course was badly taught;[49] but they also found it excessively theoretical. They sensed, perhaps, that the arts of the Gunner and the Engineer had been somewhat marginalised by Napoleon's new art of mobile war,[50] even despite the fact that the campaigns fought by the French from 1823 to 1855 had very often been narrowed down to a decisive siege rather than a decisive battle. The combination of Polytechnique followed by Metz still offered the best education available anywhere in those arts; but the pupils were becoming restless with what increasingly seemed a dry technicality.

The scientific arms had particularly good regimental schools, with permanent staff and facilities for practical work. As such, they were completely different from the amateur primary schools established intermittently in infantry regiments, even though they acted as a model for them. More than in the Infantry, the schools of the technical arms were attended by officers as well as other ranks, and could often provide the sort of experience in practical engineering that Metz and Polytechnique were criticised for lacking. Scientific experiments were also carried out: they had more time for such things than the crowded Metz timetable would allow.[51]

The Engineer schools each had three full-time professors, in Reading, Writing and Drawing. A library and workshops were attached, and there was plentiful practice in digging. Although the object was to impart literacy to would-be officers, however, the digging often seems to have prevailed over the 'Three Rs', at least in the beginners' class. At Arras in 1850 there were some bitter complaints about the poor standard of orthography.[52]

The Artillery's schools were older than the Engineers', dating from the *Ancien Régime*, and since they were commanded by Maréchaux de Camp they also enjoyed greater prestige. Their academic appointments on occasion even posed political problems for the Minister.[53] Each school had a professor and assistant in Mathematics, and a professor in Drawing. In addition to a library and a map room, they were intended to have facilities for Chemistry, Physics and Metallurgy. Although the success of the latter courses is not recorded, their very existence is eloquent of the seriousness with which the army approached the latest developments in science.

The Staff and Geographical Engineers' Schools

The equivalent of Metz for those destined for the Staff Corps was the school of that arm in Paris, in the Rue de Grenelle. It was there that the most successful graduates from St Cyr, and later also a few from Polytechnique, went for a further two-year course in the techniques of Staffwork. These men were usually from the social cream of the army, and a significant number of them were related to generals.[54] The school was small, exclusive and consciously an élite. Its members were allowed freer discipline and received more personal attention than they had at St Cyr, or would have in a regiment, and this rankled with the rest of the army. On the other hand the school was not politically neutral, since it supported both the Revolution of 1830 and the Coup d'État of 1851. To some extent this may be attributed to the Bonapartism endemic to the Staff Corps as a whole.[55]

In common with other military schools, that of the Staff was faced with the dilemma of choosing between a theoretical and a strictly practical syllabus. Its role as a depository of an overview of the military art meant it could not afford Polytechnique's brand of narrow speculative education. However the compromise which it drew between a 'liberal education' and the practical details of staff service tended to be weighted in favour of the latter. This in turn produced complaints that the course was merely repeating the syllabus of St Cyr, although that in itself may have been no bad thing. Better teaching staff were available at the Rue de Grenelle, and their course undoubtedly had greater depth than at St Cyr. Repeated demands from the Dépôt for greater practicality also spurred them to frequent revisions of content,[56] and replacements for the teaching staff were scrutinised more for their ability to teach than for their theoretical grasp of the subject.[57] On the other hand it was in the nature of the work itself that pupils should be required to make a detailed study of the regulations of every arm, and there was a temptation to concentrate on these rather than on more general considerations. In 1833 the course nevertheless included Administration, Geography, German, Drawing, Drill, Artillery, Military Art, Fortification, Descriptive Geometry and Topography.

Although a certain evolution away from a more general view may be detected in the content of the syllabus, it never became the excessive immersion in detail that was perhaps seen at Saumur. The series of pamphlets for Staff School pupils which appeared in 1824 made more play with general considerations than one would have gathered from the syllabus as revised in 1843; but Fix, writing of his experiences eight years after that, still extolled its virtues in terms of its 'general mental training' through such courses as Economics or Cosmography.[58] The staff officer had to understand all aspects of the life and resources of the countryside through which he passed, and Odier's course of Military Administration, for example, talked of 'hidden social motors' behind military phenomena. Later even some Civil Law was added.

The course in Military Art was started by Colonel Koch, an old associate of both Jomini and Pelet. It was very modern in its isolation of 'Grand Tactics' as the essential science of the general, and its corresponding relegation of Drill to a subordinate status as 'Minor Tactics'. The attempt to find a set of 'rules' behind the operations of war was particularly characteristic of the era, and had its value; although the range of examples invoked in support perhaps left something to be desired. Koch rested his work largely on that of the émigré officer Ternay, who had been writing in 1808 – before some of the most important lessons of the Napoleonic era had been properly understood.[59] In common with Jomini and Chantreau, also, he looked as much to the Seven Years' War as to the Napoleonic experience, and tended to build up his 'principles' from lessons of detail. He was well aware that the action of fate, or chance, might upset even the best-founded 'rules'.

There were several suggestions for the establishment of a separate school of 'Strategy' or Grand Tactics, or even that a university department should be created for them. Other nations, such as Sweden, were cited as already possessing such a school,[60] and the variety of subjects embraced within the modern art of war was urged as a basis for making it a 'universal' academic discipline in its own right. Beyond that, furthermore, there was a felt need to make the French Staff Corps into a more integral part of the army as a whole, as was the case in some other countries.[61] Against this, however, too many of the demands for a higher war school, or for opening the Staff more widely, were seen as levers for undermining Staff privileges, admitting ncos as well as officers, or linking promotion too tightly to examination results.[62] Such a development was unacceptable, and it was unfortunate that for many generals the more enlightened conception of the war school became tainted in this way.

One other institution of advanced education should be mentioned here: the *École d'Application* of the Geographical Engineers. It had only three professors, and usually no more than a dozen pupils, fresh from Polytechnique. Its purpose was exclusively to teach the science of cartography, but even so it managed to give riding lessons and in 1818 even asked for a training observatory to be installed. As an academic discipline with great military relevance Topography certainly merited its outlay of scientific talent; but it is reported that the pupils of the Geographical School were often bored by the dryness of their course.[63]

École de Saumur

The one *École d'Application* that remains to be discussed is that of the Cavalry at Saumur, which started as a 'Normal' school in riding and horse care for nco instructors taken from each mounted regiment. This gave it a distinctly Bonapartist flavour until, from 1823 onwards, cavalry officers started to be sent sent there on graduation from St Cyr. The school immediately became as much a centre of royalist privilege as the Guard,[64] and until 1833 it even included a class of gentlemen–amateurs who joined as ncos in the hope of obtaining a commission outside the normal channels. The problem, however, was that since St Cyr itself already had some of the features of an *École d' Application* for the Infantry, it was found to be somewhat difficult to fill the Saumur syllabus with pertinent technical instruction. Instead, it laid more emphasis on 'Military Spirit' than any other school, with a peculiar narrowness that was all its own.

The reforming Restoration General La Roche Aymon deplored the uneconomic use of time involved in using two years to teach officers to ride, when it could have been done just as well within the regiments.[65] Admittedly there were some new developments in horse care and breeding which lent a little credibility to Saumur's claim to be a centre of new technology; but to a large extent these rested on pseudo-science rather than real science. The school was defended more convincingly as an institution for creating group loyalty, and in a reply to La Roche Aymon one anonymous writer argued that the officer should belong to a vocational caste at the national level, rather than to a regimental or 'Prussianised' profession.[66]

La Roche Aymon perhaps went too far when he wanted to convert Saumur into an *École de la Grande Tactique* similar to the War School proposed for the Infantry and Staff. His 'Prussian' ideas saw this as a way to prepare all ranks for their wartime roles in making split-second decisions; but the conservatives made the slightly unconvincing reply that their method – the memorisation of the regulations – had always been envisaged as having the same purpose. La Roche Aymon's higher tactical school would also surely have imposed an inappropriately advanced level of education on the subaltern, and might have distracted him from more pressing problems of horse care, map reading and 'little war'. More serious still, in the eyes of many, was the idea of linking the higher school to promotion by examination at each rank. This was no more popular in the Cavalry than in any other arm.

Saumur saw itself in a humbler role than the reformers would have liked, and the grandiose syllabus of 1823 was gradually reduced to fit regimental needs rather than any broad ideal of 'general knowledge'. Even Military Art and History was all but abandoned in 1833, leaving a course pitched no higher than those of regimental schools. By 1845 pupils were studying only the Regulations, Equitation, Horse Care and various types of Gymnastics.[67]

While it lasted, the Military Art and History course was probably well taught. Jacquinot de Presle's book[68] was surprisingly advanced in its recommendation of a close fusion between moral and technical aspects in war, and particularly in his realisation of the practical difficulties which this would imply. Like La Roche Aymon, he followed the Prussian stress on the importance of 'Leadership' guided by a rational 'Theory'. In common with Rocquancourt he combined a full and intelligent discussion with a lack of positivist excess, and presented the reader with a full bibliography on which to base subsequent studies. He resisted the temptation to portray war as the exclusive preserve of the Cavalry, and explained many of the demands of the general military reform movement.

In stark contrast was the course in Military Theory that was attempted at Saumur in 1861 by Chef d'Escadron Humbert. After thirty years without such a course, it seemed as though the school had lost all sense of proportion, since Humbert strayed from the judicious commentaries of the Napoleonic generation and immersed himself in all the speculations of an age of change. He thought, for example, that improved weaponry would lead to closer formations and more fighting hand to hand. The school authorities, at least, were quick to see his incompetence and soon reverted to their former intellectual apathy.[69]

'Theory' at Saumur was taken to stand not for the general ideas which broadened the judgement, but for the standardisation of regulations in all aspects of cavalry life. As in other arms, this was both a preoccupation of the age, and a source of many abuses. It was nevertheless a necessary part of the transformation of a small dynastic army into a national, scientific one. It was essential to effective organisation and control that one regiment should be more or less the same as another. Saumur's origins as a 'Normal' school, and its rejection of the intellectualism of the reformers, predisposed it to embrace this function with exceptional zeal. It would point to its published works on the regulations as its proudest achievement.[70]

9

National strategy and the ministry of war

Wars, reform and the ministry

Like every other great continental power, France was a leading runner in the 'arms race', and a central player in that game of universal deterrence which we today call 'the balance of power' – but which Humboldt more graphically described as 'Europe's mutual education in fear'.[1] In an age when armies were thought capable of crossing any obstacle and reducing any permanent fortification, a strong military posture was seen as a more effective guarantee of peace than any of the many schemes for international co-operation that were currently in the air.

When they were first set up, the régimes of 1830, 1848 and 1851 each experienced acute pressures to fight a major war in central Europe as a means of establishing their legitimacy – but each of them wisely shied away from such a dangerous policy. Instead, a prudent and effective system was developed whereby limited diplomatic or military action was often taken, but only after careful scrutiny of the intentions of 'the northern powers'. Thus for their operations of 1831–32 in Belgium the French mustered a second army to cover the Rhine against possible Prussian intervention; while in 1859 the Italian campaign was called off as soon as Prussian mobilisation had been reported. France's liability in these operations was always intended to be essentially 'limited' or 'political', and no one believed that she should even think of fighting more than one opponent at a time unless, of course, she had sufficient allies.

Few of its members had ever heard of Clausewitz, but the army nevertheless had a strong practical awareness of its political role in all the military operations of this period, externally as well as internally. In Spain in 1823, for example, looting was forbidden and propaganda directed against the essential clergy and nobility who controlled local life, just as efforts had to be made to preserve the troops from republican indoctrination.[2] At Ancona in 1832 the tiny occupation force knew it had been placed in an exposed position just to send a diplomatic signal to Austria; while at the sieges of both Antwerp and Rome the line of attack was determined mainly by the need to avoid the main centres of population.

Nor did the French politicians of our era adhere to the ideal that war was a condition clearly distinct from peace, or that it should always be an intense national effort that might be contemplated only in the direst of emergencies. In 1831 Thiers – in the event very perceptively – assumed that a *Grande Guerre*, in which the whole French 'Nation in Arms' would have to be called out to reinforce the regular troops, would occur only once every forty to a hundred years.[3] In most normal times the sustained underpinning of diplomacy could be entrusted to the regulars alone – and indeed we find that throughout this period the army was used for limited operations probably more successfully and intelligently than by any other nation. No great power in this era spent such a relatively small amount on defence – yet defeated more internal unrest and simultaneously staked out a greater network of neighbouring 'buffer states' – than France. Until his great error of declaring war in 1870, indeed, Louis Napoleon could even be said to have brought the technique to a new peak of perfection.

Some of the hidden implications of this system were perhaps best described by Thiers in his speech on the fortification of Paris in 1841;[4] a speech which contains many chilling resonances for students of both the Maginot era and of contemporary nuclear strategy. He argued that because the first objective of modern 'wars of invasion' was the soft target of the enemy capital, any attempt to attack France could be defeated if Paris were made impregnable for at least as long as it took to mobilise the ultimate weapon of the nation in arms. Even in the worst case of a French failure on the frontier, an attacker would still find himself immobilised in a siege of the capital, during which the whole force of France could be organised in his rear for an inevitably crushing counter-blow or, in modern parlance, a 'second strike'. If Paris were 'hardened', therefore, no sane aggressor would ever wish to cross the frontier, and *La Grande Guerre* would be made entirely obsolete. Limited or political wars would be the only ones which remained possible or conceivable: they would take place under what we would today call an 'umbrella of mutual great power deterrence'.[5]

Thiers perhaps took logic at least one step too far, and few officers followed him all the way in his assumption that a major war would be completely impossible. Contingency plans were certainly made for such a war on a number of occasions, although they were moulded by a fascinating interplay of interest between the different arms, services and ministerial departments. As time passed, the balance of advantage slipped gradually away from the Engineers, who had been the guardians of strategic knowledge for over a century, and more towards the bureaucracy of the ministry of war and the newly-created Staff Corps. These debates also acted as a focus for many of the reformist demands of half-pay officers and others who were excluded from the inner circles of power. They wanted to use their technical expertise as a lever for their own advancement, and saw the existing decision-making structure as an obstacle to be overcome or at least changed in its nature. The debate about national strategy thus became intimately commingled with a debate about the shape of the ministry of war and about the role of the minister.

The minister himself was often a man of mediocre military standing, overshadowed by his political masters in Parliament and by his permanent staff within the ministry. Despite the occasional Soult, the minister was quite likely to be a court puppet lacking military experience, like Damas, or an effective soldier who was politically naïve, like Lamoricière. However the only complete set of internal ministerial minutes – those of the legitimist Clermont Tonnerre from 1824–27,[6] shows that despite the weight of these pressures the minister could influence many details of army organisation on his own initiative, and much was felt to rest on his personal abilities.

Perhaps ten of the twenty-seven ministers who held office in our period were enthusiastic for reform, of which three were from the political right. The 'reforming' ministers tended to be those with experience of active command in war, while the less enthusiastic tended to be from noble backgrounds, from the Cavalry or from the Staff. Not even the best minister of war, however, could hope for a term of office longer than that of the government he served, which in the turbulent atmosphere of the time would usually be short. There was therefore little real opportunity for any extensive programme of reform to be pushed through, and this led to demands for authority to be vested in some more permanent institution than the minister. Inevitably, perhaps, such demands were rejected by successive ministers as a challenge to their own hierarchical supremacy.

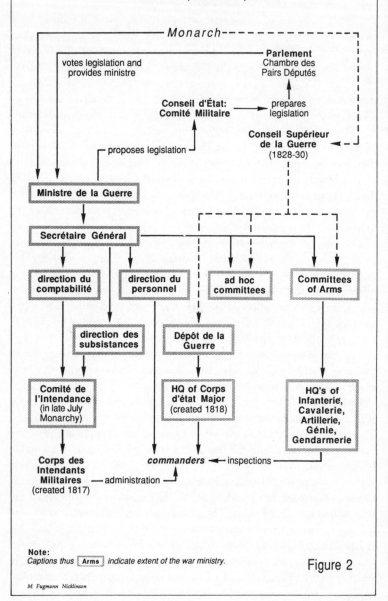

Higher organisation of the French army 1815-48 (schematic)

Monarch

votes legislation and provides ministre

Parlement
Chambre des
Pairs Députés

Conseil d'État:
Comité Militaire → prepares legislation

Conseil Supérieur de la Guerre
(1828-30)

proposes legislation

Ministre de la Guerre

Secrétaire Général

direction du comptabilité

direction du personnel

ad hoc committees

Committees of Arms

direction des subsistances

Dépôt de la Guerre

Comité de l'Intendance
(in late July Monarchy)

HQ of Corps d'état Major
(created 1818)

HQ's of Infanterie, Cavalerie, Artillerie, Génie, Gendarmerie

Corps des Intendants Militaires
(created 1817)

commanders ← inspections

— administration —

Note:
Captions thus [Arms] *indicate extent of the war ministry.*

Figure 2

M Fugmann Nicklinson

The Intendance and the *Conseil Supérieur de la Guerre*

In many parts of the army there was a feeling that administrative conservatism was nowhere more deadening than inside the ministry itself. Its bureaucracy was manned partly by soldiers, but partly by members of the *Corps des Intendants Militaires* which had been formed in 1817 to control all parts of military administration. The power of the latter body on the minister was as real as that of the court and the politicians, and it was resented by the army every bit as strongly as its pretentions within regiments. When the *Conseil Supérieur de la Guerre* was set up, for example, its role as an alternative source of authority was systematically reduced by the bureaucracy, and even the ministers themselves sometimes failed in their attempts to prevent such practices.[7]

The patronage exercised by the Director of Personnel in promotions was considerable, and the delays imposed in other departments on such reforms as the new penal code were notorious. Préval, who for many years had been attempting to reform the administrative and field service regulations, was particularly incensed by the obstruction he experienced from the Intendance, and went as far as to see it at the root of all military ills – an idea that was to be happily purloined by critics after 1870: 'In proportion as this corps [i.e. the Intendance] is elevated, the Ministry of War successively descends in the eyes of the army, which at present no longer considers it as anything more than a bureaucratic assemblage.'[8]

As such, however, the ministry was extremely efficient at maintaining the status quo, and mastering the details of pay, promotion and recruiting. The real difficulty was that it stifled attempts at reform, even when they came from the minister himself. Its personnel enjoyed an inordinate continuity in office which was not shared by the officers seconded from the army for a year or two at a time. The names of Martineau, Tabarié, Genty, Melchion, Petitet and Brahaut recur in ministerial documents from one decade to another. Such men made their entire careers in the corridors of power, and it was scarcely surprising if they became more dextrous in manipulations than could any officer coming in from outside.[9]

The active army had cause to resent the bureaucracy for its power, but often preferred to couch its attack in less basic terms, diverting political arguments into appeals to the mystique of military honour and nobility. The Intendance was seen as a collection of civilians in uniform who not only undermined the 'dogma and mores' of the military canon, but also obstructed that special relationship between the king and the army which underpinned the theory of military professionalism:

It is quite enough that the press and parliamentary intervention harrass and interrupt the royal initiative towards the army: must the crown also deliver up its influence and its action into the hands of men who have no sympathy with it? . . . The bureaucracy is at the opposite pole from true administration . . . it uses the time and intelligence of its functionaries to make tables, diagrams and statistics; not to solve problems, but to state them and describe them. It creates nothing, invents nothing, produces nothing; but prevents creation, invention and production, under the pretext of opposing abuses of power.[10]

Préval clearly hoped that if these duties were given to the men who did the actual fighting, the administrative machine would bring more security to France and more authority to the officer class.[11] Although widely debated, however, such a radical change in military structure was beyond the power of anyone to achieve.

Each successive minister had a personal idea of how the ministry itself should be organised, but all were forced to leave power in the hands of the professional bureaucrats. Under Napoleon the situation had been somewhat less acute, since he not only combined political and military power in his own person but also used two war ministries which could be played off against each other. The ministry of war material was kept separate from that of war personnel until they were brought under one roof in 1814.[12] The new 'ministry of war' nevertheless remained divided into two parts until 1817,[13] under the hand of a General Secretary. This man quickly became the most important member of the administration, and despite several attempts to abolish it, his office remained secure. He worked through between three and eight administrative divisions at different times, either directly or through between two and four General Directors. These usually supervised Personnel, Accounts and Supply as separate departments, with Algeria coming to importance after 1840. The detail of ministerial organisation changed almost annually, however, as ministers came and went.[14]

Apart from the executive bureaucracy, the ministry also contained a variety of consultative agencies which were manned almost entirely by soldiers. It was from these that demands for reform usually emerged, although by the same token they were usually least well placed to implement it. There were the committees of inspectors from each arm which met at the start of each year to see what changes were required within their own specialities: there was the *Dépôt de la Guerre,* effectively the headquarters of the Staff Corps and the intelligence services: and there were various committees specially appointed for specific tasks – most notably the *Comité de Défense,* which sat intermittently to discuss the strategy of national defence. All these institutions were composed of soldiers chosen for their ability to advise the minister, and for their technical expertise. With the possible exception of the *Dépôt*, none of them was supposed to have any executive or political weight, although it was only natural that, as the highest corporate expressions of the active army, they should have made several attempts to obtain both.

The members of these bodies felt that their agenda was too unsystematic and their meetings too little co-ordinated to produce a reasoned programme of military reform. Agitation for such a thing remained largely a matter of individual crusades in Parliament or the press, although it eventually crystallised into a quite widespread demand for a new *Conseil Supérieure de la Guerre*.[15] The idea was as much for soldiers to organise themselves, in face of bureaucrats and politicians, as it was a genuine call for military efficiency. It looked less at the Prussian concept of a General Staff, or even at those structures 'in the English manner'[16] that were claimed as models, than at some respected home-grown precedents such as Guibert's *Conseil de la Guerre* of 1789 or Napoleon's military committee of the *Conseil d'État*. The legislative authority of the latter body had been attenuated by the Emperor's personal supremacy, but it had been a useful forum for the discussion of military affairs between soldiers and politicians, bypassing the bureaucrats. In the constitutional monarchies the *Conseil d'État* had been reduced to an occasional consultative role on legal technicalities, and its reforming inclinations were lost. A brief attempt was made in 1814 to recreate a proper *Conseil de Guerre* for the great task of rebuilding the post-war army, but in common with all subsequent attempts this was ultimately vetoed by the minister and the court.[17]

There were many ideas current about the form a new *Conseil Supérieur* should take. Some thought that its role was already nearly filled by the generals of the Royal Guard, who had a powerful collective influence at court.[18] Others believed that united sessions of the committees of the various arms would serve just as well.[19] The *Conseil Supérieur de la Guerre* that was finally set up in 1827, however, was forced on the court by liberal victories in Parliament, and rested on a misunderstanding by the Dauphin of the implications of his resulting take-over of military appointments. He saw the new body chiefly as a means of bypassing the government and its minister of war, which naturally offended both Caux, the minister in question, and the *Conseil Supérieur* itself. When it transpired that appointments were still effectively run by the bureaucracy, furthermore, the Dauphin was also disappointed in turn.[20]

No one viewed the *Conseil Supérieur* with the sort of reverence that was to be reserved for its memory by subsequent reformers, and many of its members were either opposed to change or ambivalent. Thus the aristocratic cavalryman Préval opposed attempts to widen the basis of recruitment or shorten the length of service, yet was led by his Bonapartism, and role as prime mover of the new administrative code, to mount a sustained demand to reform the Intendance. Although he had no thought of using the *Conseil Supérieur* for radical change, he was still a staunch supporter of its existence as a political outlet for army opinion.

Apart from one Intendant, the *Conseil Supérieur* of 1827 was composed of sixteen soldiers, of whom two cavalrymen and two engineers were known to be opposed to reforming the recuitment law in the direction of a trained reserve, but about half were known to favour it. None of the reformers were from the Cavalry; only three had risen through staff appointments; only their two leading spokesmen, Marmont and Ambrugéac,[21] were from old noble backgrounds; and most of them were more or less Bonapartist in sympathy. The known opponents of reform, on the other hand, although they included two members of the 'third estate', had all risen through staff appointments – a fact which perhaps helps to confirm that reformism grew out of command experience. Of the remaining four members of the *Conseil Supérieur* whose views on reform are unknown, all except Molitor probably opposed it. Three of them were royalists, including two who had risen by service as staff officers.[22]

Caux, the minister of war, had originally intended that discussion within the *Conseil Supérieur* should be restricted to such immediate problems as army morale, the half pay officers, and some minor ways of saving money. Progressive members nevertheless soon extended their deliberations to wider issues of recruitment and the length of service, such as a normal ministerial committee could not have addressed.[23] Comprising three marshals and the leading generals of every arm, the *Conseil Supérieur* was sufficiently robust to impose upon the minister. A reaction was nevertheless quick to follow from many different directions, with the court objecting to attacks on the Guard, conservatives objecting to the very idea of reform,[24] and the minister closing ranks with his entrenched bureaucrats. Three successively less radical programmes had to be abandoned in face of this combined opposition, and the *Conseil Supérieur* gradually fell into disuse.[25] In 1830 it was dissolved completely, being replaced by the pious hope that a strengthened Committee of Infantry and Cavalry would be an acceptable substitute.

The committees of the arms

After the *Conseil Supérieur* had failed, the demand for its revival continued, and had to be placated. Préval was particularly interested in the possibilities offered by the Infantry and Cavalry Committees, and of linking them to a 'Central Committee' which would include delegates from other arms. In this concept he was looking back to Clarke's united Infantry and Cavalry Committee of 1816, which had been established to discuss wide reforms in administration, but which had been emasculated by Gouvion St Cyr.[26] Various combinations of Infantry and Cavalry Committee had been attempted during the Restoration, but had never achieved much prominence, hence Préval's envisaged central co-ordinating role for this committee would have represented a major promotion.[27] He was supported at first by Soult in 1832, but his agitation for wider powers quickly alienated much of the army, and when Soult left office in 1834 the 'Central Committee' was effectively abandoned. After that, Préval found increasing difficulty in keeping the Infantry and Cavalry elements united in the same committee, and they were finally separated in 1841.[28] As a reforming agency the combined committee had always been a compromise, and failed to give an unambiguous lead. As the press put it, 'A thick cloud covers what it has done and what it ought to do; it's lucky it was set up to innovate and conserve, both at the same time . . .'[29]

It was also criticised for its relative lack of members with established positions at court, and characterised as a collection of upstarts trying to undermine vested interests: 'It is only a miniature version of the ministry, which seeks only to obstruct the minister's action; a sort of 'camarilla' of officers that is better at upsetting the army's general welfare than at furthering it.'[30] Pelet, one of the committee's chief opponents, would have preferred his own organisation, the Staff Corps, to have had a separate committee which – since the staff alone took an overview of the whole art of war – could have achieved a privileged position next to the minister and could advise him on all these subjects.[31]

The strength of an arm's committee was something of an index to that arm's importance, and certainly of its degree of centralisation, since the inspectors who sat on it would be constantly struggling to retain their patronage against that of the court, the Intendance and the minister. They could do this partly by exerting strong control over their subordinates, imposing regularity and uniformity throughout the dispersed regimental garrisons, and thereby removing opportunities for direct appeals to politicians or bureaucrats. In the Restoration such appeals had been almost encouraged in the Infantry and Cavalry, as a weapon against Bonapartism; but by the July Monarchy the inspectorate had successfully asserted its authority. Préval's campaign for revised regulations had played an important part in this evolution, although an unfortunate price was paid in pedantic emphasis on dry detail.[32]

Among other arms which might have had committees, the Chasseurs à Pied failed to establish their claim to be separate from the Infantry, and were given no committee. The Gendarmerie's committee never had more than secondary importance, while those of both the Intendance and Staff Corps were eclipsed by the more visible other activities of their arms within the ministry. The two technical arms of the Artillery and the Engineers, on the other hand, each had especially strong committees and were backed by extensive private bureaucracies independent of the Intendance. Especially in the Restoration, they were each given a 'First Inspector General' with wide powers over their respective administrations, while their attached Intendants were given subordinate employment rather than the independent, and implicitly equal, offices that were the more normal arrangement.[33] Some of this predominance was lost in the July Monarchy as a result of the rise of the Staff Corps, but the Artillery and Engineers still enjoyed a privileged position. Unlike any other arm, they had their own separate 'sections' in the ministry which were run by their own members and exempted from the operations of the Director of Personnel.

The high status of the technical arms had an historical basis, since in the eighteenth century they had required an advanced organisation long before it had been claimed by, let alone granted to, the Infantry and the Cavalry. As a result the gunners and engineers had enjoyed a head's start in the ministry, and had accumulated an experience of departmental politics which allowed them, uniquely, to at least hold their own against the bureaucrats.

All this, however, made the technical arms almost as obstructive to the idea of a *Conseil Supérieur* as the bureaucrats themselves, and for much the same reasons. Any assault on the ministry by outsiders to its normal working was – quite naturally – resented. The idea of a body designed to unify the army, and represent its interests as a single whole, was also generally anathema to most soldiers anyway, and at any level from the inter-regimental café brawl upwards. The corridors of the ministry were certainly no exception to the general rule of 'cap badge exclusivity',[34] and every arm had its own self-image ready to hand as either 'the mainstay of the throne' or 'the democratic arm *par excellence*', depending on the political requirements of the case. Even those who lamented the disunity which such attitudes produced were ultimately caught up in their own polemic. Fabvier, for example, apparently wanted a *Conseil Supérieur* as much as a weapon against the Engineers as against the Intendance.[35]

One of the fundamental factors in the predominance of the special arms was the monopoly of education and 'military science' which they had enjoyed in the eighteenth century. At a time when warfare had been largely a matter of sieges, it had been natural to entrust its higher planning to the experts in that activity. During the early Revolution, too, many of the best officers remaining in French service from the *Ancien Régime* had come from the Third Estate, and had won promotion through their technical expertise in the Artillery or Engineers. Only in later times had the role of siegecraft receded before more mobile operations, and the Staff Corps science of 'Strategy' began to be recognised. Education, moreover, was rapidly widening its scope in both society and army, with even ncos being expected to be literate after 1818. The particular science, numeracy and literacy of the gunner and the engineer were thus being outflanked from several directions, and they could no longer claim to be the sole guardians of the military mystery. Their institutional hold on the formation of policy, however, took rather longer to be relaxed.

The Committees of Defence

Contingency planning for national strategy was conducted in a 'Committee of Defence' that was called at irregular intervals whenever the minister thought a revision was due. The three régimes between 1815 and 1851 each held one series of meetings to decide on the military needs of their new status quo, and there were additional partial meetings in the intervals. The committee's decisions were extremely influential on the way contemporaries viewed strategic questions, and although many of their recommendations would never be fully implemented due to lack of funds, they in fact lay at the very root of all planning for possible large future wars. The difficulty was that with the exception of that of 1848, these committees restricted their investigations to the fortifications of France, and were composed almost entirely of members of the 'technical arms'. The repeated plea that new forms of conscription and a new – reduced – role for fortification should be discussed, were doomed to failure. It was paradoxically felt both that the traditional role of the technical arms in deciding strategy should be maintained, yet precisely because the committee was drawn only from those arms, not all aspects of strategy should be discussed. The only sensible alternative was some form of *Conseil Supérieur*, which was a generally unacceptable option.

There was nevertheless a weakening of the rigid hold of the technical arms upon successive Committees of Defence, which can be traced in the evolution of the type of war that they expected to fight. The original terms of reference given to Maréscot, the president of the committee which started work in 1818, included an assumption of an attack by 600,000 allies against 300,000 French troops – a less serious threat than could be mounted by a full coalition such as those of 1814 or 1815, but the worst that the Bourbons felt they might face in the diplomatic circumstances of the time.[36] From this it was but a short step back to the old view of wars as limited affairs on the frontier. Some generals refused to accept this view, however, and continued to see the future in terms of the national mobilisations witnessed in the recent past. Pelet especially saw any system based on fortification as the perpetuation of the hold of the special arms on an area which by rights belonged to the Staff. He had great faith in 'Strategy' as a staff science which transcended siegecraft, and in the Committee of Defence he provoked Andréossy, a champion of the independence of each arm, into an angry demand of 'What does this word "Strategy" mean?'[37] Whenever possible, Pelet would try to show that a fortress should be built at some unlikely spot indicated by the interests of strategy, or of the National Guard's mobilisation, rather than by the limited topographical obsessions of the Artillery or the Engineers. His personal acerbity in favour of a defensive republican war, however, was often at odds with the general feeling of an age when even Clausewitz was talking of a reversion to the professional fortress wars of the *Ancien Régime*.

Most members of the committee were divided or ambivalent in their views, and preferred to treat each problem individually rather than be tied to some general system. For example, they wanted the armament factories moved from their exposed sites on the frontier, but were reluctant to downgrade frontier fortresses in favour of large entrenched camps in the interior. In so doing, however, they implicitly rejected the claims of 'Strategy' to speak for a wider whole, and Maréscot was quick to state this openly. Equally Dode, Valée and Guilleminot, although men of broad vision, were present as presidents of their respective arm committees, and hence suspicious of the Defence Committee's potential to extend its powers into their own areas.[38]

At a less elevated level, the committee was keen to keep abreast with changes in the art of fortification. There were many new ideas in the air, ranging from Carnot's idea that defences held by conscripts should be held by repeated counter-attacks, to Paixhans' penchant for automatic steam artillery and other wonders of modern science. Perhaps the most influential writer in the field was Rogniat, who was actually a believer in large entrenched camps rather than Vauban's chequerboard of relatively small forts.[39] Since the latter could be masked by large armies advancing past them, he argued that the defender needed to keep his reserves in greater concentrations than hitherto, for disruptive counter-attacks into the enemy's rear. The Committee of Defence held long arguments over this issue.

Paradoxically, Pelet himself preferred a national defence that was conducted by numerous small National Guard posts held 'in the spirit of Saragossa'. He also believed in holding the frontier zone as a base for offensive operations – themselves a contingency which few of his colleagues on the committee were prepared to contemplate. In taking these positions, however, Pelet found himself in an uneasy alliance with the traditionalists who opposed Andréossy from the opposite side, and who wanted to continue the Vauban system almost unchanged. Chief of these was Maréscot, who saw his duty as president in terms of reducing Vauban's triple cordon to a double one, with little need to turn either Paris or Bitche into entrenched camps. He felt that maybe Tours would be a better choice as an interior redoubt, since it was closer to the Bourbons' ultimate fallback position in the Vendée, and he was ready to upgrade the interior fortress of Langres. Apart from that, however, his only concessions were to reduce a few of the exposed posts on the extreme frontier in Alsace and Lorraine.

When the next Committee of Defence was called in 1836, its members made a more homogenous group from the technical arms, more tightly united against the other arms. This was partly a reaction to the growth in influence of the Staff Corps, and to a lesser extent to that of the Infantry and Cavalry. Since the war scare of 1830–31, furthermore, the very idea of a technically exclusive professional force itself seemed to be under threat, bringing all parts of the army to its defence – but none more so than the Artillery and Engineers. This argument was effectively won by the time of Thiers' 1841 doctrine for the fortification of Paris, which made an elegant combination of advanced technology, a theoretical mass mobilisation and enhanced opportunities for limited action on the frontier. Thiers' concern to deter a major war not only made plentiful work for the technical arms in the massive scheme to fortify the capital, but also made an unspoken assumption that the professional army would be

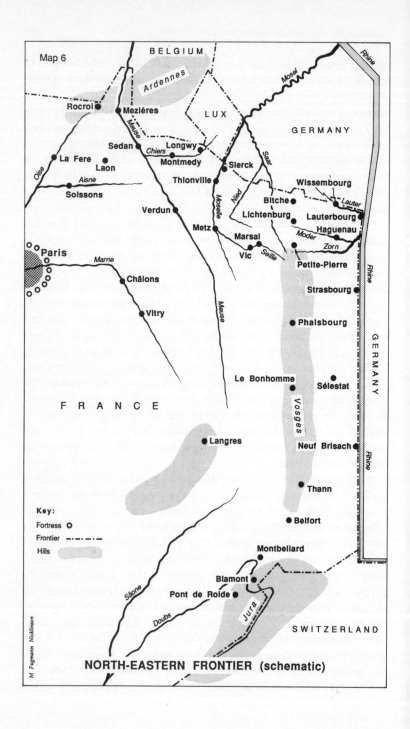

Map 6

BELGIUM

Ardennes

LUX

GERMANY

Rhine

Rocroi

Mezières

Mosel

Sedan
Chiers
Longwy

Meuse

La Fere
Laon

Montmedy

Slerck

Saar

Wissembourg

Oise

Thionville

Nied

Bitche

Lauter

Soissons

Aisne

Lichtenburg

Lauterbourg

Moselle

Haguenau

Verdun

Moder

Zorn

Metz

Marsal

Paris

Marne

Vic
Seille

Petite-Pierre

Rhine

Châlons

Strasbourg

Vitry

Phalsbourg

GERMANY

Meuse

Le Bonhomme

Sélestat

FRANCE

Vosges

Langres

Neuf Brisach

Rhine

Thann

Key:
Fortress O
Frontier —·—·—
Hills

Belfort

Montbellard

Blamont

Saône

Pont de Roide

Jura

Doubs

SWITZERLAND

M. Fagmann Nicklinson

NORTH-EASTERN FRONTIER (schematic)

all the more free to pursue its small wars without the need for a *levée en masse*.[40]

The 1836 Committee of Defence marked a step along the road to Thiers' formulation of 1841. It wanted increased fortifications for the extreme front line in Alsace and Lorraine,[41] thereby emphasising the role of the professional standing army, and incidentally reversing Maréscot's 1818 decision to step back to regroup before mounting a counter-attack. Within its general agreement on forward defence, however, the committee found many issues to debate.

The peace treaty of 1815 had deprived France of some of her fortresses on the left bank of the Rhine, opening a sector between Metz and Bitche and thrusting Wissembourg into the front line. The question therefore revolved on the degree to which this area should be strengthened, and how. Haxo favoured a strong line on the Lauter supported on its flank by the then relatively weak fortress of Bitche, but with no corresponding defence in Lorraine north of the Seille.[42] Rogniat's conservative 'Committee of Fortifications', the arm committee of the Engineers, also wanted to convert Bitche into an entrenched camp as a dépôt to cover Lorraine,[43] and succeeded in having the Lauter reinstated as a serious defensive line. Officers on the ground, however, continued to regard these advanced works as dangerously exposed, and they were supported by politicians who were reluctant to convert any more land to military use than was absolutely necessary.

The 1836 committee also accepted the fortification of Paris more readily had that of 1818, although there was still a controversy over the best method to be used. Dode, the president of the committee and eventual supervisor of the works, favoured detached forts – and was supported by Rogniat and Caraman, while Valazé and Haxo preferred the more 'democratic' continuous *enceinte*.[44] This question generated considerable heat, and was finally settled only by Thiers' compromise of using both types of fortification.

The next debate on strategy took place in 1848, when a 'Commission of Defence' was convened on a very different basis from its two predecessors.[45] It was no longer an exclusive gathering of the technical arms, and its scope was specifically extended well beyond the question of fortification. It also sat at the very height of an official realisation that a war was probably imminent, and that the nation was ill prepared to fight it. The commission suggested reforms in every part of the military system, not least in the controversial sphere of recruiting, where the scale of the impending crisis seemed to demand a temporary abandonment of the 'professional' ideology. Gone were Maréscot and Dode's frontier wars, and Thiers' logical solutions. The new revolution gave new life to the idea of a mass mobilisation, and did so in a body which looked remarkably similar to a *Conseil Supérieur*. It was scarcely surprising that this body was rapidly put in abeyance, or that its early unanimity soon dissolved as its underlying radicalism became obvious.

Pelet was a member of the commission, as he had been of its two predecessors, although he was now officially in retirement. He had become more shrill and pedantic than ever, although his demands for reform were more in harmony with the real world than those of conservative opponents such as the royalist Courtigis. Other members of the commission included Oudinot, Bedeau and Lamoricière from the African army, and Schramm, the influential doyen of the Infantry Committee.[46] On paper this should have made a sufficiently weighty and reformist body to achieve important changes.

The commission was ultimately unsuccessful in part because the war crisis itself diverted effort away from structural reform and into the pressing business of organising men and material. The revolutionary atmosphere of the moment also made generals hesitant to 'innovate' in the one institution which might save the state from anarchy. Bedeau and Oudinot were particularly identified with the *reprise en main* which followed the June Days. Finally there was the opposition of the minister, who saw the commission as a challenge to his authority. After only six weeks he downgraded it to the status of merely a 'Consultative Commission on Organisation', in which guise it lingered on for a few months more. It was followed by a reforming impetus given by Lamioricière when he became minister in turn, but although this produced a parliamentary 'Commission on the Public Force', it never approached the same level of military independence as had been foreshadowed by the earlier institution.[47] As the nation and the army slipped back into conservatism and 'order', so the possibility of military reform also evaporated, and no true *Conseil Supérieur* was set up until 1871.

The rise of the Staff Corps

The Commission of Defence in 1848 was the first strategic planning body which included fewer members of the technical arms than of the others, and was particularly noteworthy for its predominance of Staff Corps members. This marked a victory for which the Staff had been working since their creation in 1818: the recognition that they were competent to deliberate on higher military policy rather than to act merely as office boys for commanders. Indeed, the commission of 1848 went as far as to provide special light cavalry units for that service.

The generalised view of strategy that was the hallmark of the Staff Corps grew in importance in proportion as progress was made in civil and military centralisation on Paris, and also by the advent of the railway. Pelet, as head of the corps during the July Monarchy, was quick to see the need for a unified national plan of mobilisation and manoeuvre, making use of new technology. As early as 1842 he issued a directive for the corps which outlined future defensive plans in terms of railways, telegraphs, and 'the powerful centralisation which should save the homeland'.[48] Unfortunately this plan lost some of its revolutionary force through its obsession with esoteric and geometrical calculations of a pedantry quite equal to those of the technical arms that Pelet condemned. Indeed, he was later forced to admit that his own geometry should not be taken too seriously,[49] although he did at least have the satisfaction of seeing a continuous growth in the influence of his corps.

As a new creation in 1818, the Staff Corps had faced hostility from many entrenched interests, and all the more so because Gouvion St Cyr had used it as a means for bringing many Bonapartists back into the officer corps. Generals resented the Staff demand to appropriate the choice of their adcs; while colonels were horrified to see their subalterns elbowed aside, including in promotion, by staff officers visiting their regiments on fleeting 'sandwich courses'. On campaign the gulf between the Staff and the Line was as notorious as it was inevitable, just as in society the staff officers always seemed to be more brilliant and better connected. This gulf was never healed, and the time spent by staff officers in regimental duties remained low. The practical necessity for a Staff Corps, on the other hand, was an idea which did gradually gain favour. A succession of writings, and its increasing organisational authority, helped convince many soldiers of its essential place in warfare. A series of clashes with the other arms also helped to define its place in the workings of the army, although at the same time they appear to have produced a store of grudges against the Staff that were not forgotten after 1870.[50] Friction was especially acute with the Intendance and the technical arms, some of whose functions the Staff was appropriating, although in the case of the Intendance the bitterness was somewhat modified by the inclusion of several former staff officers in its ranks.[51]

The *Dépot de la Guerre*, as an ancient establishment created to deal with intelligence, cartography and the minister's archives, was occasionally included in the formal organisation of the ministry, although it was more normally left on the fringes. When the Staff Corps and its *École d'Application* were created, they brought a new lease of life to the *Dépot,* being loosely under the command of the *Dépot's* director. An annual 'Staff Commission' was established under his presidency to fill the role of an arm committee, although apart from a brief interlude in the Restoration the prestige of the latter title was conferred only after 1841.[52] It is noticeable that this happened at the same time as Pelet found himself able to use 'strategy' and railways as an effective argument against the technical arms, and when even Orleans' manoeuvre camps were starting to take proper account of staff functions. At this point the Staff appeared to be well on the way to asserting itself as an arm which dictated policy to others.

The *Dépot,* however, remained largely on the fringes of power and, apart from a brief moment of glory in the Defence Commission of 1848, continued to be purely consultative rather than exercising the full political influence which was potentially within its grasp. Perhaps the reason for this is to be found in Pelet himself, who was an awkward political operator. Having raised the Staff further than he could have hoped when he took it over in 1830, he was also possibly inclined to be cautious in the 1840s. To have aimed any higher would have enmeshed him in politics, and he felt very strongly that his personal role was merely military. At some point around 1832 he had even told the minister that he had a horror of exposing himself to the hurly-burly of political existence: 'Far from wishing for an extension in the scope of my directorate, I would rather have hoped to see it restricted, in order to spare you, as much as me, from political responsibility and odious accusations which respect neither the purest of intentions nor the most loyal and candid of conduct.'[53] Here in a nutshell was the reason why the army of the constitutional monarchies failed to produce an equivalent to the Prussian General Staff. 'Simple soldiers' like Pelet felt they should defer to the minister, and ultimately had no business setting up any equivalent of a *Conseil Supérieur* that might seem to challenge his authority.

10

Conclusion: a mature yet innovative army

The French army of the constitutional monarchies was a perfectly-forged instrument for the roles it was intended to fulfil. It was relatively small, cheap and unobtrusive in everyday life; yet normally obedient and fully prepared to defend order against anarchy. As it shook itself free from the political tensions of 1815, and gained expertise in the crises of 1830–31 and 1848–51, the army developed an appropriate set of philosophic attitudes and tactical doctrines for the suppression of internal disturbances, riots and – indeed – mutinies.

The army was also an ideal weapon for a judicious series of limited wars on the frontier and in Algeria. It had dash, *attaque* and high military science. Its leaders were uniquely experienced, and its men were hard-bitten professionals. What they might lack in aristocratic or scholarly culture, they more than made up for in 'military nobility', straightforwardness and high morale. Between them, they picked up the nation's honour from the mud of Waterloo and – apparently effortlessly – restored it to a position of international pre-eminence. France was thus enabled to dictate the evolution of its neighbouring countries, no less than to lay the foundations of a novel African empire.

Government policy was consistently designed to avoid *La Grande Guerre* on the Rhine, but the army was nevertheless always acutely conscious that such a war might one day occur. Its network of fortresses and garrisons was orientated towards Alsace and Lorraine, and many of its most active intellects were drawn from those regions. They studied the problem in all its aspects, and devised a new set of prescriptions to keep abreast of changing circumstances.

In the higher echelons of the army there was a growing awareness of the importance of the Staff and of the Jominian sciences associated with the word 'Strategy'. Napoleon and his lessons were studied and digested, and usually with rather more constructive criticism of his mistakes than blind admiration of his successes. Pelet and Koch at the *Dépôt*; Rocquancourt, La Roche Aymon and Jacquinot de Presle in the officer schools – and a welter of lesser names besides – gradually updated the army's thinking on these subjects. Rogniat, Paixhans and Haxo also pushed forward the arts of gunnery and fortification, while Thiers and Orleans also produced a burst of reforms around 1840.

Although the attempt to create a *Conseil Superieur de la Guerre* was ultimately a failure, and a fully 'Prussian' conception of staffwork was never quite achieved, the French did at least make some progress in the right directions. They by no means stood in the sort of total antithesis to the Prussians' efficiency that has often been alleged, but were perhaps fifty per cent well organised as against their opponent's fifty-five per cent. In 1870–1 the victory went one hundred per cent to the side which enjoyed only a marginal edge; but that should not blind us to the many excellent ideas and achievements on the side of the loser.

The army was not left small by accident, but as a logical result of its deliberate emphasis on high quality. It always expected to fight outnumbered, if it had to fight 'the northern powers' at all – and the wonder is not so much that Bazaine fielded fewer troops than the Prussians at Gravelotte, but that St Arnaud contrived to meet the Russians on terms of equality in the Crimea, and Napoleon the Austrians at Solferino. The French certainly did multiply their numbers by tactical efficiency, taking the lead in new thinking about the soldier's role in combat no less than in the technology of his weapons.

The *Chasseurs à Pied* became a focus of tactical speculation and firearms design, in somewhat the same way as the *Dépôt de la Guerre* was a centre of strategic thinking. Metropolitan theories were then complemented by the practical experiences of the *Zouaves* and the rest of the African army, making for a rounded whole. A Combes, a Canrobert or a MacMahon would move freely back and forth between the test ranges at Vincennes and the gorges of the Atlas, just as Bugeaud, Lamoricière and Cavaignac saw no contradiction in coming from the war in Africa to the 1848 revolution in France. Only a few drill masters, notably Castellane at Perpignan, shook their heads at the way the war was spoiling the army – but then drill masters usually see things in this light. Besides, Castellane himself made an enormous contribution to the symbiosis between the metropolitan and the African armies, since many of the units arriving in Algeria had been trained by him in a distinctly 'European' manner.

The professionalism of the French army allowed it to stress mobility and manoeuvre, even in the days before the railway, just as its high morale allowed it to contemplate frontal assaults even after the rifle had become universal. These features were seen as keys to the Napoleonic past no less than guides for the future, and they quickly took hold as what we can today see as the characteristically French military ethos of the nineteenth century. This ethos perhaps became bloated beyond measure in the age of Dreyfus and de Grandmaison – but in the earlier period at least it was realistic and useful.

The appearance of a new ethos for combat was accompanied by a novel concern for the soldier's welfare and education in peacetime. Many of the social ideas propagated during the Revolution finally found their way into training curricula, and were complemented by a wave of military Saint Simonianism which anticipated Lyautey's 'social role of the officer' by half a century. There was a proliferation of regimental schools, libraries and gymnasia; there were efforts to make a 'Peaceful Utilization of Military Forces', and calls to soften the discipline. A vocabulary was deployed which stressed the paternal nature of the regimental family; a family which would struggle to save its members from the evils of 'the lazy life of the garrison', from 'nostalgia' and from 'reasoning'. The golden age of scientific progress and political reform thus brought a wealth of moral advances in its train for those members of the nation's youth who were privileged to serve with the colours. France could see that it had an army to be proud of – an innovative and yet compassionate army which could take on all comers.

Appendix I

The military budgets

(All figures in millions of francs)

Year	General Budget of France	Army Budget	As % of General Budget
1815	547.7	200.0	36.5
1816	839.1	180.0	21.4
1817	1,069.3	157.5	14.7
1818	1,098.4	162.8	14.8
1819	869.5	184.8	21.3
1820	737.4	180.0	24.4
1821	882.2	174.7	19.8
1822	899.3	187.3	20.8
1823	899.8	189.7	21.1
1824	895.9	189.7	21.2
1825	898.9	190.0	21.1
1826	914.5	195.0	21.3
1827	915.7	196.0	21.4
1828	922.7	196.0	21.2
1829	974.2	193.7	19.9
1830	972.8	186.8	19.2
1831	825.0	172.6	20.9
1832	1,106.6	309.0	27.9
1833	1,120.4	305.5	27.3
1834	981.9	220.3	22.4
1835	1,009.0	230.2	22.8
1836	998.9	226.7	22.7
1837	1,027.0	226.6	22.1
1838	1,039.3	226.3	21.8
1839	1,063.7	238.9	22.5
1840	1,099.9	247.7	22.5
1841	1,187.8	251.5	21.2
1842	1,276.3	325.8	25.5

Year	General Budget of France	Army Budget	As % of General Budget
1843	1,318.5	330.6	25.1
1844	1,389.2	333.0	24.0
1845	1,363.5	326.0	23.9
1846	1,434.4	325.6	22.7
1847	1,458.7	324.8	22.3
1848	1,446.2	322.0	22.3
1849	1,572.6	346.3	22.0
1850	1,461.5	318.5	21.8
1851	1,367.2	307.5	22.5

Note there were additional funds voted for specific campaigns, e.g. 100 million for the Spanish war of 1823, and 80 million for Greece in 1828. The booty won by the Algerian expedition of 1830 more than paid for its extra cost, although the same could scarcely be said for the remainder of that war, especially when the number of troops committed to it rose sharply in the 1840s.

During the period between 1822–26 and 1857–61, France's Gross National Product increased by about 70%, including a rise in Gross Domestic Product of 80%. This rise is reflected by the rise in the General Budget, and hence of the army's budget. Throughout this period, therefore, the army seems to have taken about the same share of an ever-growing cake.

Source: AHG cartons MR 1985–86, with additional details from Asselain, *Histoire Économique*, p.81.

Appendix II

Military crime

Out of a third of a million soldiers, perhaps 5,000 would stand trial for serious offences each year. Of these nearly a third might be acquitted, and a tenth convicted of the worst categories of offence. Between 1833 and 1851 a total of eighty-four French soldiers were formally executed for military crimes, mostly in Africa. One or two thousand men would be pardoned each year, and around fifty would escape from detention. A dozen or so would be transferred to civil courts, while a third of the remainder would have to wait for more than two months for their trial. Among the most common crimes were desertion, either before or after call-up; various types of theft, and insubordination – in that order of frequency. Political crimes were negligible, running at less than a hundred a year, of which the majority were cases of degrading monuments. It should be remembered, however, that many political dissidents were punished informally, since courts martial would attract too much unwelcome publicity.

Unlike political subversion, ordinary crimes seemed to occur most frequently in the units which changed garrison most often, being proportionately most common in the Infantry, followed by the Artillery, the Cavalry and finally the Engineers. In the Pontonniers – notoriously the most static and therefore most subversive unit in the army – crime was actually comparatively rare. The special African units, on the other hand, had far more crime than any other troops, with usually as many executions in a year as the whole of the French element in the army. Over two-thirds of crimes were committed by volunteers or replacements, as opposed to conscripts, while graduates of military schools were responsible for a mere three or four per year. Approximately one officer in 1,500, one nco in 200 and one private soldier in 50 would come to trial, and those usually in their first two years of service.

Source: Ministry of War, *Comte Général de l'Administration de la Justice Militaire Pendant l'Année 1833*, and each year to 1851 (Paris 1835–53), and anon., *Notes sur l'Administration,* in AHG MR 1979.

Appendix III

Bibliographical note on secondary sources

There are many excellent general histories of France between 1815 and 1851 – e.g. De la Gorce, Thureau-Dangin, and the less voluminous but more modern Ponteil, and Jardin and Tudesq. For the *Grande Bourgeoisie* Lhomme is stimulating, while Johnson gives us the essential Guizot. On the level of *mentalités*, Nora and Zeldin have each produced an exciting – and lengthy – window on to a France that is all too rarely reported.

The most vivid broad outlines of the army between the two Napoleons may be found in Carrias, *La Pensée Militaire Française*, and in the more partisan general histories by Weygand, de Gaulle and to a lesser extent Revol. Thoumas has many details of administration and organisation, as seen by the generation of the *Débâcle*, although few writers look far into the *Dépôt de la Guerre* or the *Conseil Supérieur de la Guerre*. Monteilhet's splendidly Jaurèsien *Institutions Militaires de la France* has exerted great influence in the twentieth century, mainly on matters of recruitment policy. More recent treatments of this army in English include the articles by Chapman, Kovaks and Holroyd.

To fully understand the flavour of many of the above works, it is essential to understand the depth of the historiographical bias occasioned by the defeat of 1870. Digeon's *Crise Allemande* puts this into its best general perspective, with Girardet's *Idée Coloniale* and Sternhell's *Droite Révolutionnaire* making splendid companion volumes. Pungent contemporary examples include Renan's *Réforme Intellectuelle et Morale (1871)* Gobineau's *Guerre des Turcomans* (1875) and Zola's *Débâcle* (1892). For military aspects of 1870, Bonnal and Irvine are eloquent on 'the French Discovery of Clausewitz' while Howard, supported by Holmes, Adriance and Ascoli, has modern discussions in English that are nevertheless still based on the consensus view.

For the eighteenth-century French military background see especially Léonard, and Corvisier's modern sociological studies; but also Duffy's *Military Experience in the Age of Reason* and Colin's whole *oeuvre*, including its compact summaries in English by Spencer Wilkinson and Quimby. For the 1790s, Cobb's *Armées Revolutionnaires* explains the social context of the armed mob; while Bertaud, Scott and Lynn each have good modern perspectives on different aspects of the field army. Reinhart's *Le Grand Carnot* and Phipps's *Armies of the First French Republic* also still have much to tell us.

So much has been written on the army of Napoleon that it is futile here to attempt a list; but volumes 29 to 32 of the Emperor's official correspondence contain some influential post-1815 debates. Tulard and Chandler have excellent general summaries of his career – to which we may add Geyl and Dubreton for the evolution of the Napoleonic legend, and Vachée, De Philip, Lechartier and Escalle for staffwork.

Essential for tracing individual careers throughout our period are Six on the Napoleonic generals, supported for the rising generation by the series of official *Annuaires,* and by personnel dossiers from the *Archives Administratives de la Guerre.* Volumes of biography are naturally still more revealing, where they are available, especially Debidour on Fabvier, Azan and Ideville on Bugeaud, Keller on Lamoricière, De Luna on Cavaignac and Bapst on Canrobert. Among the authors of memoirs, Castellane and La Motte Rouge stand out as particularly full – although almost all the others have valuable insights to offer, too.

The 'social role of the officer' was already a central theme for the military writers of de Vigny's generation, long before Lyautey had been born. It was also addressed to some extent by novelists such as Stendhal or Balzac, and by political theorists such as de Maistre or de Tocqueville – not to mention the military St-Simonians described by Collinet and Pinet. In recent times this whole subject-area experienced an understandably great revival during the Algerian crises of the 1950s and 1960s, when it became the focus of two modern military classics – Chalmin's *L'Officier Français* and Girardet's *La Société Militaire dans la France Contemporaine.* Monteil's *Les Officiers* is also useful, albeit less deep, whereas the works of Croubois and Serman represent a 'second generation' which seems to owe rather more to the first than it is prepared to admit. Associated with similar themes, the plight of Restoration half-pay officers is well covered by Vidalenc; military voting rights are in Charnay; and the governmental involvement of officers is instructively treated by Ornano.

Also on the political plane, the army's role in major revolutions is covered in all good general histories of France; but see especially Girard for the National Guard. The baffling changes of loyalty come through in personal memoirs such as those of Castellane, Barrès and Commissaire, while among modern writers Montagne is excellent for the Lyon riots; Bouillon and Zaniewicki for 1848; Gooch for 1851. Cobb's *The Police and the People* looks into the more low-level internal security background, and Spitzer's *Old Hatreds and Young Hopes* gives an exemplary analysis of higher police organisation no less than of Carbonarist conspirators up to about 1823. Porch takes the story on to 1835, while both Guillon and Savigear provide excellent general treatments of the Restoration's plots and mutinies.

Recruiting policy may be followed in Duvergier's collection of laws, and through the parliamentary debates reported in the *Moniteur Universel.* It is extensively discussed in Monteilhet and in Challener's musings on the nation in arms, with an interpretation of the *Loi Soult* in Porch. Schnapper's thesis is essential for the whole question of replacement, while Forrest helps us to understand the draft dodger.

Beyond general histories, magazine articles and personal memoirs, the campaigns between Waterloo and the Alma are relatively little reported. This era was so far overshadowed by the epic events of Napoleonic times that the wider public – which was later to thrill to Joffre's march on Timbuktu at the head of a mere 1,000 troops, or Marchand's to Fashoda with only 120 – could remain unmoved by feats such as the Duc d'Angoulême's capture of Cadiz with 100,000 men.

Bittard des Portes discusses the small wars of the Restoration, and is interestingly supplemented by Clayton on the various African involvements. Bugeaud, Aumale, Orleans and many others have material on Algeria – although Julien is still the best modern source, supported by Yacono on the Arab bureaux and Regnault on cohorts of officers. Castellane's memoirs and the Appendix to Duffy's *Fire and Stone* are revealing on Antwerp; while Trevelyan provides a handy account, albeit slanted against the French point of view, on the Italian involvements. Pemberton has a useful succinct summary of the Crimean War, as does Wylly of the 1859 war.

Apart from Carrias, French military thought at this period is covered briefly in Mordacq and Wanty, with idiosyncratic sidelights from Karcher and Jonquière. Both the Earle and Paret editions of *Makers of Modern Strategy* have very valuable articles on Jomini in particular – by Gilbert and Shy respectively – and on military thought in general by many other pens. Jomini's life is also laid bare by de Courville, and stimulatingly discussed by Howard, although it is mightily overshadowed in the literature by that of Clausewitz – notably in the various works by Paret. For parallel developments in other countries, see Christiansen and Carr on Spain; Curtiss on Russia and, especially, Strachan on Britain.

For the French military schools, see Pinet on Polytechnique and Titeux on St Cyr, not forgetting Spivak on the gymnastic schools. The significance of the *Chasseurs à Pied* seems to have been largely overlooked since the days of Aumale and Engels, and Hicks merely lists their weaponry without comment.

Bibliography

Manuscript sources

(a) Archives Historiques de la Guerre, Château de Vincennes
Inspection reports for the infantry 1831–45: Chasseurs à Pied Xb 716–21;
Zouaves Xb 723; Légion Étrangère Xb 725–7; Tirailleurs Indigènes Xb 724;
Infanterie de Ligne Xb 626–94; Infanterie Légère Xb 695–715; Infanterie Légère
et Tirailleurs d'Afrique Xb 728–9.

Other documents on inspections 1815–51: Xs 23–6, 95–6, Xb 625, 736–8 and
(overall reports on Artillery inspections) Xd 370.

Bureaucracy of the Ministry of War: Infantry Commission Xs 138, 140–2, MR
2127; Committees of Defence Xs 135, MR 1995–6, 2076–9, 2096–8; Dépôt de la
Guerre MR 2070 and uncatalogued Dépôt cartons A35, B12, D42; Conseil
Supérieur de la Guerre MR 2050–1; other administration Xb 161, Xe 283–4, 470–
1, 359, Xem 21, Xd 387, 400, 402, 452; MR 1910, 1953–4, 1979, 1984–6, 1988,
1999, 2019, 2013, 2038, 2198.

Training camps: Xj 1, 42, MR 1799, 1987, 2068–9, 2118.

Tactics and regimental training: H 226, Xj 54, Xs 143, MR 1844, 1946–7, 1962,
1990, 2004, 2008, 2010-i3, 2022, 2029, 2034, 2041, 2043, 2057, 2071, 2073, 2129,
2140–1, 2151.

General correspondence, where consulted: Catalogue of General Correspondence, July – December 1835, and D (3) 97; E (4) 27–9; E (5) 50, 59, 69, 71, 78,
80–1, 183.

Military schools: H217, Xae 19, Xem 12, Xo 1, 8, 11–15, 18, Xs 139, MR 1945,
1955–6, 1978, 1986, 1989, 1997–8, 2009, 2177, 2189–90, Xae 58.

Personnel: MR 2134, 2142.

(b) Archives Administratives de la Guerre, Château de Vincennes
The personal career dossiers of some 217 generals or marshals were consulted,
and those of some 719 other officers – although the latter are often very deficient
in detail.

Printed sources

P.A.J. Allent, *État du Corps du Genie Suivi du Précis de l'Histoire des Arts et des Institutions Militaires en France*, Paris, 1836

Gen. J. Ambert, *La Colonne Napoleone et le Camp de Boulogne*, Paris, 1839

Gen. J. Ambert, *Esquisses Historiques de l'Armée Française*, new edn, Brussels, 1841

Gen. J. Ambert, *Soldat*, Paris, 1854

Gen. J. Ambert, *Études Tactiques pour l'Instruction dans les Camps*, Paris, 1865

Official publication, *Annuaire de l'Armée Française*, Paris, annually, 1815–51

B. Appert, *Manuel Théorique et Pratique de la Méthode d'Enseignement Mutuel pour les Écoles Régimentaires*, Paris, 1821

B. Appert, *Du Ministère de la Guerre, des Sous-Officiers, et des Écoles Régimentaires d'Éducation Mutuel*, Paris, 1827

Col. C.J.J.J. Ardant du Picq, *Battle Studies* Trans. and ed. Greely and Cotton, New York, 1921

Duc d'Aumale, *Les Institutions Militaires de la France*, Paris, 1867

Duc d'Aumale, *Les Zouaves et les Chasseurs à Pied*, new edn, Paris, 1896

Chef de Bn. J.B. Avril, *Avantages d'une Bonne Discipline et Moyens de l'Entretenir dans les Corps*, Paris, 1824

J. Aymard, *Exemples de Vertu, Traits de Courage, de Grandeur d'Ame, d'Héroisme, de Piété Filiale, Offerts à la Jeunesse*, Lille, 1827

'B.G.', *Théorie Militaire du Pas de Course*, Paris, 1841

Gen. E.A. Bardin, *Dictionnaire de l'Armée de Terre*, ed. Oudinot, 4 vols., Paris, 1851

J.B.B. Billaudel, *Quelques Aperçus sur la Théorie des Chermins de Fer*, Bordeaux, 1837

Capt. Le Blanc d'Eguilly, *Prospectus d'un Plan Militaire Concernant les Attaques Nocturnes*, Paris, 1808

L.A. Blanqui, *Textes Choisis*, ed. Volguine, Paris, 1955

Sgt-Maj. J. Boichot, *Aux Électeurs de l'Armée*, Lausanne, 1850

Chef de Bn. Bonjouan de Lavarenne, *Mémorial de l'Officier d'État-Major en Campagne*, Paris, 1833

M. de Bonnal, *La Force et l'Idée – Lettres au Général Cavaignac sur les Réformes d'Émile de Girardin*, Paris, 1848

Capt. G.C.J. Braccini, *L'Armée et le Socialisme: Simples Réflexions sur la Question du Moment*, Paris, 1849

Gen. F. Brack, *Avant Postes de Cavalerie Légère*, 6th edn, Paris, 1880

Mal. T.R. Bugeaud, *Les Socialistes et le Travail en Commun*, Paris, 1848

Mal. T.R. Bugeaud, *Aperçus sur Quelques Détails de la Guerre*, 24th edn, Paris, 1873

Mal. T.R. Bugeaud, *Par l'Épée et par la Charrue*, ed. Azan, Paris, 1948

J. du Camp, *Histoire de l'Armée*, new edn, 4 vols., Paris, 1850

L. Carnot, *De la Défense des Places Fortes*, Paris, 1810

A.F.V.H. de Carrion Nisas, *Les Peuples et Leurs Armées*, Paris, 1820

Gen. M.F.H.E. Carrion Nisas, *Essai sur l'Histoire Générale de l'Art Militaire de son Origine, de ses Progrès, et de ses Révolutions*, 2 vols., Paris, 1824

Gen. M.F.H.E. Carrion Nisas, *Observations sur l'Ouvrage de M Le Lt Gen M Lamarque, 'De l'Esprit Militaire'*, Paris, 1827

Gen. Don M. Cavallero, *Défense de Saragosse*, Paris, 1815

Gen. G. de Chambray, *De l'Infanterie*, Montpellier, 1824

Gen. G. de Chambray, *Philosophie de la Guerre*, Paris, 1827

Gen. G. de Chambray, *Les Deux Derniers Chapitres de ma Philosophie de la Guerre*, Paris, 1835

Gen. G. de Chambray, *De l'École Polytechnique*, Paris, 1836

Gen. G. de Chambray, *De la Transformation de Paris, Ville Ouverte, en Place Forte*, Paris, n.d.

P.N. Chantreau, *Éléments d'Histoire Militaire*, Paris, 1808

Col.(Paris National Guard) F.C. Chapuis, *Quelques Observations sur Diverses Manoeuvres de l'École de Bataillon et des Évolutions de Ligne*, Paris, 1840

Archduke Charles, *Principes de la Stratégie*, trans. Jomini and Koch, 3 vols and atlas, Paris, 1818

Capt. P.M.T. Choumara, *Mémoires sur la Fortification*, Paris, 1847

Gen. C. von Clausewitz, *On War*, ed. P. Paret, B. Brodie & M.E. Howard, Princeton, 1976

Gen. A.L.A. Clouet, *De la Composition et de l'Organisation de l'Armée*, Paris, 1828

Capt. P. Colonjon, *De l'Armée Devant le Socialisme*, Paris, 1849

Capt. P. Colonjon, *La Force et l'Idée*, Paris, 1851

Official publication, *Comte Général de l'Administration de la Justice Militaire Pendant l'Année* (annually, Paris 1835–53, covering the years 1833–51)

A. Comte, *Catéchisme Positive*, ed. P. Arnaud, Paris, 1966

Anon., *Coup d'oeil Historique sur la Société des Débris de l'Armée Impériale*, Paris, 1845

C. von Decker, *The Three Arms, or Divisional Tactics*, trans. Jones, London, 1849

Chef d'Escadron A. Delorme du Quesney, *Du Tir des Armes à Feu*, Paris, 1845

Capt. J. Delvalz de Caffol, *Statistique Militaire des Officiers de l'Armée Pendant la Période Décennale 1831–41*, Paris, 1843

Dr. E. Dufour, *De la Folie Chez les Militaires*, Paris, 1872

Gen. G.H. Dufour, *Cours de Tactique*, Paris, 1840

Gen. P.G. Duhesme, *Essai Historique sur l'Infanterie Légère*, 3rd. edn, Paris, 1864

Lt-Col. L. Duparc de Locmaria, *De l'État Militaire en France Avant et Après la Révolution de 1830*, Paris, 1831

C. Dupin, *Éloge de M. le Maréchal Moncey, Duc de Conegliano, à l'Usage des Écoles Régimentaires de l'Armée Française*, 2nd. edn, Paris, 1843

C. Dupin, *Voyages dans la Grande Bretagne (depuis 1816)* 2nd. edn, 2 vols., Paris, 1843

Capt. F. Durand, *Coup d'oeil sur l'Ordre Social Actuel: l'Organisation Industrielle de l'Armée*, Lunéville, 1834

Capt. F. Durand, *Des Tendances Pacifiques de la Société Européene et du Rôle des Armées dans l'Avenir*, Paris, 1841

Capt. F. Durand, *De la Nécessité de Fonder des Bibliothèques Militaires*, Paris, 1845

J.B. Duvergier, *Collection Complète des Lois, Décrets, Ordonnances, Règlements, et Avis du Conseil d'État (de 1788 à . . . 1851) 51 vols., becoming annual*, Paris, 1834–58

Éloquence Militaire, ou l'Art d'Émouvoir le Soldat, by 'Une Société de Militaires et d'Hommes de Lettres' (Ymbert?), Paris, 1818

F. Engels, *Engels as a Military Critic*, eds. Chaloner and Henderson, London, 1959

L.A. d'Esmond, *Esquisse de la Puissance Occulte ou les Manoeuvres Avant et Après la Bataille*, Montluçon, 1844

Anon., *Essai sur l'État Militaire en 1825*, Paris, 1825

Gen. C.N. Fabvier, *De l'Armée et de la Nécessité de Créer un Conseil Supérieur Permanent et Consultatif de la Guerre*, Paris, 1849

C. Fallet, *Conquête de l'Algérie*, Rouen, 1856

Capt. J. Favé, *Histoire et Tactique des Trois Armes, et Plus Particulièrement de l'Artillerie de Campagne*, Paris, 1845

Capt. J. Favé and Louis Napoléon, *Études sur l'Artillerie*, 6 vols., Paris, 1846–71

Gen. A.C.D. de Firmas-Periés, *Le Jeu de Stratégie, ou les Echecs Militaires*, 2nd. edn, Paris, 1815

Gen. M.S. Foy, *Discours du Général Foy*, ed. M.P.F. Tissot, 2 vols., Paris, 1826

Gen. H.T.M. Gazan de la Peyrière, *École Spéciale Militaire de Fontainbleau*, Paris, 1847

E. de Giradin, *Abolition de l'Esclavage Militaire*, Paris, 1851

A. de Gobineau, *Le Guerre des Turcomans*, in his *Nouvelles Asiatiques*, ed. R. Gérard, *1018* edn, Paris, n.d. (1970?)

Mal. L. Gouvion St Cyr, *Maximes de Guerre Extrait de ses Oeuvres*, new edn, Paris, 1875

H. de Guibert, *Écrits Militaires 1772–1790*, ed. E.R. Ménard, Copernic, Paris, 1977

Anon., *Instruction sur l'Esprit des Manoeuvres à l'Usage de l'École d'Application d'État Major*, 2 vols., Paris, 1824

Anon., *Instruction sur le Figuré du Terrain à l'Usage de l'École d'Application d'État Major*, Paris, 1824

Official publication, *Instruction Provisoire sur le Tir à l'Usage des Bataillons de Chasseurs à Pied*, Paris, 1854

Anon., *Instruction pour les Sous Officiers*, Lyon, 1834

Capt. C. Jacquinot de Presle, *Cours d'Art et d'Histoire Militaires*, Saumur, 1829

Gen. A.H. Jomini, *Précis de l'Art de la Guerre*, new edn., 2 vols., Paris, 1855

Anon., *Journal du Camp de Châlons sur Marne en 1857, Publié par Ordre de l'Empereur*, Paris, 1858

Capt. N.E. Labarre du Parcq, *Éléments d'Art et d'Histoire Militaires*, Paris, 1858

Gen. A. Laborde, *Plan d'Éducation pour les Enfants Pauvres d'Après les Deux Méthodes Combinées du Docteur Bell et de M. Lancaster*, 2nd edn, Paris, 1816

Capt. J.G. Lacuée de Cessac, *Guide de l'Officier Particulier en Campagne*, new edn, 2 vols, Paris, 1823

Capt. J.L. Laisné, *Aide Mémoire Portatif à l'Usage des Officiers du Génie*, Paris, 1861

Gen. M. Lamarque, *Nécessité d'une Armée Permanente, et Projet d'une Organisation de l'Infanterie plus Économique que Celle qui est Adoptée dans ce Moment*, Paris, 1820

Gen. M. Lamarque, *De l'Esprit Militaire en France, des Causes qui Contribuent à l'Éteindre, de la Nécessité et des Moyens de le Ranimer*, Paris, 1826

P.S. de Laplace, *System of the World*, trans. Truscott and Emory, London, 1902

Prince C. de Ligne, *Préjugés Militaires*, ed. Hensch, Paris, 1914

C. Liskenne & Sauvanne (eds.), *Bibliothèque Historique et Militaire, Dédiée à l'Armée et à la Garde Nationale de France*, new edn, 3 vols., Paris, 1854

Col. F.P. Le Louterel, *Essai de Conférences sur l'Emploi des Manoeuvres d'Infanterie*

180   *Bibliography*

Devant l'Ennemi, Paris, 1848

Gen. N. Loverdo, *Considérations sur l'Organisation de l'Infanterie Française et sur la Formation d'une Réserve*, Paris, 1833

Gen. M.E.P.M. de MacMahon, *Note Rédigé dans un Intérêt Historique, dans le Courant de Janvier 1858, d'Après les Souvenirs de Plusieurs Officiers Généraux et Supérieurs Ayant Pris Part à l'Assaut de Malakoff et Réunis en Conférence*, Autun, 1861

Mal. M.E.P.M. de MacMahon, *Instruction sur les Manoeuvres, par le Maréchal de MacMahon, Camp de Châlons 1864*, Lyon, 1868

J. de Maistre, *Les Soirées de St Pétersbourg*, new edn, ed. P. Mariel, Paris, 1960

Mal. A.F.L. Marmont, *De l'Esprit des Institutions Militaires*, 2nd. edn, Paris, 1848

Capt. H. de Mauduit, *Révolution Militaire du Deux Décembre 1851*, Paris, 1852

Anon., *Military Character of the European Armies*, French edn. 1805, trans. (anon.) London, 1806

Gen. C.A.L.A. Morand, *De l'Armée Selon la Charte*, Paris, 1829

Napoleon I, *La Correspondence de Napoléon 1er*, 32 vols., Paris, 1858–70, Vols.XXIX-XXXII

Napoleon I, *The Military Maxims of Napoleon*, English edn. 1831; new edn, ed D.G. Chandler, London, 1987

Napoleon I, *Maximes Napoléoniennes*, new edn., ed. P.A. Grisot, Paris, 1897

Louis Napoleon, *Projet de Recrutement de l'Armée*, Arras, 1843

Mal. M. Ney, *Mémoires*, 2 vols., Paris, 1833; Vol.II, *Études Militaires*

'A British Officer', *Observations on the French Army*, London, 1810

Anon., *Observations sur l'Armée Française de 1792 à 1808*, ed. Gen. Dragomirow, Paris, 1900

S/Intd. Mil. F.A. Odier, *Cours d'Études sur l'Administration Militaire*, 7 vols., Paris, 1824

'Un Officier Français', *Essai sur le Mécanisme de la Guerre, ou Application des Premiers Principes de Mécanique au Mouvement et à l'Action des Corps d'Armée*, Paris, 1808

'Un Officier des Voltigeurs de la Garde Royale' (Gustave Delvigne?), *Essai sur la Carabine Rayée et sur les Avantages que Présenterait la Formation d'un Corps de Chasseurs Carabiniers*, Paris, 1825

Col. N. Okouneff, *Mémoire sur les Principes de la Stratégie et sur ses Rapports Intimes avec le Terrain*, Paris, 1831

Gen. N. Okouneff, *Use of Artillery in the Field*, trans. anon., London, 1856

Official publication, *Ordonnance du Roi sur l'Exercise et les Manoeuvres de l'Infanterie*, Paris, 4 March 1831

Lt-Gen. V. Oudinot, *De l'Armée et son Application aux Travaux d'Utilité Publique*, Brussels, 1847

Chef de Bn. H.V. Paixhans, *Observations sur la Loi de Recrutement et d'Avancement de l'Armée Française*, Paris, 1817

Lt-Col. H.V. Paixhans, *Force et Faiblesse Militaires de la France*, Paris, 1830

Gen. H.V. Paixhans, *Constitution Militaire de la France*, Paris, 1849

Gen. F.J.P. Pamphile de Lacroix, *Raisons d'État pour Fortifier le Système Militaire en France, et Rétablir le Conseil de la Guerre*, Paris, 1824

Cap. L. Panot, *Cours sur les Armes à Feu Portatives*, 4th edn., Paris, 1851

C. Pecqueur, *Des Armées dans leurs Rapports avec l'Industrie, la Morale et la Liberté*, ou les Devoirs Civiques des Militaires, Paris, 1842

C. Pecqueur, *De la Paix, de son Principe, et de sa Réalisation*, Paris, 1842

Cmdt. B. Poumet, *Instructioin sur l'Artillerie de Campagne à l'Usage des Élèves du Corps Royal d'État Major*, Paris, 1824

Gen. C.A.H. de Préval, *De l'Avancement Militaire*, Paris, 1824

Gen. C.A.H. de Préval, *Projet de Règlement de Service pour les Armées Françaises tant en Campagne que sur le Pied de Paix*, Paris, 1812

F.-V. Raspail, *Le Bon Usage de la Prison*, new edn, Paris, 1968

Anon.(ed.), *Receuil des Pièces Authentique sur le Captif de Ste Hélène*, 12 vols., Paris, 1821–25

Anon., *Réfutation de Toutes les Calomnies Imprimées Contre l'Ex-Société des Débris de l'Armée Imperiale*, Paris, 1846

Official publication, *Réglement Concernant l'Exercise et les Manoeuvres de l'Infanterie 1791*, new edn, 2 vols., Paris, 1812

B. von Reisswitz, *Kriegsspiel, Instructions for the Representation of Military Manoeuvres with the Kriegsspiel Apparatus*, London, 1824; Bill Leeson's new edn., Hemel Hempstead, 1983

Gen. V.U. Rémond, *Tactique Approprié au Perfectionnement des Armes à Feu Portatives*, Paris, 1853

E. Renan, *La Réforme Morale et Intellectuelle de la France*, first published 1871; new edn J.-F. Revel, Paris, 1967

Capt. B.E.C. Renard, *Cours Abrégé de Tactique Générale: Étude sur les Origines des Batailles Stratégiques*, Brussels, 1878

Gen. B.J.B.J. Renard, *L'Art de la Guerre*, pamphlet in British Public Record Office, *WO 33/15*

British War Office, *Report on the Training of Officers for the Scientific Corps*, London, 1857

Gen. C. de La Roche Aymon, *Des Troupes Légères, ou Réflexions sur l'Organisation, l'Instruction, et la Tactique de l'Infanterie et de la Cavalerie Légères*, Paris, 1817

Capt. J.T. Rocquancourt, *Cours Élémentaire d'Art et d'Histoire Militaires à l'Usage des Élèves de l'École Royale Speciale Militaire* 2nd. edn, 4 vols., Paris, 1831

Gen. J. Rogniat, *Considérations sur l'Art de la Guerre*, 2nd edn, Paris, 1817

Gen. J. Rogniat, *Mémoire sur l'Emploi des Petites Armes dans la Défense des Places*, transcribed by his ADC, Capt. Villeneuve, Paris, 1827

Chef de Bn. C.M. Roguet, *De la Vendée Militaire*, Paris, 1833

Gen. C.M. Roguet, *Avenir des Armées Européenes ou le Soldat Citoyen*, Paris, 1850

A. Sala, *De l'Instruction dans l'Armée et des Moyens de l'y Répandre*, Paris, 1828

Mal. M. de Saxe, *Mes Rêveries*, new edn, Paris, 1757

Mal. M. de Saxe, *Ésprit des Lois de la Tactique*, new edn, Paris, 1762

J.B. Say, *Cours Complet d'Économie Politique Pratique*, 3rd. edn, Paris, 1852

Stendhal, *Mémoires sur Napoléon*, new edn., Paris, 1937

Col. E.G. Stoffel, *Military Reports Addressed to the French War Minister 1866–70*, trans. Capt. Home, London, 1872

A.L. Suasso, *The Theory of Infantry Movements*, London, 1825

Col. C.G. d'A. de Ternay, *Traité de Tactique*, ed. Lt-Col. Koch, Paris, 1832

Col. C.G. d'A. de Ternay, *La Défense des États par les Positions Fortifiées*, ed. Prof-Capt. Mazé, Paris, 1836

M.J.L.A. Thiers, *Les Pyrénées et le Midi de la France Pendant les Mois de Novembre et Décembre 1822,* Paris, 1823

A. de Tocqueville, *Democracy in America,* Fontana translation, 2 vols., London, 1968

A. de Tocqueville and G. de Beaumont, *On Social Reform,* trans & ed. S. Drescher, Harper, New York, 1968

Col. A.W. Torrens, *Notes on the French Infantry,* London, 1852

Gen. L.J. Trochu, *L'Armée Française en 1867,* 20th. edn, Paris, 1870

Chef de Bn. M.L. Vacca, *Mémoires sur les Manoeuvres d'Infanterie et sur la Fortification,* Grenoble, 1806

Col. S.F. Gay de Vernon, *Traité Élémentaire d'Art Militaire et de Fortification,* 2 vols., Paris, 1805

Victoires, Conquêtes, Désastres, Revers et Guerres Civiles des Français de 1792 à 1815, by 'Une Société de Militaires et de Gens de Lettres' (ed. Gen. Beauvais?), 34 vols., Paris, 1817

A. de Vigny, *Servitude et Grandeur Militaires,* ed. R Matignon, Paris, 1965

Memoirs and biography

A. d'Antioche, *Changarnier,* Paris, 1891

B. Appert, *Dix Ans à la Cour du Roi Louis Philippe, et Souvenirs du Temps de l'Empire et de la Restauration,* 3 vols., Paris, 1864

C.G. Bapst, *Les Premières Années du Maréchal MacMahon,* Paris, 1894

C.G. Bapst, *Le Maréchal Canrobert,* 6 vols., Paris, 1898–1913

Gen. F.C. du Barail, *Mes Souvenirs, 1820–51,* 3 vols., Paris, 1894–96

Lt. J.B.A. Barrès, *Souvenirs d'un Officier de la Grande Armée,* 11th. edn, Paris, 1922

S. Batten, 'Napoleon III as Military Commander', unpublished undergraduate dissertation, Oxford University, 1985

S-Lt. A. Bernard, *Souvenirs de la Promotion de l'Empire, 1852–4,* Paris, 1916

Capt. M. Blanc, *Souvenirs d'un Vieux Zouave,* 2nd. edn, Paris, 1880

Sgt-Maj. J. Boichot, *La Révolution dans l'Armée Française: Éléction des Sous Officiers en 1849,* Brussels, 1865

Mal. E.V.E.B. de Castellane, *Journal,* 5 vols., Paris, 1895

Capt. P. de Castellane, *Military Life in Algeria,* trans., 2 vols., London, 1853

P. Chalmin, *Un Aspect Inconnu du Général de Lamoricière le Saint Simonien,* Paris, 1954

D.G. Chandler (ed.), *Napoleon's Marshals,* Macmillan, New York, 1987

M.A. de Comminges, *Souvenirs d'Enfance et de Régiment,* Paris, 1910

Sgt. S. Commissaire, *Mémoires et Souvenirs,* new edn, 2 vols., Lyon, 1888

X. de Courville, *Jomini ou le Devin de Napoléon,* Plon, Paris, 1935, reprinted Centre d'Histoire, Lausanne, 1981

A. Debidour, *Le Général Fabvier, sa Vie Militaire et Politique,* Paris, 1904

Gen. R.A.P.J. de Fézensac, *Souvenirs Militaires,* new edn., Paris, 1863

Col. T. Fix, *Souvenirs d'un Officier d'État Major,* Paris, 1898

Mal. L. Gouvion de St Cyr, *Mémoires sur les Campagnes des Armées du Rhin et du Rhin et Moselle de 1792 jusqu'l la Paix de Campo Formio,* 4 vols., Paris, 1829

D. Horward, 'Le Géneral Jean-Jacques Pelet, homme de guerre, humaniste et homme d'état', in *Revue Historique des Armée*, 1988, no.2, pp.22–42

Gen. J.-L. Hulot, *Souvenirs Militaires*, Paris, 1886

H.A.L. de Idéville, *Le Maréchal Bugeaud de la Piconnerie, d' Après sa Correspondence Intime*, 2 vols., Paris, 1881–82

E. Keller, *Le Général de Lamoricière: sa Vie Militaire, Politique et Religieuse*, 2 vols., Paris, 1874

Gen. M. Lamarque, *Mémoires et Souvenirs, Publiés par sa Famille*, 2 vols., Paris, 1835

J. Lucas-Dubreton, *Aspects de Monsieur Thiers*, Fayard, Paris, 1948

F.A .de Luna, *The French Republic under Cavaignac*, Princeton, 1969

Gen. M. de Marbot, *Mémoires*, new edn, 3 vols., Paris, 1891

Mal. A.F.L. Marmont, *Mémoires du Maréchal Marmont, Duc de Raguse, 1792 à 1841, Imprimés sur le Manuscrit Original de l'Auteur*, 9 vols., Paris, 1857

Capt. P. de Molènes, *Les Commentaires d'un Soldat*, Paris, 1877

Gen. J. de la Motte Rouge, *Souvenirs et Campagnes*, 3 vols., Paris, 1895

Duc d'Orléans, *Lettres, 1825–42*, Paris, 1889

Duc d'Orléans, *Récits de Campagne*, ed. by his son, Paris, 1890

Mal. N.C. Oudinot, *Memoirs of Marshal Oudinot*, trans. Steigler, London, 1896

P. Paret, *Yorck and the Era of Prussian Reform, 1807–15*, Princeton U.P., 1966

P. Paret, *Clausewitz and the State*, Oxford, 1976

Gen. V. de Pelleport, *Souvenirs Militaires et Intimes du Général Vicomte Pelleport, 1793–1858*, ed. by his son, 3 vols., Paris, 1857

Capt. L. Robatel, *Mémoires, 1788–1877*, ed. Donnet, Paris, 1966

Gen. O. de Saint Chamans, *Mémoires du Général Comte de Saint Chamans, Ancien Aide de Camp du Maréchal Soult, 1802–32*, Paris, 1896

Mal. J. de D. Soult, *Mémoires du Maréchal-Général Soult, Duc de Dalmatie*, ed. by his son, 3 vols., Paris, 1854

M. Spivak, 'Le Colonel Amoros, un promoteur de l'éducation physique dans l'Armée Française, 1770–1848' in *Revue Historique de l'Armée*, 2, 1970, p. 65

Mal. L.G. Suchet, *Mémoires du Maréchal Suchet sur ses Campagnes en Espagne Depuis 1808 Jussqu'en 1814, Écrits par Lui-même*, 2 vols., Paris, 1828

Contemporary periodicals consulted

Bulletin des Sciences Militaires, Paris, 1824

La France Militaire, Lyon, 1845

Journal de l'Armée , Paris, 1833, 1836–37

Journal de l'Infanterie et de la Cavalerie, Paris, 1834–35

Journal des Sciences Militaires, Paris, 1825–26, 1830, 1844–47, 1849–51

Mémorial du Dépôt de la Guerre, Vol.I, Paris, 1829

Moniteur de l'Armée, Paris, 1840–41, 1847, 1849–50

Moniteur Universel, Paris, 1817–18, 1824, 1831–32, 1836–39, 1840–45, 1848–51

Le Musée Militaire, Journal de Littérature Militaire, Paris, 1845

Revue Militaire, Journal des Armées de Terre et de Mer, Paris, 1833–34

Sentinelle de l'Armée, Paris, 1835–36,1841,1848

Spectateur Militaire, Paris, 1826–29, 1842–43 (also many reprinted articles deposited in AHG cartons, MR series)

Le Vétéran, Journal du Temps Passé, Paris, 1839

Modern works

E.H. Ackerknecht, *Medicine at the Paris Hospital, 1794–1848*, Johns Hopkins University Press, 1966

T.J. Adriance, *The Last Gaiter Button – a study of the Mobilization and Concentration of the French Army in the War of 1870*, Westport, Conn., 1987

C.-R. Ageron, *Histoire de l'Algérie Contemporaine*, first publ. 1964, new edn Paris, 1983

D. Ascoli, *A Day of Battle, Mars-La-Tour 16 August 1870*, London, 1987

J.-C. Asselain, *Histoire Économique de la Révolution Industrielle à la Première Guerre Mondiale*, Paris, 1985

C.G. Bapst, *Essai sur l'Histoire des Panoramas et des Dioramas*, Paris, 1891

C. Barnett, 'The education of military élites' in *Journal of Contemporary History*, Vol.II, No.3, July 1967, pp.15–35

V.L.J.F. Belhomme, *Histoire de l'Infanterie en France*, 4 vols., Paris and Limoges, 1893–99

I. Berlin, *The Hedgehog and the Fox*, 2nd. edn, London, 1967

J.-P. Bertaud, *La Révolution Armée: les Soldats-Citoyens et la Révolution Française*, Paris, 1979

J.-P. Bertaud, 'Napoleon's officers' in *Past and Present*, 112, 1987, pp. 91–112

R. Bittard des Portes, *Les Campagnes de la Restauration*, Tours, 1899

B.J. Bond, *The Victorian Army and the Staff College*, London, 1972

H. Bonnal, *De la Méthode dans les Hautes Études Militaires en Allemagne et en France*, Paris, 1902

J. Bouillon *et al.*, *L'Armée et la Seconde République*, Vol.XVIII of *Bibliothèque de la Révolution de 1848*, La Roche sur Yon, 1955

F. Boyer, 'L'Armée des Alpes en 1848', in *Revue Historique*, Vol. CCXXXIII, no.1, 1965, pp.74–100

J. Brunon, 'Algérie, terre d'évocation et souvenirs' in *Revue Historique de l'Armée*, Vol.IX, no.2, 1953, pp.125–136

R. Caillois, *Quatre Essais de Sociologie Contemporaine*, Paris, 1951, No.IV, *Le Vertige de la Guerre*.

H. Camon, *La Bataille Napoléonienne*, Paris, 1910

R. Carr, *History of Modern Spain*, Oxford, 1966

E. Carrias, *La Pensée Militaire Française*, Paris, 1960

O. Cederlof, 'The battle painting as an historical source' in *Revue Internationale d'Histoire Militaire*, XXVI, 1967, pp.119–44

R.D. Challener, *The French Theory of the Nation in Arms, 1866–1939*, New York, 1955

P. Chalmin, *L'Officier Français de 1815 à 1870*, Paris, 1957

D.G. Chandler, *The Campaigns of Napoleon*, London, 1967

G. Chapman, *The French Army and Politics*, in M.E. Howard (ed.), *Soldiers and Governments*, London, 1957

J.-P. Charnay, *Société Militaire et Suffrage Politique en France Depuis 1789*, Paris, 1964

E. Christiansen, *Origins of Military Power in Spain, 1800–54*, Oxford, 1967

A. Clayton, *France, Soldiers and Africa*, Brassey's, London, 1988

R.C. Cobb, *Les Armées Révolutionnaires*, 2 vols., Paris, 1961–63

R.C. Cobb, *The Police and the People*, Oxford, 1970

J. Colin, *La Tactique et la Discipline dans les Armées de la Révolution*, Paris, 1902, Preface

M. Collinet, 'Le Saint Simonisme et l'armée' in *Revue Française de Sociologie*, April-June, 1961

I. Collins, *Government and the Newspaper Press in France, 1814–81*, Oxford, 1959

G.A. Craig, *The Politics of the Prussian Army 1640–1945*, Oxford, 1955

C. Croubois and J.-P. Surrault, *L'Officier Français de 1815 à 1870*, in C. Croubois, ed., *L'Officier Français des Origines à Nos Jours*, St Jean d'Angély (Charente Maritime), 1987

J.S. Curtiss, *The Russian Army Under Nicholas I, 1825–1855*, Durham, N.C., 1965

R. Debenedetti, *La Médecine Militaire*, Paris, 1967

K.H. Doig, 'War in the reform programme of the Encyclopédie,' in *War and Society*, Vol.VI, No.I, May 1988, pp.1–10

C.J. Duffy, *The Military Experience in the Age of Reason*, London, 1987

E.M. Earle, ed., *Makers of Modern Strategy*, Princeton, 1943

J.R. Elting, 'Jomini, disciple of Napoleon' in *Military Affairs*, 1964, No.1, pp.17–42

Lt. C.-P. Escalle, *Des Marches dans les Armées de Napoléon*, Paris, 1912

A. Forrest, *Déserteurs et Insoumis sous la Révolution et l'Empire*, Paris, 1988

J.G. Gallagher, 'Marshal Davout and the Second Bourbon Restoration', in *French Historical Studies*, Vol.VI, no.3, 1970, pp.351–64

D. Gates, *The Spanish Ulcer, a History of the Peninsular War*, London, 1986

D. Gates, *The British Light Infantry Arm, c.1790–1815*, London, 1987

C. de Gaulle, *La France et Son Armée*, London, n.d.

P. Geyl, *Napoleon For and Against*, trans. London, 1949

N.H. Gibbs, 'Armed forces and the art of war: armies' in *New Cambridge Modern History*, Vol.IX (1793–1830), Ch.3, section A, Cambridge, 1965

L. Girard, *La Garde Nationale 1814–71*, Paris, 1964

R. Girardet, *La Société Militaire dans la France Contemporaine, 1815–1939*, Paris, 1953

R. Girardet, *L'Idée Coloniale en France de 1871 à 1962*, Paris, 1972

B.D. Gooch, *The New Bonapartist Generals in the Crimean War*, The Hague, 1959

P. de la Gorce, *La Restauration*, 2 vols., Paris, 1926

P. Griffith, *French Artillery 1800–1815*, London, 1976

P. Griffith, *Forward Into Battle*, 1st. edn. Chichester, 1981

E. Guillon, *Les Complots Militaires sous la Restauration*, Paris, 1895

J.E. Hicks, *French Military Weapons 1717–1939*, New Milford, Conn., 1964

E.R. Holmes, *The Road to Sedan – The French Army 1866–70*, Royal Historical Society Studies in History Series, 41, 1984

R. Holroyd, 'The Bourbon army, 1815–30' in *The Historical Journal*, Vol.XIV, 1971, pp.529–52

A. Horne, *A Savage War of Peace*, London, 1977

J.A. Houlding, *Fit for Service; the Training of the British Army 1715–1795*, Oxford, 1981

M.E. Howard, *The Franco-Prussian War*, London, 1960

M.E. Howard, 'Jomini and the classical tradition in military thought' in his *The Theory and Practice of War*, London, 1965

J. Huizinga, *Homo Ludens*, first publ. 1938, Paladin edn. London, 1970

D.D. Irvine, 'The French and Prussian staff systems before 1870' in *Journal of the American Military History Foundation*, Vol.II, No.3, 1938

D.D. Irvine, 'The French discovery of Clausewitz and Napoleon' in *Journal of the American Military Institute*, Vol.IV, No.3, 1940

A. Jardin and A.J. Tudesq, *La France des Notables 1815–1848*, vols. VI and VII of *Nouvelle Histoire de la France Contemporaine*, Paris, 1973

D. Johnson, 'The foreign policy of Guizot, 1840–48' in *University of Birmingham Historical Journal*, Vol.VI, 1957, pp.62–87

D. Johnson, *Guizot*, London,1963

C. de la Jonquière, *L'Armée à l'Académie*, Paris, 1894

C.A. Julien, *Histoire de l'Algérie Contemporaine*, Paris, 1964, vol.I (1827–71)

S. Kanter, 'Exposing the myth of the Franco-Prussian War' in *War and Society*, Vol.IV, No.1, May 1986, pp.13–30

T. Karcher, *Les Écrivains Militaires de la France*, London, 1866

E. Keyser, 'Société Philanthropique des Anciens Frères d'Armes de l'Empire Française à Gand' in *Bulletin de la Société Archéologique, Historique, et Artistique*, Auxerre, 1953, p.3ff.

A.F. Kovacs, 'French military institutions before the Franco-Prussian War' in *American Historical Review*, January 1946

W. Laqueur, *Guerrilla*, Boston, 1976

M. Lauerma, *L'Artillerie de Campagne Française Pendant les Guerres de la Révolution*, Helsinki, 1956

G. Lechartier, *Les Services de l'Arrière à la Grande Armée, 1806–7*, Paris, 1910

E.G. Léonard, *L'Armée et ses Problèmes au XVIIIe Siècle*, Paris, 1958

J. Lhomme, *La Grande Bourgeoisie au Pouvoir, 1830–80*, Paris, 1960

B.H. Liddell Hart, 'Armed forces and the art of war: armies' in *New Cambridge Modern History*, Vol.X (1830–70) Ch. XII, Cambridge, 1960

J. Lucas-Dubreton, *La Restauration et la Monarchie de Juillet*, Paris, 1937

J. Lucas-Dubreton, *Le Culte de Napoléon* , Paris, 1960

G. Lukács, *The Historical Novel*, English edn, trans. Mitchell, London, 1962

J.A. Lynn, *The Bayonets of the Republic, Motivation and Tactics in the Army of Revolutionary France, 1791–94*, University of Illinois, 1984

J. Milot, 'Évolution du Corps des Intendants Militaires' in *Revue du Nord*, 1968, pp.399–422

P. Montagne, *Le Comportement Politique de l'Armée à Lyon*, Paris, 1966

V. Monteil, *Les Officiers*, new edn, Paris, 1966

J. Monteilhet, *Les Institutions Militaires de la France*, Paris, 1932

H. Mordacq, *La Stratégie, Histoire et Évolution*, Paris, 1912

P. Nora (ed.), *Les Lieux de Mémoire*, 4 vols., Gallimard, Paris, 1984, Vol.I, *La République*

P. O'Brien and C. Keyder, *Economic Growth in Britain and France 1780–1914*, George, Allen & Unwin, London, 1978

R. d'Ornano, 'Gouvernement et haut commandement en régime parlementaire français, 1814–1914' unpublished thesis, University of Aix en Provence, 1958

P. Paret, *Internal War and Pacification, The Vendée 1789–96*, Princeton, 1961

P. Paret 'Colonial experience and European military reform at the end of the eighteenth century' in *BIHR Journal*, Vol.XXXVII, 1964, pp.47–59

P. Paret, *French Revolutionary Warfare from Indochina to Algeria*, London, 1964

P. Paret (ed.) *Makers of Modern Strategy*, Oxford, 1986

W.B. Pemberton, *Battles of the Crimean War*, first published 1962, Pan edn, London, 1968

De Philip, *Étude sur le Service d'État Major pendant les Guerres du Premier Empire*, Paris, 1900

R.W. Phipps, *The Armies of the First French Republic*, 5 vols., Oxford, 1926–39

G. Pinet, 'L'École Polytechnique et les Saint Simoniens' in *La Revue de Paris*, Vol.III, 15 May, 1894, pp.73–96

G. Pinet, *Histoire de l'École Polytechnique*, Paris, 1887

F. Ponteil, 'L'Eveil des Nationalités' in *Peuples et Civilisations*, Vol.XV, Paris, 1968

D. Porch, 'The French Army Law of 1832' in *Historical Journal* Vol.XIV, 1971, pp.751–69

D. Porch, *Army and Revolution, France 1815–48*, London, 1974

J. Regnault, 'Les Campagnes d'Algérie et leur Influence de 1830 à 1870' in *Revue Historique de l'Armée*, Vol.IX, no.4, 1953, pp.23–38

M. Reinhard, 'L'Historiographie Militaire Officielle sous Napoléon Ier' in *Revue Historique*, Vol.CXCVI, no.2, 1946, pp.165–84

R. Rémond (ed.), *Atlas Historiques de la France Contemporaine, 1800–1965*, Paris,1966

P. Renouvin (ed.), *Histoire des Relations Internationales*, 8 vols., Paris, 1954–58, Vol.V (1815–71)

J. Revol, *Histoire de l'Armée Française*, Paris, 1929

D. de Rougemont, *Passion and Society*, first publ. 1938; Faber edn, London, 1962

R. Rudirff, *War to the Death : The Two Sieges of Saragossa*, London, 1974

P. Savigear, 'Carbonarism and the French Army, 1815–24' in *History*, June, 1969

B. Schnapper, *Le Remplacement Militaire en France*, Paris, 1968

L.C.B. Seaman, *From Vienna to Versailles*, first publ. 1955, University Paperbacks edn, London, 1964

N.W. Senior, *Conversations with M. Thiers, M. Guizot, and other Distinguished Persons During the Second Empire*, 2 vols., London, 1878

W. Serman, 'Les Généraux Français de 1870' in *Revue de la Défense Nationale*, 1970

W. Serman, *Les Officiers Français dans la Nation 1848–1914*, Paris, 1982

G. Six, *Dictionnaire Biographique des Généraux et Amiraux Français de la Révolution et de l'Empire*, 2 vols., Paris, 1934

A.B. Spitzer, *Old Hatreds and Young Hopes – The French Carbonari Against the Bourbon Restoration*, Harvard, 1971

M. Spivak, 'Le Colonel Amoros, un promoteur de l'education physique dans l'Armée Française' in *Revue Historique de l'Armée*, 1970

Z. Sternhell, *La Droite Révolutionnaire, les origines françaises du fascisme 1885–1914*, Paris, 1978

H. Strachan, *European Armies and the Conduct of War*, London, 1983

H. Strachan, *Wellington's Legacy, the Reform of the British Army 1830–54*, Manchester, 1984

Sun Tzu, *The Art of War*, ed. S.B. Griffith, Oxford, 1963

J. Terraine, 'Big Battalions, the Napoleonic Legacy' in *History Today*, 1962

C.A. Thoumas, *Les Transformations de l'Armée Française*, 2 vols., Paris, 1887

D.H. Thomas, 'The reaction of the Great Powers to Louis Napoleon's rise to power in 1851' in *Historical Journal*, Vol.XIII, 1970, pp.237–50

P. Thureau-Dangin, *Histoire de la Monarchie de Juillet*, 7 vols., Paris, 1884

E. Titeux, *Saint Cyr et l'École Spéciale Militaire en France*, Paris, 1898

L. Tolstoy, *War and Peace*, trans. L.A. Maude, new edn, London, 1941

S. Toulmin and J. Goodfield, *The Discovery of Time*, new edn, London, 1967

G.M. Trevelyan, *Garibaldi's Defence of the Roman Republic*, 1907, new impression, London, 1928

E. Turbiana, 'La Nostalgie dans les Armées de la Révolution' unpublished thesis for *doctorat en médicine, Diplôme d'État*, Paris, 1958

A. Vachée, *Napoleon at Work*, trans. London, 1914

A. Vagts, 'Battle scenes and picture politics' in *Military Affairs*, 1941

A. Vagts, *A History of Militarism, Civilian and Military*, London, 1959

J. Vidalenc, *Les Demi-Solde*, Paris, 1955

J. Vidalenc, 'Quelques Remarques sur les Rapports Entre Officiers et Soldats dans l'Armée Française de la Révolution à 1914' in *Revue Internationale d'Histoire Militaire*, 1955

E. Wanty, *La Pensée Militaire des Origines à 1914*, Paris, 1962

M. Weygand, *Histoire de l'Armée Française*, Paris, 1938

T.H. Williams, 'The Military Leadership of North and South' in D. Donald (ed.), *Why the North Won the Civil War*, Louisiana, 1960

A. Wilson, *Wargaming*, new edn, London, 1970

M.D. Wright (ed.), *Science, Technology and Warfare*, proceedings of the 3rd. Military History Symposium, USAF Academy, 1969, pp.51–85

H.C. Wylly, *1859, Magenta and Solferino*, London, 1907

X. Yacono, *Les Bureaux Arabes*, Paris, 1953

X. Yacono, 'La colonisation militaire par les Smalas de Spahis en Algérie' in *Revue Historique*, Vol.CCXLII, no.2, 1969, pp.347–94

W. Zaniewicki, 'L'Armée au lendemain de la Révolution de Février, 1848' in *Cahiers d'Histoire*, Vol.XIV, no.4, 1969, pp.393–419

T. Zeldin, *France 1848–1945*, 2 vols., Oxford, 1973

Sites visited:

The present work has drawn considerable inspiration from tourist visits to a number of historical sites and art galleries, although no claim can be made to any application of that exciting new pair of scientific disciplines: military archaeology and military iconography. Sites visited include the following:

'*La Colonne Napoléone*' in Boulogne; The *École Spéciale Militaire* at Coetquidan;* *La Ministère de la Défense Nationale, Le Panthéon* and the Louvre in Paris; *Le Musée des Beaux Arts* in Rouen, and the – not yet then burned – *Salon des Batailles* in the Château de Versailles.*

The battlefields of Austerlitz,* the Peninsular War, the 1814 campaign, Waterloo,* Magenta and Solferino,* Sadowa, Gravelotte* and Sedan.*

The fortifications of Besançon, Briançon, Bayonne, Cadiz, Givet, Langres, Laon, Metz, Montmédy, Paris,* Phalsbourg,* Pontarlier,* Saumur,* Vincennes*

– and the architectural models in the gallery of *Plans Reliefs* in the Paris *Musée de l'Armée.**

Centres of pilgrimage at Domrémy, Farnborough Abbey, Montmartre, Paray le Monial, *Les Invalides* in Paris,* and Le Puy.

(Asterisks indicate a military museum. See also A. Chappet *et al., Guide Napoléonien*, Lavauzelle, Paris, 1981; and J.-M. Humbert and L. Dumarche, *Guide des Musées d'Histoire Militaire*, Lavauzelle, Paris, 1982.)

Notes

Most of the notes refer to items which are listed more fully in the Bibliography and are therefore expressed in a shortened form of their title, or merely by the author's name. 'AHG' refers to cartons in the Archives Historiques de la Guerre; 'AAG' to the Archives Administratives de la Guerre – both at Vincennes.

Chapter 1

1 Alfred de Vigny's phrase, from *Servitude et Grandeur*, p. 33; compare also his pp. 231–3.

2 My Appendix 'Bibliographical note on secondary sources' gives general orientations in the historiography of this army.

  Correlli Barnett's *Bonaparte*, London, 1978, is a telling modern indictment of Napoleon and his art of war, just as Julien is damning on the army's later comportment in Algeria. Chalmin, Girardet, Croubois and Porch each in their own way echo de Vigny's bleak view of the peacetime garrison army, while Chapman, Kovacs, Howard, Holmes and Adriance are no less unanimous in their condemnation of the various institutional legacies which the French brought to the war of 1870. Holroyd and Thoumas each find an essentially good army 'spoiled' at some particular moment in its development (1830 and 1854 respectively); while Weygand would have waxed almost enthusiastic – were it not for the lack of a trained reserve (p. 279).

  Compare the views of Bittard des Portes and Liddell Hart, who each praise this army highly – albeit for their own personal reasons. Bittard is interested in its royalism and successful wars of *Révanche* (but see Trevelyan's strictures on his 1849 book in *The Roman Republic*, pp. 331–3); while Liddell Hart is fascinated mainly by its implied antithesis to the hated Clausewitz!

3 Although the golden age of French anti-militarism was destined to arrive only during the Third Republic, there had always been a significant groundswell of opposition to the pre–1870 army: from such groups as draft-resisters, revolutionaries and liberals; socio-economic or religious pacifists; owners of requisitioned land; town councils upon whom rowdy garrisons had been stationed . . . and taxpayers in general.

  For the campaign medals issued in recognition of the 1851 *coup*, see

Monteilhet, p. 32.

4 Carrias, p. 237. A typical modern view is in Croubois, pp. 184–94 for officers'
   lack of study, and p. 184 for Trochu as 'clairvoyant'. On Castellane, however,
   Croubois is more ambiguous – praising him on p. 187, but condemning him
   on p. 192!

5 Sanford Kanter makes a challenging case against the *Franc Tireur* in his
   fashionably anti-French 'Exposing the myth of the Franco-Prussian War' in
   War and Society, Vol. 4, No. I, May 1986, pp. 13–30. Digeon, by contrast, asks
   the rather more constructive question of how and why the *Franc Tireur*
   should have seemed such an attractive myth-figure to the French public in the
   years following the *Débâcle*.

6 Paradoxically the concerted study of Gravelotte by French staff historians in
   the 1890s laid bare the fact of Bazaine's near-success while simultaneously
   concealing its significance behind a mass of secondary indictments of the
   military system. We should remember that at 113,000 men Bazaine's army
   was still small enough to be commanded 'personally' in the Napoleonic
   manner, just as Napoleon III had been able (see Batten's thesis) to articulate a
   force half as big again very successfully at Solferino in 1859. Even if the extra
   men required to give parity with the Germans had been available to Bazaine
   in 1870, there is little evidence to suggest that he would have felt any more
   free to use them effectively.

   For a clear analysis of how the personality of a commander was often
   demonstrably more important than either numbers or institutions in the
   American Eastern battles of the 1860s, see Michael Adams's *Our Masters the
   Rebels*, Harvard UP, 1978. The point is made with still greater clarity for 1870
   by Captain Folliet in *Vouloir! . . . La Volonté à la Guerre*, Paris, 1915.

7 E.g. Holmes, p. 1; 'The war was lost not so much on the battlefields of
   Alsace, Lorraine and Champagne in 1870 itself, as in the French cabinet and
   Ministry of War, in the regiments and military academies, in the years before
   1870.'

   The assumptions behind this view are in many ways equivalent to those of
   the medieval ordeal by combat: they see the result of battle as a
   comprehensive moral judgement rather than the avoidable accident of a
   single afternoon. Compare also the 1988 FA Cup Final, in which Liverpool –
   the unquestionably dominant British football side of the 1980s – chanced to
   be humbled by the relatively lightweight Wimbledon. Are we to conclude
   that the Liverpool club was thereby shown to be rotten to the core, and that
   suburban teams from Southeast England have always understood the central
   essence of football? Of course not!

8 Chalmin, pp. 224–6. USA paid the supreme compliment of modelling her
   army almost entirely on the French, while British awe of their allies in the
   Crimea, even in adversity, is well reflected in Pemberton, pp. 29–31, 35, 207,
   221, 224. Conversely Croubois, pp. 195, 200, is scarcely fair when he
   complains that 13.5% of French officers had seen no action – in Prussia the
   figure was surely nearer 99.5%!

9 Bardin's *Dictionnaire*, Vol. 4, p. 4993, claimed that by 1851 130 books on
   tactics had been produced by the French, as compared to 69 by the Germans
   and Swiss, 22 by the British and Americans, 15 by the Italians, 13 by the

Greeks and Turks and 10 by others.

Kathleen Doig's article gives a modern summary of the encylopaedists' position, while General Ménard's selective new edition of Guibert adds an extra dimension to R.R. Palmer's article in Paret, *Makers of Modern Strategy*, pp. 91–119.

10 The French gap in general coverages of mid-nineteenth-century military literature is resoundingly evident in Paret's *Makers of Modern Strategy*. See also Theodore Zeldin's apparent assumption, in *France 1848–1945*, Vol. II, pp. 876–905, that army debates about 'the social role' began only in the age of Lyautey.

11 These have mainly been soldiers smarting from the Algerian dilemmas of the 1950s, or scholars who have found themselves professionally or ideologically committed to redefining armies in sociological terms.

12 Bonald's political theory summarises the ideal society of the legitimists, while Rogniat's *Considérations sur l'Art de la Guerre*, 1817, p. 113 *et. seq.*, gives one among several contemporary visions of the reborn legion – albeit a vision that was instantly criticised both by Napoleon from St Helena and by Paixhans in his 1817 *Observations sur la Loi de Recrutement*. I am especially grateful to John Naylor for showing me his exhaustive notes on the Departmental Legions, from AHG cartons MR 2015, 1944, 1884, Xp4, Xs66, 116, 117, 128, and from other sources. The Legion experiment was ended in 1820.

13 Lhomme, p. 111 *ff.*, and Asselin pp. 80–81, for the rise in GNP and the concentration of economic power in a few hands. Army salaries did not rise in the same proportion as general wealth.

14 See Schnapper, *passim*, on replacement. The text of the Loi St Cyr is in Duvergier, Vol. XXI pp. 288, 436, but see also p. 294 for 'veterans', and p. 411 for promotion arrangements. The parliamentary discussion is in *Moniteur Universel* for 1817, p. 1318, and for 1818, much of pp. 30–330.

15 Military budgets are shown in Appendix I. The low pay scales are discussed in Porch, pp. 22–33 and Serman, pp. 203–26.

16 Napoleon in 1814 had called for battalions of only 400 men, but had been forced to accept 200. In his *Esprit des Institutions Militaires*, p. 34, Marmont assumed that a battalion starting with 1,000 men would soon be reduced to 500 by the rigours of campaigning.

17 The Clausewitzian critique (*On War*, p. 194 *ff.*) was supported by Marmont, *Esprit*, p. 11; but rejected by Morand, p. 90, Lamarque, *Nécessité d'une Armée Permanente*, p. 22 *ff.*, Chambray, *Philosophie de la Guerre*, p. 68 *ff.*, and Captain Laporte, ms, *Mémoire sur Quelques Modifications à Introduire dans l'Organisation, la Solde, l'Habillement, l'Equipement et l'Armement de l'Infanterie*, in AHG MR 2088. La Roche Aymon, *Des Troupes Légères*, p. 4, and Carrion Nisas, *L'Art Militaire*, Vol. II, p. 436, both specifically link the rejection of gigantism to a desired restoration of the military values of the Ancien Régime.

18 See Turbiana, *passim*, for nostalgia. Among others Bugeaud, *Par l'Épée et par la Charrue*, p. 124, echoes the emphasis placed on the legs by de Saxe; while Marmont's *Esprit*, p. 11, echoes Napoleon on the disproportionate advantages conferred by cohesion in fighting against irregular opponents.

19 Préval's speech to the Peers, 16 June 1840, in AHG MR 1910.

20 Porch, *passim,* discusses both the political necessity for and effect of unit rotations, while Girardet, *Autour de Quelques Problèmes,* in Bouillon (ed.), *Études,* pp. 3–16, shows how the process was accelerated in the crisis of 1848. Against this we have complaints by soldiers against the disruption of constant moves, e.g. *Journal de l'Armée,* 1835, Vol. I, No. 11, pp. 342–4. Compare the not dissimilar eighteenth-century British experience described by Houlding.

For the military ideal of a large training camp, see, e.g., the inspection of the 55th Line, 1831, in AHG Xb 680; Le Louterel, pp. 87–9; La Motte Rouge, Vol. 1, p. 286.

21 The vicissitudes of the National Guard are fully traced by Girard, *passim.*

22 Lamarque, *De L'Esprit Militaire;* and compare Foy's opinions in his collected speeches. Lamarque was an infantryman born in 1770 and compromised for his suppression of the Vendée during the Hundred Days. He became a popular liberal politician, and his funeral in 1832 became the occasion for a major anti-government riot. Foy (1775–1825) was a gunner with a very similar political evolution and, if anything, a still higher political profile. Dossiers in AAG.

23 The spontaneous National Guard mobilisation of 1831 was alleged to have produced three and a half million men, and to have maintained that figure for several years. Such claims, however, are deeply suspect.

24 Inspection of 53rd Line, 1831, in AHG Xb 678; and Castellane, Vol. I, pp. 121, 131.

25 The parliamentary debate on the abolition of the 'veteran' reserve is in *Moniteur Universel,* 1824, pp. 588–91, 667–710. That on the Loi Soult is in 1831, pp. 1561–2, 1949–2077; 1832, pp. 19–32, 148, 262–325, 702, 765. Soult's final arrangements are in his report to the crown, 1 May 1833, with an afterthought in the *Moniteur* for 1841, p. 186. Porch discusses all these issues on pp. 9–16, 61–78.

26 Porch, p. 67, misleadingly states that 'The absence of a trained reserve was the real failing of the Soult law and largely accounted for the 1870 defeat.'

27 Spitzer, pp. 228, 254 believes the Carbonari were consciously inspired by Napoleon's French military coup of 1815 and by the various Spanish *pronunciamientos* between 1815 and 1820. On p. 281 he estimates that 23.3% of all the Carbonari were serving soldiers, and 17.2% were retired or half-pay soldiers.

28 Cohorts of officers have been identified especially by Commandant Chalmin in both his seminal *L'Officier Français* and in his article on 1848 – *La Crise Morale de l'Armée Française,* in Bouillon (ed.), *Études,* pp. 28–76. However the latter is moderated by Girardet in his article in the same collection, pp. 5–8, where he highlights the homogeneity of the officer corps alongside its divisions. For other versions of the officer cohorts, see General Regnault's analysis of the Algerian army; Croubois's examples on p. 171; and Serman's article on the 1870 generals which he later elaborated in his book.

29 See Porch's Appendix I for a list of the ministers of war. Bardin and Ornano each provide additional details and vignettes of the individua concerned.

30 Lamarque in his memoirs, Vol. 2, p. 84, is very critical of Angoulême; but Préval's letter of 21 April 1830, in AHG MR 2019, suggests that the prince

later became more constructive. Orleans was more liberal in his outlook, and often sought out leading officers – see his *Letters* and *Récits de Campagne*. Lamoricière, however, was cynical: see Keller's biography, Vol. I, pp. 325–6.

31 Ornano discusses this question, which is elaborated in Chapter nine, below. See also the distinctly 'post-1870' views of Bonnal and Irvine.

32 See Ornano's appendix, and De Luna for Cavaignac.

33 The figures may be calculated from the official parliamentary journals, and are summarised in *La Sentinelle de l'Armée*, 1 March 1837. Croubois, p. 240, however, believes there were fewer soldiers in Parliament by 1848 – only 4% of the Deputies, 25% of the Peers and 8% of Departmental assemblies.

34 Colonel Fabvier (1782–1855: dossier in AAG, and biography by Debidour) led a most astonishing life during the early Restoration as a proscribed Bonapartist Liberal and chief activist in Carbonarist anti-government demonstrations. His liberalism then chanced to coincide with official policy towards Greece, where he was re-employed, soon promoted general, and even warmly embraced by the Establishment. For comparably brilliant careers built on opposition activism, one is forced to turn to such figures as Smuts, De Valera or Makarios.

35 *Moniteur Universel*, 1848, p. 683. See also Charnay, *passim*, and Serman, Chapter Two, pp. 21–43, for the military 'servitude' of the vote; Gossez and Bouillon for detailed psephology – both in Bouillon's 1848 *Études*, pp. 77–120; and the memoirs of sergeants Boichot and Commissaire for ground-level views of what it all meant to the other ranks.

36 See, among others, the constitution of 29 June 1815 in Duvergier, Vol. XIX, p. 437. The Second Republic did not have an oath, and the Restoration and July monarchies were themselves less specific in their formulae than the 1791 constitution – see Croubois, p. 237, and especially Serman, pp. 22–5.

37 Serman, 'Les faux-semblants de l'apolitisme militaire', Ch. 4, pp. 65–84, and Ornano, p. 25. Compare eye-witness agonisings by St Chamans, p. 282; Barrès, p. 269; and Marmont, *Mémoires*, Vol. VIII, p. 237 *ff*.

38 The polemic attaching to pay scales is in the anonymous *Essai sur l'État Militaire en 1825;* Clouet's *De la Composition et de l'Organisation de l'Armée;* Lamarque's *Esprit Militaire;* Paixhans's *Constitution Militaire*, and Préval's *De l'État des Officiers Généraux en France*, October 1828, in AHG MR 1953. Compare Léonard's eighteenth-century precedents for a similar line of argument.

  Related to the above, Fabvier in 1815 (Debidour's biography, p. 102) and Changarnier in 1848 (Antioche's biography, p. 191) shared the desire to serve on the frontier, rather than the interior, during troubled times. Compare Lamoricière in Keller, Vol. II, p. 17: 'When princes desert us, we still have the soil and the *patrie* to preserve.'

39 Chalmin and Croubois both stress this point, and 'de' Brack's fraudulent attempt (see AAG dossier) to appropriate a particule seems to bear them out!

40 Gooch's *Bonapartist Generals* is eloquent on the military contribution to the 1851 coup. See also Captain Hippolyte de Mauduit's (embarrassingly) more than enthusiastic *Révolution Militaire*.

41 Carrion Nisas, *Observations sur l'ouvrage de M le Géneral Max. Lamarque*, p. 23; and compare Vaudoncourt in *Journal de l'Infanterie et de la Cavalerie*, September 1835.

42 Marmont's memoirs, Vol. VII, p. 185. Cf. the more successful industrial activities of Soult, Clausel and Brun de Villaret.

43 The officer's daily life is well covered in Serman, pp. 125–83. For some abortive attempts to introduce unified messes on the English pattern, see inspections of 19th Light Infantry, 1834, in AHG Xb 712 and the Dépôt of 24th Line,1837, in Xb 649; also *Journal des Sciences Militaires*, 1830, p. 287. For the need to avoid debt, see inspection of 38th Line, 1838, in Xb 663, and especially the recent analysis of personal budgets by Serman, pp. 185–226.

44 For statistics on promotions see *Moniteur Universel*, 1849, p. 2414, and the study made by captain Devalz de Caffol.

45 Castellane comments on lack of education in Vol. III, pp. 242, 345, 365 – a point picked up with enthusiasm after 1870.

46 This point is discussed by Vidalenc in his 1955 article, and see *Sentinelle de l'Armée*, 16 April 1836; Lecouturier in *Spectateur Militaire*, 1827, p. 601; General Simon ms on nco promotion, 7 July 1844, in AHG MR 1947.

47 De Tocqueville, *Democracy in America*, Vol. II, pp. 845–8, for an 'abstract' discussion of nco revolts which is clearly based on French experience.

48 Du Barail, Vol. I, p. 334.

49 Examples are in E.Keyser, 'La Société Philanthropique des Anciens Fréres d'Armes de l'Empire Francaise'; Anon, 'Coup d'oeil Historique sur la Société des Débris de l'Armée Impériale'; *Réfutation de Toutes les Calomnies Imprimées contre l'Ex-Société des Débris de l'Armée Impériale;* and cf. the officers' friendly society in Seine et Oise mentioned in the AAG dossier of the Duke of Orleans.

50 See Vidalenc, *passim*, on half-pay officers, who in the Restoration were as numerous as the employed officers. By locating 'the return to normality' only in the Second Empire, Croubois, p. 204, surely puts it too late.

51 AHG MR 1948, and see the promotion debates in *Moniteur Universel*, 1818, p. 32; 1832, p. 215; 1849, p. 1522, with final texts of the laws in Duvergier. Holroyd's article is useful for the 'personal' nature of command in the Restoration . . . and for the colonel who issued personal badges to his men in 1822.

52 Croubois, p. 238, on censorship, and see, e.g. Heudetot's order demanding clearance before publication, 14 July 1835, in the AAG dossier of Colonel Beaux de Lebeau – to which we are tempted to add '*plus ça change* . . . '. For the promotion-orientated press see Chapter three, below – and Holmes, pp. 97–125, for a somewhat gloomy view of the situation it described.

53 La Motte Rouge, Vol. I, p. 290; inspections of 21st Line,1841, in AHG Xb 646, and 13th Light, 1839, in Xb 706.

54 Inspections of 13th Light, 1845, in AHG Xb 706; 41st Line, 1832–39, in Xb 666; 24th Line, 1832–33 in Xb 649.

55 Ministerial report on inspections, 23 July 1817, in AHG Xs 23, shows that many half-pay officers would never have qualified for a commission if so many vacancies had not occurred between 1811 and 1815. Cf. Préval, 15 March 1821, in AHG MR 2019, who can see no such virtue in the purges.

56 Inspectors often complained of this, e.g. instructions for the inspections of 1821, in AHG Xs 24, pp. 3, 8, 9.

57 Chalmin, pp. 52–62, and Croubois, pp. 140, 211–12 for duels. The *Journal de*

l'Armée, 1835, Vol. I, No. 7, p. 214, gives a breakdown by region of mortality due to duelling, 1820–26, showing that 6% of all military deaths in the North and East were for this cause: 4.5% in the centre, 5% in the Midi and over 10% in Gascony!

For attacks on civilians see Cobb, *The Police and the People*, pp. 57, 238. Rullière's letter to General Rapatel, 29 November 1822, shows that the latter assaulted the postmaster at St Malo (see his AAG dossier); while even the normally urbane Castellane, Vol. IV, p. 267, hit a chaplain for wanting to be received on equal terms with officers!

58 Serman, pp. 48, 50, lists a few officers who did, specifically, relish the prospect of repressing a riot. Croubois, pp. 230–1 for indebtedness; p. 183 for the increasingly rural base of officer recruitment.

59 E.g. Serman, p. 101; cf. Chalmin – in Bouillon's *Études*, p. 75 – who traces the polarised attitudes of the 1890s to the traumas and fear of disorder engendered in 1848–51.

60 It was perhaps no coincidence that Bonaparte himself had at one point embraced Islam! See Croubois, pp. 162–4, 234–5 and Serman, pp. 93–7 for anti-clericalism; Spitzer, pp. 56, 224, 232 for the Masonic roots of Carbonarist mutiny.

Anti-semitism can be found, e.g., in Keller's *Lamoricière,* Vol. I, p. 32; Fézensac, p. 134; du Barail, Vol. I, p. 40; Castellane *père,* Vol. I, p. 116 and *fils,* p. 256. However in 1848 in Alsace the army was called out specifically to protect Jews from attack: Chalmin, p. 331.

61 Croubois, pp. 171, 179.

Chapter 2

1 Bittard des Portes, pp. v–vii.

2 La Motte Rouge, Vol. I, pp. 257–8.

3 The background is in Christiansen: see also Thiers's 1822 pro-republican report on the Pyrenees; Guillon, pp. 254–323; Bittard des Portes, pp. 1–378. A wide-ranging coverage which I have not used is G. de Grandmaison, *L'Expedition Français d'Espagne en 1823*, Paris, 1928.

4 Bittard des Portes, p. 29 *ff*. See also St Chamans's memoirs, pp. 398–432.

5 Guillon, pp. 286–90; Bittard des Portes, pp. 68–73; Spitzer, pp. 199–200.

6 But cf. St Chamans' complaints – Bittard des Portes, p. 106. Despite the claim in Chandler, *Marshals*, p. 518, there remains plenty of room to doubt that Victor was 'falsely' blamed for the army's logistic difficulties.

7 Opinion of Guilleminot, 2 May, in Bittard des Portes, p. 124.

8 *Ibid.*, pp. 125–36, 149–65, 195–203, 247–52, 356–64. A modern claim, in Chandler's *Marshals*, p. 306, that Moncey 'defeated' Mina, seems to be something of a simplification!

9 Spitzer, p. 200, for a list of the French Carbonari who fought in Spain.

10 See Bittard des Portes: for the fall of Madrid, pp. 137–48; for mobile operations in the South pp. 171–90, 287–320; for Corunna, pp. 211–26, 262–3; for the Cadiz siege pp. 233–433, 267–9, 274–86, 329–41.

11 *Ibid.*, pp. 379–423.

12   *Ibid.*, pp. 424–67.

13   *Ibid.*, pp. 468–520.

14   La Motte Rouge participated in both campaigns: Vol. I, pp. 334–41; 357–72. (See p. 336 for the French desire to destroy the lion monument at Waterloo!)

15   Duffy, C.J., *Fire and Stone*, Newton Abbot, 1975, pp. 174–7; *Journal de l'Armée*, Vol. I, No. 2, 1835, pp. 33–46.

16   La Motte Rouge, Vol. I, pp. 361, 363–4.

17   *Journal de l'Armée*, Vol. I, No. 2, 1835, pp. 42–3 and diagram, opposite p. 33, for specifications and cut-away of the *Mortier Monstre*. It had a range of up to 2 km and produced craters 8 feet in diameter and 3.5 feet deep. Each shot cost 446 francs, or approximately the total maintenance cost of the average army member for an entire year. See also Castellane, Vol. III, pp. 31–57; La Motte Rouge, Vol. I, p. 362.

18   Castellane's correspondence from Perpignan, 1841–42, in AHG E5 183, E4 28, for an example of the regular monitoring of Spanish affairs. See Boyer's article for the *Armée des Alpes;* and for an unauthorised invasion of Piedmont, see Brahaut's report on the partisan adventurer Vasseur, March 1831, in MR 2029.

19   Trevelyan, pp. 127–34, 165–236. Other sources that I have not used include Bittard des Portes's *Expédition Française de Rome,* Paris, 1849, 2nd. edn, 1905; and Vaillant's official history, *Le Siège de Rome en 1849,* Paris, 1851.

20   Paradoxically, the censorious and anti-military Veuillot served for a time as secretary to the anti-clerical Bugeaud – Ideville, Vol. I, p. 392, Julien, pp. 159, 253, 261–2, 289, 310–12, 442, also p. 585 for Veuillot's bibliography.

21   Bittard des Portes, p. 595.

22   *Ibid.*, pp. 608–752, for the Restoration's operations, and Ageron, p. 7, for the numbers at Staouëli – a battle fought on what was to be the site of 'Operation Torch', November 1944. For all military operations in Algeria between 1827 and 1871 see Clayton, *passim;* Julien, *passim*, and especially Julien pp. 271–341 for an excellent portrait of the African army.

23   The French had, of course, considerable Napoleonic experience of fighting guerrillas, from Spain and elsewhere: see the article on Suchet in Chandler's *Marshals*, pp. 479–508, and D.W.Alexander's *Rod of Iron: French Counter-insurgency Policy in Aragon during the Peninsular Wars*, Wilmington, NC, 1985.

24   Bittard des Portes, p. 750. A similar instinct was to re-emerge on later occasions in Algiers, not least during the last four years leading up to final withdrawal.

25   Turbiana, *passim*, and cf. *Journal de l'Armée*, Vol. I, No. 7, p. 213.

26   For a summary of indigenous regiments see Weygand, p. 271 *ff.*; Clayton *passim*, and cf. the inspections of African Light Infantry units in AHG Xb 723–9. Three battalions of *Récompensés de Juillet* were created in 1830 specifically to remove revolutionary elements from the capital: see Keller's *Lamoricière*, Vol. I, p. 57, for their gradual evolution into the 67th Line Regiment. We eagerly await Douglas Porch's forthcoming scholarly work on the Foreign Legion, which is a subject that has in the past received a quite excessively journalistic type of coverage.

Castellane called the Zouaves a 'Band of Harlequins', and was generally contemptuous of African *laisser-aller* under Valée and then Bugeaud: Vol. III, pp. 135–59, 219, 231, 264, 351, and see Julien, p. 314. Fabvier was also violently opposed – see Debidour, p. 447 *ff.* – while Blanc's *Souvenirs d'un vieux Zouave* is critical of almost everyone except MacMahon. Cf. Regnault's article, which correctly downplays the African army's role as a source of inefficiency in 1870 – a point echoed in Holmes, pp. 51–4, 81, 215–16.

27 The bibliography of the present work contains a selection of contributions to these debates, and see both Chalmin's Annexe no. 11, p. 384, and Julien's discussion of military art and literature, pp. 256–64, for sketch-maps of just who held which points of view. For the Algerian debates of the 1950s see Alistair Horne, and Paret's *Guerre Révolutionnaire*.

28 Yacono on Arab Bureaux, and note especially Lamoricière's role.

29 Cavaignac's AAG dossier shows him often in trouble for his 'exalted' ideas, but he served as an engineer in Greece and Algeria before, like Lamoricière, transferring to the Zouaves for their faster promotion. Da Luna explains his achievements in 1848, and see Spitzer, p. 244n. for his carbonarism at Polytechnique, and pp. 4, 8, 265, 266, 277 for discussions of his St Simonian brother.

30 It was largely the 'Africans' who would have commanded the mobile metropolitan formations if there had been a war in 1848 – see Pelet's notes for 1 and 14 December 1848 in AHG MR 2070, and compare the thoughts of Ornano and Regnault. For French officers' 'Arabism' see e.g. Tanski, *Mémoire*, 10 August 1835, and other mss in AHG H 226.

31 Keller, *passim*, for Lamoricière, especially Vol. I, pp. 55–75 on the Zouaves; pp. 238, 253, 265 for his fanaticism for living off the land. *Ibid.*, p. 269, and Blanc's memoirs, pp. 151–5, on the practical effects of this approach. Keller, pp. 162, 335, and Chalmin's pamphlet *Un Aspect Inconnu du Général Lamoricière le Saint Simonien*, Paris, 1954, for Lamoricière's desired social-catholic ideology in Algeria.

32 The Third Republic's right-wing and colonial ideologies are vividly described by Sternhall on the Boulangist movement and Girardet on the colonial idea. Compare Paret's *Guerre Révolutionnaire* for the 'Maoist' generals of the Fourth Republic.

33 Julien, p. 156, for casualties in 1840, and the memoirs of Castellane *fils* for small unit tactics. See also the books written by the dukes of Orleans and Aumale at around this time, since each of them helped to achieve the change in metropolitan attitudes towards Algeria.

     Valée was the son of a gamekeeper who became an artillery general in 1809 under the patronage of Suchet. By 1827 he had re-designed French artillery equipment, and in 1830 he became a peer.

34 Dossier in AAG, and the works on Bugeaud by Azan and Ideville. See Azan, pp. 69, 77, 158, for Bugeaud's concept that France had no alternative apart from total invasion. For his ideas on veteran colonies, and the way in which his creative liberal authoritarianism gradually turned into an attack on all socialists, see Collinet's article on military St Simonians; Yacono, p. 128 *ff.*; and Bugeaud himself in *Les Socialistes et le Travail en Commun*.

35 Bapst on Canrobert, p. 376. In Azan, p. 162, Bugeaud claims to spare the enemy's women and children; but on p. 193 he admits to leaving his reports

'incomplete' because he does not want to alienate the philanthropists. Julien, pp. 314–20, for the argument on how the razzia should be conducted and how, despite his moralistic posturing, Lamoricière himself was associated with some of the worst excesses.

36 Julien, pp. 174–8.

37 Keller, Vol. I, p. 318.

38 S. Coquerelle, *L'Armée et la Répression dans les Campagnes*, in Bouillon's collection on 1848 – table on pp. 151–9.

39 Sarragossa was a notorious reference point in every debate on popular resistance and street fighting. See Rudirff, *passim*, and Cavallero's first-hand account of the siege.

40 Marmont's memoirs, Vol. VIII, p. 274 *ff.*.

41 Montagne, pp. 139–41; Zaniewicki, p. 396.

42 St Chamans, p. 502; Roguet, p. 239; Keller, Vol. II, p. 34.

43 See Montagne, p. 138 for the mutilation of the army's wounded by the Lyon mob in 1831, and p. 182 for the army's incendiarism and murders in 1834. De Luna, p. 148, says two million shots were fired by the army during the June Days in Paris, to produce some 5,000 civilians killed, plus an unknown number of wounded and 11,000 jailed or deported. Against this 708 soldiers were killed, of which six were generals – to which Croubois, p. 246, adds that a total of fifty-three were officers.

44 E.g. Azan, pp. 206–11, 233; Ideville, Vol. I, pp. 389, 393, 399.

45 Roguet, *Avenir des Armées*, p. 81; Beik, p. 103.

46 Roguet, *Avenir des Armées*, p. 187. He was adc to Louis Napoleon in 1851, and the son of the commander of Lyon in 1831. For his work see also Holmes, pp. 143–51.

47 For police structure and methods see Cobb, *The Police and the People, passim*; Spitzer, pp. 50–75, 143–89.

48 Ideville, Vol. I, p. 279.

49 Roguet, *Avenir des Armées*, p. 88 on the June Days.

50 La Motte Rouge, Vol. II, p. 65 *ff.*, for the minister's orders to fire at 100 metres, December 1851.

51 Girard, p. 305 *ff.* for the National Guard. Roguet, *Avenir des Armées*, pp. 147–63, 190–1, 235 for statistics of the man-hours required for different tasks . . . on each side of the barricades.

52 Roguet, *Avenir des Armées*, p. 87.

53 Ideville, pp. 275–9, shows Bugeaud had very similar ideas to those in Roguet's pp. 91–101, 302–8. Unfortunately I have been unable to find the 1848 formal treatise on street fighting by Bugeaud which is cited in Azan's preface and in Clayton's footnote 3 on page 393.

   Castellane, commanding in Lyon at about the same time, apparently also shared the same general view to the two sources cited above – see his memoirs, Vol. IV, pp. 287–9. Apparently not dissimilar are Subervie's (1848) *16th March System*, cited in Da Luna, p. 163; and Changarnier's *16th April System*, re-issued in his instructions for Paris, 16 August 1848 – quoted in Antioche, p. 222.

   Note, however, that Roguet's manuscript of December 1848 – from which his 1850 book was written, in AHG MR 2151(1) – was not as influential as

Holmes suggests on his p. 146. The original was annotated within the ministry in terms which – probably quite correctly – dismissed the author as 'too theoretical'. Roguet *fils* was also noted in his AAG dossier, by Bugeaud, as over-intellectual and lacking in the essential quality of 'communicative energy'.

54   Discussion in Montagne, pp. 192–4; and see Chapter nine, below.

55   Monfalcon, quoted in Montagne, p. 172.

56   Castellane, *Journal*, Vol. IV, p. 248, says that in 1848 there had been too many forts in Lyon, requiring too many troops to hold. However in February 1848 at Le Havre he had himself evacuated the city in order to take up a defensive position outside the town (*ibid.*, p. 24).

57   Roguet, *Avenir des Armées*, pp. 114–34, for discussion of retreats to a fortress outside the capital city.

58   Coquerelle in Bouillon *passim* for 1848, and the inspection reports for the effect of rural dispersion on training – e.g. 3rd Line, 1831–35, in AHG Xb 628. Castellane, Vol. I, pp. 329, 341, recommends cavalry should charge rather than shoot in suppressing the 1817 grain riots; p. 373 for the need to disarm the Morbihan National Guard in 1819; and pp. 353–7 for his cultural contempt for the Morbihan peasants and all their ways.

59   Roguet, *Vendée*, pp. 167–73 *ff.*

60   *Ibid.*, pp. 154, 176–7.

61   Walter Laqueur, *Guerrilla*, p. 113, has claimed the work of the Breton officer and composer Le Mière de Corvey, *Des Partisans et des Corps Irreguliers*, Paris, 1823, as 'in some respects the first truly modern work on the guerrilla'. Equally Roguet's *Vendée* can be seen as one of the earliest works about countering the guerrilla, although it was by no means the first. The Spanish Marquis of Santa Cruz had already produced an analysis of counter-insurgency in 1724–30 that apparently included many of the recommendations put forward by the counter-insurgency experts of the 1950s (Duffy, *Military Experience*, pp. 306–8).

62   Quoted in Roguet, *Vendée*, p. 196.

63   For the class analysis in Scott, see G.Lukács's *The Historical Novel*. A number of military memoirs show that Scott was very well known to the French army in this era.

64   Roguet's *Vendée, passim*, but especially pp. 223–71 for the strategic routes. Also see 'Un officier supérieur', 'Observations sur les routes stratégiques de l'ouest' in *Journal de l'Infanterie et de la Cavalerie*, February 1834; Lamarque on Suchet in *Spectateur Militaire*, 1826 p. 153 *ff.* .

65   For Blanqui see his *Textes Choisis;* and Spitzer, pp. 230–41, 290–93 for the Carbonarist background to his revolutionary theories. Cf. Marx and Engels's military analyses of the same era – see *Engels as a Military Critic*, and Neumann and von Hagen in Paret's *Makers of Modern Strategy*, pp. 262–80. On p. 266 the latter are wrong to say Cavaignac in 1848 'first' broke the myth of the barricades, since this had already been done in the early 1830s – but they are right to see 1848 as the starting point of 'scientific' socialism.

66   The diplomatic background to military action may be traced through Renouvin, Vol. V, De la Gorce, and Thureau-Dangin. See also Seaman, and the articles by D.Johnson and D.H.Thomas.

67 Bugeaud, 5 April 1843 in Azan, p. 141, perceptively realised that his African army could conquer Austrian Italy – but not Algeria!

Chapter 3

1 Croubois, p. 236, does correctly note that the army was astonishingly prolific in technical literature – but airily dismisses this in a phrase, as making no advance over the ideas of the preceding century. Chalmin, pp. 351–6, and Serman, pp. 216–18 also each fail to notice that the existence of an extensive nineteenth-century debate may actually have been a reflection of perceptive contemporary professionalism.

2 The idea that 'France is shrinking' was *not* a novelty in the 3rd Republic, since the loss of the Rhineland and its fortresses in the 1815 Vienna treaty had already been widely resented in patriotic circles.

3 E.g. de Vigny is still celebrated in the army for his *Servitude et Grandeur*, while Stendhal's evocation of Waterloo in *La Chartreuse de Parme* must surely rank highly in that marvellous series of battle-pieces that runs from *Candide* and *Soirées de St Pétersbourg* through Tolstoy, Zola and Crane to Remarque and Hemingway.

4 Julien, p. 304, concedes that the African officers were far from intellectual, yet on p. 300 he alleges that many of them saw literary activities as an aid to promotion, and that many of their garrisons had libraries.

5 Serman, p. 218.

6 This view is expressed in, e.g., Ambert, *Soldat*, p. 479; Sala, p. 19; J.R. de St Aubain, *Tribut Filial*, 1831, in AHG MR 2141, p. 42; and Fabvier's inspection of the 38th Line, 1845, in Xb 663.

7 Karcher, *passim*, and see especially N.Tomiche, *Napoléon Écrivain*, Paris, 1952, in which the cynical reader is, despite everything, still left suspecting that the Emperor's literary reputation is based on such masterpieces as *Marengo*, *Austerlitz* and *Jena*, rather than on anything he actually wrote!

8 Hugo's Waterloo is in *Les Misérables*: Balzac has the crossing of the Berezina in *Adieu*, and some highly 'Napoleonic' passages in *Le Médecin de Campagne* (taken from an abortive novel called *La Bataille*), not to mention a wide variety of military men all the way from *Cromwell* through *Les Chouans* to *Le Colonel Chabert*.

9 Even Jomini wanted to write a novel *à la* de Maistre (De Courville, p. 284) – and see Berlin's *The Hedgehog and the Fox* for the influence of de Maistre (see especially his pp. 226–7) on Tolstoy.

10 De Gaulle, p. 103, deploring the lack of these things in France . . .

11 De Courville's biography, drawing on the work of Jean Lecomte, is rare for its adulatory tone. Elting's article borrows its title – but is somewhat less enthusiastic. Perhaps Carrias, pp. 241–2, and Shy in Paret's *Makers of Modern Strategy*, pp. 143–85, are the fairest and most charitable recent treatments.

12 The 'Reform Era' was particularly rich in military theory – see especially Paret's *Yorck* – but the succeeding decades also produced such figures as Rüstow and Willisen, not to mention the whole General Staff apparatus as a matrix for study.

13 Writers after 1870 have been quick to imply that Jomini failed to equip

France with a mass army – e.g. Irvine on *The French Discovery of Clausewitz*.

14   This is a common theme running through Modacq's and Strachan's books, Howard's article on Jomini, Gilbert's chapter in Earle's *Makers of Modern Strategy*, and Williams's article on the strategists of the American Civil War. For something of a corrective see Shy in Paret's *Makers of Modern Strategy*, pp. 158, 171–2, 177–9; reinforced by Paret on Clausewitz in the same volume, pp. 211–13.

15   The author is signed merely as 'a French officer'. Cf. Paret on Napoleon, in his *Makers of Modern Strategy*, p. 134, who shows that the Emperor had seized the relationship between war and mechanics at least as early as 1809 – although this point must surely have been self-evident, at that time, to almost anyone with a 'technical arms' education.

16   Koch was a Bonapartist who had been Jomini's adc, and had helped him produce the French edition of the Archduke Charles's work on Strategy. He wrote a vibrant history of the 1814 campaign, left a deep mark on the military history courses at the Rue Grenelle and later at St Cyr, and worked in Pelet's *Dépôt*, editing Ternay's work, among other projects. Dossier in AAG.

17   Shy gives an excellent summary of the influences on Jomini in Paret's *Makers of Modern Strategy*, although on p. 148 he misses the stress that de Courville, p. 18, had laid on Lloyd as early as 1935. We may even suspect that, as renegades who each came from small countries and who each eventually found high rank in the Russian service, Lloyd and Jomini perhaps had still more in common than has yet been documented?

18   Tactical manuals will inevitably be outdated for any given campaign, since that campaign will always be simultaneously a 'unique' event and the 'latest' event. No one will ever be able to catch up with its specifics, in a widely-distributed manual, until it is over. More questionable, however, is the common failure to issue a manual for some fairly new technique that promises to have a wide *general* application; e.g. Napoleon's gunners failed to produce an official manual for the concentration of large numbers of cannon on the battlefield – even though this was the accepted solution to a frequently-recurring problem – until a decade after the wars had ended (see my *French Artillery*, p. 15).

19   His Boulogne drills are printed in Vol. II of Ney's memoirs as *Études Militaires*. De Courville, pp. 21–4, discusses the headquarters intrigues at this time between General Dutaillis (Ney's Chief of Staff and a protégé of Berthier), Colonel Passinge (Ney's old companion and first adc), and Jomini himself. De Courville believes Passinge wrote the drills, Jomini corrected them radically, and Dutaillis was shown up as incompetent. Non-believers in Jomini, however, may perhaps wish to rearrange this pecking-order in their own manner.

      As for battlefield practice, Ney invariably used column formations, preferably without any firing by the assault troops: e.g. at Friedland, Krasnoi, Bautzen and Montmirail.

20   Colonel Ternay, 1771–1813, had emigrated from France during the Revolution, and served under Wellington in the Peninsular War.

21   As, indeed, did Clausewitz himself. If Jomini can be criticised for looking only at small manoeuvrable armies, then Clausewitz can be criticised for

failing to see the mounting pace of technological development and the ways in which future warfare might change as a result.

22 See his many, more or less well-authenticated, writings from St Helena: notably the official *Correspondence*, Vols.XXIX–XXXII.

23 Only two out of the projected five parts of Soult's memoirs ever appeared. Suchet gives us only 1808–14; while Gouvion offers only 1792–97. Since these three officers stood very much at the head of the military profession, their lack of systematic analysis makes a particularly disappointing gap in the literature.

24 See the volume of extracts from Gouvion St Cyr's memoirs, and of course the many editions of Napoleon's 'maxims'. Chandler's 1987 edition of the latter, p. 17 *ff.*, is hard-pressed to deny the despair which they can provoke in the serious student!

25 Duhesme led a chequered and active career – not without scandals – during the Revolutionary and Napoleonic wars. His *Essai Historique de l'Infanterie Légère* appeared a year before his death at Waterloo, and immediately became the standard source for this very important subject. It was read by French officers quite as often as the works of those other two purveyors of psychology and paradox, Guibert and de Saxe.

Morand and Marmont each covered a wider subject-area than Duhesme, but laced it with no less originality – from an 'infantry' and an 'artillery' point of view, respectively. It is noteworthy that each of them took up the pen after their military employment had been ended for political reasons.

26 Pelet, 1777–1858, was a star in the 'second generation' of Napoleonic officers, rising from the ranks in the Infantry to become a general in 1813. See his dossier in AAG; his extensive *fonds* in AHG, and Donald Horward's article on Pelet.

27 Vaudoncourt was the son of a mathematics teacher in the Metz artillery school, rising first through the Infantry, then the Artillery. He helped found the *Journal des Sciences Militaires* in 1825 (No. I, p. 1) and was prolific in the Restoration military press.

Rogniat had not fallen from favour after 1815 but – like Haxo – combined continuing influence at the top of the engineers with the residual prestige of having led the engineers of the *Grande Armée*.

Chambray had a less elevated career, but was an ardent royalist as well as a prolific writer. He retired from the army due to ill-health in 1826.

Carrion Nisas, on the other hand, was a staff officer on half pay from 1815 to 1824, when he was eventually found a niche in the historical section of the *Dépôt de la Guerre*.

Finally, Mathieu Dumas had been an exceptionally highly qualified and noted staff officer for Napoleon, becoming one of the most noted historian-analysts of the Napoleonic Wars. He survived half pay during the Restoration, to become a *Conseiller d'État* (dossiers in AAG).

28 Clouet was an engineer who had served in that hotbed of military theory – Ney's staff. In 1815 he was on Bourmont's staff, followed him into royalism, and in the July Monarchy became an active leader of revolt in the Vendée.

Allix was a gunner, an ingenious inventor, prolific self-publicist and such a pure Bonapartist that he was totally unemployable in the Restoration – and even beyond.

Lecouturier, from the Infantry, had a similar career, such that not even the liberal-minded *Dépôt de la Guerre* would employ him, even as a librarian.

29 Trochu was a career staff officer, born in the year of Waterloo. In a letter of 21 March 1841 he expressed a desire to serve in Africa specifically because of the faster promotion there, and in 1844 he was briefly an adc to Bugeaud. In 1854 he was a.d.c. to St Arnaud, whence he was promoted brigadier general (dossier in AAG).

30 Puvis was an infantryman who had been on half pay 1815–19, then became noted for his interest in regimental education and gymnastics – but not for his skills as a practical commander.

Bléton was an infantryman who was never employed in the Restoration, but was quickly taken up by General Galbois in 1830.

Noblot started brilliantly in the 1826 *Garde du Corps*, and passed briefly through the *Chasseurs à Pied* – but he later ran into serious trouble over unauthorised publications, debts, 'exalted' political ideas, timidity and absenteeism (dossiers in AAG).

Unfortunately I have been unable to trace Beauchamps.

31 Préval's military career was already well launched before the Revolution, and he served with distinction in the cavalry throughout the Napoleonic wars. Although the Restoration employed him but rarely, he quickly became a power in the ministry of war during the July Monarchy (dossier in AAG and copious *fonds* in AHG).

32 Made an infantry general at the same time as Pelet, Aymard was equally unemployed during the Restoration. He commanded Lyon between 1832 and 1841.

Castellane rose from the ranks of Napoleon's cavalry and remained in favour with all régimes except the Second Republic. All who met him were struck by his insistence on the letter of the regulations, and he seems to have cultivated some of the mannerisms of Frederick the Great – see his own *Journal* and Bapst's *Canrobert*, Vol. I, p. 144; La Motte Rouge, Vol. I, p. 473; AHG MR 2252, 2142, and AAG dossier.

33 Second only to those who joined the African Army, officers seeking service in the *Chasseurs* tended to win promotion more rapidly than usual. It is a moot point in each case, however, how far this was because the glamour and seriousness of the outfit in question attracted the best men, and how far it merely created a self-propagating élitist clique. At least in an officer like MacMahon – first up the Atlas in 1831; designer of *Chasseur* drills and uniforms in 1841; and very nearly France's third Emperor in 1877 – we can agree with Cavaignac's 1846 assessment that he was 'one of the most distinguished colonels in the army, without any doubt' (AAG MF 57; see also Bapst's biography).

34 Captain P.F.F. Durand did not, as sometimes stated, attend Polytechnique – but entered the *Garde du Corps* from Saumur. Nor did he join the 1834 Lunéville mutiny, although present in the garrison at the time. He was more noted for intellectualism, and running his regimental school, than for his talents as an officer. In 1848 he was 'attached to the most extreme socialists and agitators', but retired only in 1853 (AAG dossier).

35 See Chapter Six, below.
36 AAG dossier, and compare Montagne's musings on Vigny's version of 'the military specificity', pp. vii–41.
37 Ambert was surely a unique case. He was a Protestant who married an Englishwoman and at one time resigned from the army, but returned to serve in the Foreign Legion. Nevertheless he later served as an instructor in the reactionary Saumur cavalry school, and made his name especially as a sentimental writer. He was insubordinate, unreliable and quirky – yet popular and clever enough to retire as a general and a *Conseiller d'État* in the Second Empire (dossier in AAG). His Catholic colleague La Motte Rouge, Vol. I, p. 344, is highly enthusiastic – yet the censoriously modern Serman, p. 217, considers his literary reputation 'usurped'.
38 The word 'poetic' occurs in this context in e.g. Brack, p. 7; Anon. ms, *Réflexions sur l'Application du Règlement dans les Régiments de Cavalerie*, in AHG MR 1947; Janin in *Journal de l'Armée*, 4 September 1836. Many other writers glorified war – e.g. N. Le Boeuf, in *Revue Militaire*, January 1834, delighted that 'War, war – this dreadful accumulation of confusion, of delirium, this undermining of reason – thus seems to be a constituent state of individuals and peoples . . .'
39 *Commentaires d'un Soldat*, p. 56.
40 On 25 June 1818 a subscription to the *Journal Militaire Officiel* was made compulsory for every regiment and every general officer. The *Mémorial du Dépôt de la Guerre* (16 vols., Paris, 1829–80) was successor to the *Mémorial Topographique et Militaire* (3 vols., Paris, 1804–06). See also Lamarque's view of it in *Spectateur Militaire*, Vol. I, 1826, p. 545.
41 Captain Jacquinot de Presle was a gunner who joined the Staff Corps at its formation in 1818, becoming a teacher at Saumur in 1825 until he retired in 1830 (dossier in AAG).
42 Contributors are listed in *Journal des Sciences Militaires* 1830, p. 1.
43 See *Spectateur Militaire*, Vol. 3, 1827, p. 5.
44 Dufriche de Valazé was an engineer, made general in 1813 but influential only after 1830.
   Fririon was an infantry general of 1800 and commander of Paris in 1812. He weathered the Hundred Days, but felt excluded in the later Restoration, and retired in 1832.
45 *Journal de l'Armée*, 7 February 1836.
46 De Tourreau had emigrated in the Revolution, before returning in 1802 to serve in Napoleon's cavalry. In 1825 he taught briefly at Saumur, and in 1832 took a post in the ministry of war, in semi-retirement (dossier in AAG).
47 After fighting for Napoleon, de Maudit (or de Mauduit) served in the Restoration Guard, but refused the oath in 1831 and resigned. In 1848 he stood for election on the right wing, and eventually became consul in New Grenada (dossier in AAG).
48 Colonel Itier was a Restoration Guard cavalryman, sent to Africa in 1836 for his Carlism. His career revived in 1845 when he invented a new drill system, and he retired in 1860 (AHG MR 2013).
   Colonel Mussot rose from the ranks in the cavalry and *Gardes du Corps*, was also sent to Algeria in 1836 for Carlism but in 1849 was retired for his

revolutionary activities.

Lieutenant Delvigne rose through the Restoration Guard infantry and was an expert on small arms, but resigned over difficulties with the authorities in 1830 and thereafter acted officially only as a technical designer.

Captain Beurmann also rose through the Restoration infantry, including the Guard, and was later in Africa with the 55th Line – a regiment which seems to have had an active group of intellectual officers (dossiers in AAG).

My only information on Squadron Commander L.F. Merson, apart from his taste for the antiquarian side of the army, is that he commanded a remount dépôt in 1844. Equally, H. Calais is known to me only as 'a cavalry officer'.

49 Circulars, 17 July 1833, 13 March 1837, 1 March 1841. See *Sentinelle de l'Armée*, 8 March 1841.

50 *Moniteur de l'Armée*, 8 December 1840.

51 *Le Musée Militaire*, 1 December 1845.

52 *La France Militaire*, 5 April 1845. Cf. the inspections of the regiment, AHG Xb 674, which show it to have been more intellectual than the average – although there is no mention of a library.

53 Boichot, p. 4.

54 Details based on AAG dossiers supplemented by the *Annuaire*. Members of the sample are chosen subjectively, as representing those who appear to have been active in discursive military writing, but excluding those who wrote only routine *ex officio* reports. There are also obvious problems in documenting the anonymous writers, just as there are in tracing some of the others through the idiosyncratic Vincennes archives.

55 The total number of officers in 1835 is estimated, from the *Annuaire* for that year, as 14,968.

56 Chalmin, pp. 89, 173 and *passim*.

57 See, e.g. Fézensac's memoirs, p. 8.

58 The sample includes nine members (2.6%) from French overseas possessions; eight (2.3%) Germans, and twenty-three (6.5%) non-German foreigners.

59 A classic title in this genre is J.J.H.D. Rolland's *Exposé de la Position Militaire du sr. Rolland, Ancien Lieutenant d'Infanterie et des Moyens à l'Appui de sa Requête au Roi, en son Conseil d'état à l'Effet d'Obtenir sa Réintegration*, Paris, 1840.

Chapter 4

1 Vachée is still the best evocation of Napoleon's personal methods, although for his system of staffwork Escalle, De Philip and Lechartier together create a much fuller picture. See also Ward for a comparison with Wellington's – equally 'personal' – arrangements, and Hittle for a general modern view of staffwork.

Post-war Staff Corps arguments may be found in, e.g. Rocquancourt, Vol. III, p. 47 *ff.*, and Jomini, *Précis*, Ch. 6.

2 E.g. Taverne, *Essai Raisonné*, in AHG MR 1984.

3 E.g. Rocquancourt, Vol. IV, p. 183; La Roche Aymon, *Des Troupes Légères*, p. 4.

4 E.g. Carrion Nisas, *Essai sur l'Histoire*, Vol. II, p. 427 *ff.*.

5 E.g. Captain Pagezy ms, *Plan Sommaire d'un Cours Annuel d'Art et d'Histoire Militaires*, December 1826, and Taverne, *Essai Raisonné*, both in AHG MR 1984.

6 Taverne, *Essai Raisonné*, p. 18. Note that the British tradition has been to demand 'Prussian' standards of education within a 'French' staff structure!

7 See *Victoires et Conquêtes, passim;* Lamarque in *Bulletin des Sciences Militaires*, Vol. I, p. 259; review of *Bibliothèque Portative de l'Officier* in *Spectateur Militaire*, Vol. I, p. 494 .

8 In 1912 Commandant Mordacq, pp. 37–63, memorably alleged that the French between 1815 and 1870 lacked a theory of war, and preferred *innéisme* (or 'inborn genius') instead. This has been followed by e.g. Wanty, pp. 389–90 and Croubois, pp. 184–5, 222.

9 See S.B. Griffith on Sun Tzu, preface, p. 24.

10 A point well made by Ben Pimlott, 'If You Can't Stand the Heat, Become a Pundit,' in *the Guardian*, 29 August 1985, p. 17.

11 E.g. Pelet ms, *Notes sur l'Art de la Guerre*, 1829–30, p. 69, in AHG MR 2073. Such a reaction, however, could often extend to scepticism about Jomini and his school.

12 Allent, p. 53.

13 See, e.g., Comte, p. 90.

14 Beurmann in *Sentinelle de l'Armée*, 8 September 1836; Stendhal, *Mémoires sur Napoléon*, p. 215; Jomini, *Précis*, Vol. I, pp. 26, 158. The evolution of Frederick's ideas is splendidly explained in C.J. Duffy's *Frederick the Great, a Military Life*, London, 1985.

15 For an extreme case, see Doisy, *Essai de Bibliologie Militaire* 1824, in AHG MR 1955.

16 Laplace, *System of the World*.

17 Taverne, *Essai Raisonné*, p. 10; Durand, *Des Tendances Pacifiques*, p. 81; review by 'J.P.' of Laurillard-Fallot's *Cours d'Art Militaire* in *Spectateur Militaire*, Vol. 33, p. 458.

18 Ms, *Mémoires sur l'Avancement des Sous Officiers et Soldats*, 26 April 1826, in AHG MR 1984.

19 Morand, p. 127; Marmont, *De l'Esprit*, preface.

20 Chantreau, p. 30.

21 Chalmin, p. 315.

22 Napoleon, *Correspondence*, Vol. XXXI, p. 415, and see Chantreau, p. 1; Rocquancourt, Vol. I, p. 16.

23 See, e.g., letters of 19 June 1840 and 11 January 1841, in AHG (uncatalogued) Dépôt carton B 12. Clermont Tonnerre's ambitious scheme for an index of tactical experiences is in ms minute, 2 October 1826, in MR 1979.

24 Doisy, *Essai*, in AHG MR 1955; Durand, *De la Nécessité de Fonder des Bibliothèques Militaires*.

25 Pagezy, *Plan Sommaire*, in AHG MR 1984; cf. Inspection of 12th Line, 1844, in Xb 637.

26 Both Brack's *Avant Postes* and Bugeaud's *Aperçus* first appeared as handbooks written by colonels for their regiments. For later examples see the 1842 inspection of 3rd Light in AHG Xb 697, and Le Louterel, *Essai de Conférences*.

27 Marmont, *Esprit*, pp. 133–7; Odier, Vol. I, p. 12.

28 Chalmin, p. 351, and a similar point made by Bajon, ms on military legislation, 1838, in AHG MR 2011. In 1845 the library of the 8th battalion of *Chasseurs* consisted of just one copy of Houdard's *Grammaire*, and six of Liskenne and Sauvan: Xb 720.

29 E.g. Clouet, p. 106, *Sentinelle de l'Armée*, 24 June 1836.

30 See *Moniteur Universel*, 1849, p. 1405; Oudinot, p. 107.

31 Listed in AHG Xj I; MR 1987, and MR 1799.

32 E.g. Inspection of 55th Line 1831, in AHG Xb 680; Le Louterel, pp. 87–9; La Motte Rouge, Vol. I, p. 286.

33 Anon. ms, *Notes sur les Camps d'Instruction*, 20 January 1825, in AHG MR 1987; anon. ms, 10 August 1852, in MR 2068; and *Sentinelle de l'Armée*, 8 April 1836.

34 See, e.g., De Gaulle, pp. 104–5, following Trochu, on the 1867 Châlons camp. Also contrast the tactics used in 1859, in La Motte Rouge, Vol. III, pp. 55 *ff.*, with the very different ones practised in the 1857 camp, in anon., *Journal du Camp de Châlons*.

35 *Sentinelle de l'Armée*, 16 July, 24 August 1836; *Journal de l'Armée*, 27 March 1836.

36 See Pelet's correspondence on this, 1841–42, in AHG MR 2118, especially ms note for Orleans, 9 May 1942.

37 All the camps are listed in AHG MR 1987: see also the AAG dossier of the Duke of Nemours.

38 E.g. Captain Langermann's ms translation *Du Jeu de la Guerre*, 1826, in AHG MR 1984; and Cte. de Firmas-Periés, *Le Jeu de Stratégie*. For the classic von Reisswitz 1824 war game, see Bill Leeson's 1983 translation, as well as the Wilson overview of early war games.

39 *Rapport sur les Travaux, 1841* and *1844*, in AHG Xs 141; cf. earlier and smaller competitions in AHG uncatalogued Dépôt carton A 35.

40 Duhesme, p. 151; 1842 Inspection of 33rd Line, AHG Xb 658.

41 Light Infantry officer reconnaissances in AHG Xs 141.

42 *Moniteur de l'Armée*, 11 August 1841, 25 May 1850.

43 AHG Xb 646. Compare also the *orgie buvante* of three topographically-minded sergeant majors from 12th Line Infantry in 1844, who were celebrating their honourable mention – in Xb 637.

44 See – perhaps surprisingly – Mordacq himself, p. 41.

45 General futurology is in I.F. Clarke. Steam and rockets in naval warfare are treated by Montgéry in *Bulletin des Sciences Militaires* 1824; steam machine-guns in trench warfare by Morand in *De l'Armée Selon La Charte*, p. 232 *ff.*; and other schemes in Paixhans, *Force et Faiblesse*, p. 402 *ff.* and his *Constitution Militaire*, pp. 37, 57, 224; and in Marmont's *Ésprit*, p. 74.

46 Source: AHG MR 2029, 2140, 2141.

47 Ms report, March 1831, in AHG MR 2140. Most of such annotations were made either by St Yon, a career *Dépôt* staff officer and later minister of war, or by Brahaut, an ex-infantryman who became indispensable in the *Dépôt's* archives. Both these men had experienced certain difficulties under the Restoration which seem to have intensified their unpromising interest in a mix of military history plus bureaucracy (AAG dossiers).

48 In AHG Xb 676.

49 E.g. articles in *Sentinelle de l'Armée* 1 September 1836, 1 March 1841; ms 8 December 1826 in AHG Xs 143. Bittard des Portes, p. 687, for Delvigne's unit of rampart rifles in Algiers, 1830.

50 La Motte Rouge, Vol. I, p. 362, for the poor effect of the rifles at Antwerp; Castellane, Vol. III, p. 94, and Bapst on Canrobert, p. 183, for Combes's unpopularity with the gymnastic pace. Combes had followed Napoleon to Elba in the first, and Lallemand to Texas in the second Restoration. In 1832 he led the Ancona expedition, and in 1837 was killed at the siege of Constantine.

51 The French 'Light' Infantry regiments at this time were notoriously no less 'Heavy' than the Line Infantry.

52 Tamisier, however, had first risen through the Artillery staff and was noted for his loyalty at Strasbourg during Louis Napoleon's attempted coup (letter of 24 October 1844, in AHG Xo 18 file 6, *Écoles de Tir*). Garraube's AAG dossier shows him constantly noted for his unmilitary attitude but influential aristocratic friends, whereas Minié rose from the ranks of 56th Line Infantry – Bugeaud's old regiment and source of many of the original *Chasseurs*.

53 Scheme of ex-artillery Colonel Lambert, 4 August 1831, in AHG MR 2140. The proposed officers are mostly on half pay or 'members of the circle of the *Café Americain* at Marseilles'.

54 E.g. projects of the 1790s in AHG MR 2008, 2034, 2043; projects of the Restoration era in Xs 143.

55 Paixhans's AAG dossier noted that he was allowed frequent leaves to pursue his inventing, and it took him thirty-nine years to become a brigadier-general.

56 E.g. *Journal des Sciences Militaires*, 1846, p. 289.

57 Valée's system is described in Hicks, pp. 154 *ff*.

58 Mountain artillery had been suggested in a circular of 17 May 1827 in AHG Xd 402, but was perfected in Algeria – see Favé, p. 274. Conversion of flintlocks to percussion priming was denounced as 'the castration of our best guns' in *Moniteur Universel*, 1840, p. 524.

59 Ms Valée to the minister, 30 December 1842, in AHG MR 2079.

60 Ducastel ms, *Exposé de la Conduite Tortueuse des Membres Influents du Comité de l'Artillerie*, 1832, in AHG Xd 402. Considérant served two years as an engineer before taking leave in 1832 to write a book on 'the science of industrial association' – which on 14 September 1835 was dismissed by Bugeaud as 'inexecutable due to human nature' (AAG dossier under 'Celebrités').

61 Ms letters, 11 July 1840, August 1824, in AHG MR 2129.

62 Barré note on percussion muskets, December 1830, in AHG MR 2141. See AAG dossier of General Girardin for the international competition at the Liège exhibition of 1844.

63 Thouvenin rose to be a general, although Valée's associate Captain Piobert was more influential in technical matters (AAG dossiers).

64 'Table' in *Journal Official Militaire*, 19 May 1824, for the creation of the Pyrotechnie Militaire.

65 *Spectateur Militaire*, 1843, p. 718; Favé and Louis Napoleon *Études sur*

l'Artillerie; Colonel Thuillier ms, *Note sur la Machine à Camoufler Contrepuits,* 1828 in AHG MR 2004.

66   The great *Carte de France* was completed in 1852, representing a truly gigantic technical advance over the Cassini map of 1755. For the organisation of the surveys, see AHG Xae 58. Modern military historians interested in Alpinism and mountain troops may pause to consider the case of Captain A.Durand, who first conquered Mount Pelvoux during his surveying tour for the *Carte de France* (commemorated in the stone monument still standing in Aillefroide village, Hautes Alpes).

67   Research into the telegraph was left to individual initiatives rather than contracted centrally – e.g. AHG uncatalogued *Dépôt* series D, 42–5; ms and printed brochure by the civilian Coulier, 1846, in MR 2140, or Sudre in *Moniteur de l'Armée,* 12 September 1841.

Field duplicating was pioneered in Spain 1823 by Guilleminot – see A.Desmadryl, 'Application de la lithographie à l'art militaire' in *Journal de l'Armée,* 1833, p. 237.

68   Coynart, 'Emploi militaire des chemins de fer' in *Journal des Sciences Militaires,* 1847, p. 389. The anon. ms, *Transport des Troupes sur les Chemins de Fer,* 1842, in AHG MR 2070, is almost certainly his work, although the same carton also contains many of Pelet's thoughts on railways. Cf. *Moniteur de l'Armée,* 24 January 1840, which reports a military test on the Versailles line.

69   E.g. E.A. Jullien, *Considérations sur l'ordre – Aperçus sur les Sciences des Découvertes,* reviewed in *Spectateur Militaire,* 1844, p. 90.

70   Desmadryl on lithography, and his 'Progrés de la Topographie' in *Journal de l'Armée,* 1833, p. 299; also Allent, p. 53, and review of an Austrian handbook in *Spectateur Militaire,* 1827 p. 377. For the importance of Geography as a new subject, see Gay de Vernon, p. 151 *ff.*.

71   Captain Noizet's review of Puissant's *Principes du Figuré du Terrain et du Lavis* in *Spectateur Militaire,* 1827, p. 632. See also Desmadryl on Topography, and the AAG dossier of Colonel Puissant – a Geographical Engineer through most of the Revolution and Empire, who worked in the *Dépôt* from 1810 until his retirement in 1833.

72   Gorrant, letter of 10 June 1840, complained of an administrative lack of co-ordination within the ministry (AHG *Dépôt* carton B 12); and St Yon – in the État Major Commission of 1833, AHG Xs 139 – thought the French less centralised than the Prussians.

Chapter 5

1   For the 'extreme' variant of 1890–1914, see Sternhell; Girardet on colonialism; Zeldin, Vol. II, pp. 876–905; Porch's *March to the Marne,* and the section 'Pleasure train to Berlin' in the forthcoming second edition of my *Forward Into Battle* .

2   Anon. ms, *De la Nécessité d'un Code Militaire,* 1818, in AHG MR 1979. See also inspection of 57th Line, 1835, in Xb 628.

3   The sentiment behind Morand's title is strongly echoed in Duhesme's ms, *Considérations sur la Constitution de l'Infanterie de l'Armée Française,* in AHG MR 1947.

4 E.g. in Préval's *De l'Avancement Militaire*, pp. 21, 30; Bardin, Vol. IV p. 4193, and Chambray, *Philosophie de la Guerre*, p. 86.

5 J.F.C. Fuller's book of that title appeared in London in 1924, although Moore's actual contribution to the system has recently been convincingly refuted in David Gates' book, as well in earlier private communications to the author by Joe Park.

6 The phrase recurs often in the published debate, e.g. in *Moniteur Universel*, 1824, p. 691; 1849, p. 1321. See also Colonel Lebeau on cantonments, August 1834, in AHG MR 1947; and discussion of his proposals, 9 March 1836, in MR 2140, Xs 142.

7 J.B. Avril, p. i; *Éloquence Militaire (&c)*. Note that in this and in the following notes which refer to conventional phrases, the aim is to indicate a few of the places where those phrases or sentiments are typically found – not to list all known instances of their use.

8 Brenier ms, *Observations sur l'Ordonnance de 1791*, 16 February 1826, in AHG 143, p. 13; Marmont, *Ésprit*, p. 7; Brack, p. 15; Inspection of 6th Line, 1840, in Xb 631; and Napoleon's famous mockery of 'Frederickan' methods in *Correspondence*, Vol. XXXII, p. 303.

9 *Sentinelle de l'Armée*, 16 October 1836; Lamarque, *Nécessité d'une Armée Permanente*, p. 25; Odier, Vol. II, p. 204; Rogniat, *Considérations*, p. 410.

10 Ambert, *passim*; Rocquancourt, Vol. I, p. 38; *Éloquence Militaire*, Vol. I, p. 68.

11 A pregnant text for this type of phenomenon is Berger and Luckman, *The Social Construction of Reality*.

12 Morand, p. 74, for his list of military vices; and anon. ms, 1814?, in AHG MR 1979, for a homely discussion which concludes that coffee is more dangerous to the troops than brandy.

13 Mussot in *Sentinelle de l'Armée*, 3 October 1841.

14 Captain A.Desbordeliers in *Sentinelle de l'Armée*, 1 October 1836.

15 Hulot's inspection of 1st battalion, *Chasseurs à Pied*, 1839, in AHG Xb 717; and see several examples in Porch.

16 Morand, p. 48; Fririon in *Spectateur Militaire*, 1826, p. 20; Inspection of 32nd Line, 1835, in AHG Xb 657.

17 Inspection of 21st Light Infantry, 1835, in AHG Xb 714. Meynadier rose through the infantry and staff, keeping a clean record with all régimes until his death in 1847.

18 AHG Xb 643.

19 Bapst's biography of Canrobert, Vol. I, p. 80.

20 La Motte Rouge, Vol. I, p. 306.

21 Fririon in *Spectateur Militaire*, 1826, p. 18.

22 *Éloquence Militaire*, Vol. I, p. 113.

23 E.g. for alcohol see the case of *Chef de Bataillon* Abadie, in the inspection of 3rd Line, 1831, in AHG Xb 628. For musket breaking, inspection of 29th Line, 1843, in Xb 654; and policy decision of the Infantry Committee, 1844, in Xs 141. See also Vidalenc's *Le Peuple des Campagnes*.

24 E.g. inspections by Durrieu at Nîmes, 1834, in AHG Xb 655; and Aymard at Grenoble, 1833, in Xb 640.

25 Inspection of 27th Line, 1838, in AHG Xb 652.

26 Anon. ms, *De la Baïonette*, in AHG MR 1962; *Sentinelle de l'Armée*, 10 January

1836.

27 The general directives, and such inspections as survive from the Restoration, are in AHG Xb 625, 738 and Xs 23–6. The inspections for 1831–45 are in Xb 626–729.

28 AHG Xs 23–4 show the decline of the spring inspections in the late Restoration, as well as the exceptional measures of 1831–32.

29 AHG Xs 141–2, 148; MR 1910 and 2127.

30 E.g. in Taverne ms, *Essai Historique et Raisonné sur les Manoeuvres des Trois Armes et leurs Règlements en France*, in AHG MR 2011.

31 Anon. ms in AHG MR 1947, *Réflexions sur l'Application* . . . ; and *Spectateur Militaire*, 1826, p. 541.

32 See the committee minutes in AHG Xs 141–2, 148, MR 1910 and 2127; especially Schramm on 23 April 1842 in AHG Xs 141. Also Colonel Lefaivre's ms, *Fragments d'un Mémoire d'un de nos Hommes de Guerre sur l'Infanterie*, 1846, in MR 1962.

33 *Sentinelle de l'Armée*, 20 January 1836; Paixhans, *Force et Faiblesse*, p. 24; Colonel Avigor des Fontès ms, *Considérations sur les Inspections Générales et les Revues Trimestrielles*, 1845?, in AHG MR 1946.

34 *Journal des Sciences Militaires*, 1847, p. 92; *Sentinelle de l'Armée*, 24 December 1836; and anon. reprint, *Quelques Observations sur l'Écrit Intitulé Première Lettre à l'Auteur Présumé des Changements Introduits dans l'Administration de l'Armée*, 1834, p. 11, in AHG MR 1979.

35 Préval, *Avancement*, p. 71; Captain Pecholier, ms *Mémoire sur l'État de Discipline Militaire en France*, 1830, p. 28, in AHG MR 1996; Commissaire, p. 126, and La Motte Rouge, Vol. I, p. 261.

36 This includes the Infantry side of the Infantry and Cavalry committee, when the Infantry committee did not sit alone. Sixty-nine per cent of known cases had a noble background, with the remainder from families in medicine or the law. Eighty-one per cent had attended a military school, and only 25% were identifiably politically liberal – significantly less than in the army as a whole.

37 See meetings of 9 March 1844, 27 February 1845, in AHG Xs 141.

38 E.g. Trochu's ms, *Examen du Projet d'Organisation de la Réserve*, 'around 1850', in AHG MR 2038.

39 Vichery to 33rd Line 1832, in AHG Xb 658; Lecouturier in *Spectateur Militaire*, 1827, p. 609.

40 Orleans to the minister on the *Chasseurs à Pied* cyclostyled sheets, 1840, in AHG MR 1947 and 1990, p. 10.

41 Girardin's report to Conseil Supérieur, 29 June 1829, in AHG MR 1947; Rogniat, *Considérations*, p. 106; Curial on 1821 inspection in Xs 26.

42 Inspection of 42nd Line 1832, in AHG Xb 667, and *Quelques Observations*, p. 11, in MR 1979.

43 Inspection of 11th Line 1835, in AHG Xb 636; 34th Line, 1832, in Xb 659. Cf. 26th Line, 1833, in Xb 651, which seemed to be suffering from subalterns who actively interfered in their superiors' exercise of command.

44 E.g. 42nd Line, 1840 and 1844, in AHG Xb 667.

45 Many military writers were noted in their AAG dossiers as too soft or sensitive, whereas Garraube and Combes were noted in the opposite sense.

46 Extraordinary inspection instructions 1832, in AHG Xs 24. An invaluable

list of 'unreliable' officers and their peccadilloes is in Préval ms, *Ésprit de l'Armée*, 1828, in MR 1945.

47 Infantry Committee, 12 April 1842, in AHG Xs 141, and Roguet ms, *Note sur les Dépôts des Corps en Général et sur leurs Confections en Particulier*, 1850, in MR 1996. For the general organisation of supernumerary companies, see MR 1962, letters of 1 April, 15 July 1831, and ms notes on *Compagnies Hors Rang*, in MR 1947.

48 Anon., ms report on the organisation of the Infantry 1762–1825, in AHG MR 2008; *Sentinelle de l'Armée*, 16 August 1841; *Moniteur Universel*, 1832, pp. 151–2; and Schramm in the Infantry Committee, 26 April 1842, in Xs 141.

49 Castellane, Vol. III, p. 373.

50 Ms notes on administration, 1819, in AHG *Succession Brahaut*, MR 1984; and Reports for the Conseil Supérieur – 16, 18 July, 22 August 1828 and 20 May 1829, in MR 2008.

51 Marmont, *Ésprit*, pp. 99–105; Odier, Vol. I, p. 293, Vol. VI, pp. 319–22.

52 Thoumas, Vol. II, pp. 12, 42 *ff.*, and Odier *passim*, show how the best elements in the Intendance were organised to look ahead – but Fézensac, p. 38, and Lechartier, *passim*, show how easily these plans could fall apart. Disaster seems to have dogged the logistics of almost every French campaign between 1792 and 1870, most of which were nevertheless victorious.

53 Anon., *Essai sur l'État Militaire en 1825*, p. 50; *Moniteur de l'Armée*, 10 May 1850; Commissaire, p. 160; Morand, p. 93. For the lack of a military code, see also anon. ms, *Examen du Titre IV du Projet d'Ordonnance*, February 1822, p. 24, in AHG MR 1979. Central dépôts were finally introduced in 1859 – Thoumas, Vol. II, p. 27.

54 See especially AHG MR 1885. I am especially grateful to John Naylor for bringing this to my attention.

55 J.Milot, 'Évolution du Corps des Intendants Militaires'.

56 E.g. AHG, *Succession Clermont Tonnerre*, ms, *Mémoire sur l'Intendance Militaire*, 19 August 1822, in MR 2010.

57 *Journal de l'Armée*, 8 May 1836; and ms memoir, 19 August 1822, in AHG MR 2010.

58 See Thoumas, Vol. II, p. 12; Milot, *Évolution;* Préval ms, *Examen de la Question du Défiler des Troupes et des Honneurs Militaires*, July 1839, in AHG MR 1910, p. 102.

59 E.g. D'Alton's ms, *Observations sur l'Organisation de l'Infanterie*, 10 February 1820; 1814 ms reports to the *Comité de la Guerre*, in AHG MR 1962.

60 Girardin to Conseil Supérieure de la Guerre, 29 June 1829, in AHG MR 1947; Lamarque's memoirs, Vol. I, p. 100 – but contrast La Roche Aymon, *Des Troupes Légères*, p. 85.

61 Circular to inspectors, 7 July 1820, in AHG Xs 23; inspection of 61st Line, 1839, in Xb 686; Ambert, *Esquisses*, p. 572; Paixhans, *Constitution Militaire*, p. 109; Clouet, p. 35.

62 *Moniteur de l'Armée*, 26 January 1850; cf. *Moniteur Universel*, 1849, p. 1320, and 1850, pp. 108, 561.

63 Le Louterel, pp. 74, 82–5; Gaullier, *Petit Manuel des Sous Officiers et des Caporaux*, 1825?, in AHG Xs 143; Poisson ms, *Cours d'Administration, de Legislation, et de Jurisprudence Militaires*, 29 May 1845, p. 75, in MR 1979.

64 *Moniteur Universel*, 1831, p. 2076; circular, 7 July 1820, in AHG Xs 23; Gallimand's ms, *Remarques sur l'Instruction des Corps d'Infanterie*, in Xs 143, and inspections of 26th Line, 1840 and 1842, in Xb 651. Cf. *Moniteur Universel*, 1832, p. 215, for the idea of but two years' training.

65 E.g. inspections of 28th Line, 1834, in AHG Xb 653, and 32nd Line, 1839, in Xb 657.

66 For typical daily routines see inspections of 26th Line, 1841, in AHG Xb 651; and 46th Line register for 1832–35, p. 10, in Xb 671. See also Le Louterel's proposed reforms, p. 82.

67 Rates of pay are in Porch, pp. 22–6, 31; Lamarque, *De l'Esprit Militaire*, p. 24; and Torrens, p. 62. *Sentinelle de l'Armée*, 16 April 1836, warns of the *abrutissement* that followed a pay rise.

68 E.g. Lt.-Col. Mussot's scheme in his 1849 election programme (AAG dossier), or Durand's association with the *Banque du Peuple* (AAG dossier, note of 12 November 1848); Lieutenant 'J.J.T.' in *Revue Militaire*, 1834, and inspection of 51st Line, 1839, in AHG Xb 676.

69 Grundler's reprinted article on Light Infantry, 29 August 1831, in AHG MR 2140, p. 7. Pelet's speech to the Deputies, 7 May 1835, in MR 2070.

70 Vaudoncourt, in *Journal des Sciences Militaires*, 1830, p. 287, and still less liberal allowances of space in *Moniteur de l'Armée*, 10 September 1847.

71 Anon., *État Militaire en 1825*, p. 20, and Torrens, *Notes*.

72 *Journal de l'Armée*, 1833, p. 212; cf. the less detailed retraction of these figures in *ibid.*, 27 March 1836.

73 Thoumas, Vol. II, p. 77; anon., *Réponse à la Note Inserée dans le Spectateur Militaire*, 15 December 1839, p. 7 *ff.*, in Castellane's papers, AHG MR 2252; *Journal de l'Armée*, 13 March 1836; Préval to the Peers, 16 June 1840, in MR 1910, p. 156.

74 *Moniteur de l'Armée*, 30 April 1850; Duvergier, 1850, p. 139.

75 Ackerknecht, *passim;* Debendetti, Ch. 2 .

76 Endless discussions in the Infantry Committee, AHG Xs 141.

77 Inspections of 9th Line, 1831, in AHG Xb 634; and regimental order book of 46th Line, 1832, p. 15, in Xb 671. For preventive hygiene in general, see, e.g., Sous-Lieutenant Chauchar ms, *Physiologie de la Guerre*, 1846, p. 39, in MR 2004.

78 Dr. Ducoux in *Sentinelle de l'Armée*, 24 December 1836; *Spectateur Militaire*, 1827, p. 429; and subsection on *Écoles de Natation*, in AHG MR 2189.

79 St. Chamans, pp. 478–83. Compare La Motte Rouge, Vol. I, pp. 414–15, for a contemporary explanation of sleepwalking.

80 Inspection of 56th Line, 1841, in AHG Xb 681; Register of correspondence of 16th Line, 2, 4 March 1828, in Xb 641; and anon. ms, *Observations et Propositions Concernant le Recrutement et les Dépôts des Chasseurs à Pied*, 1835, in MR 2022.

81 Tubiana, *passim;* Dufour, *De la Folie*, for statistics of military mental patients at an Armentières hospital.

82 Bugeaud in *Moniteur Universel*, 1832, p. 32.

83 Duhesme ms, *Constitution de l'Infanterie*, in AHG MR 1947; and for its application to gymnastics, anon., ms *De l'Avantage qu'il y aurait d'Établir dans les Regiments d'Infanterie une École Gymnastique*, 1828?, in MR 2004.

84 Inspection of 6th Line, 1831, in AHG Xb 631.
85 Morand, pp. 25–9, 75; Marmont, *Esprit*, p. 130, says these methods can even make soldiers out of townsmen!
86 For Algeria see Julien, Ch.6, and letter from Soult complaining to Bugeaud, 30 August 1845, in AHG MR 1996. See Chapter six, below, for the military schools.
87 AHG Xb 627.
88 Avril, p. 37.
89 Le Louterel, *Conférences*, p. 75; Préval, *Projet de Règlement*.
90 Taverne, *Essai Raisonné*, in AHG MR 1984, p. 46.
91 Infantry Committee, 4 May 1844, AHG Xs 141; Castellane, Vol. III, p. 117; *Journal de l'Armée*, 20 March 1836.
92 E.g. Boichot, p. 10, Pecqueur, p. 153.
93 Préval's report to Infantry & Cavalry Committee, 2 November 1835, in AHG MR 1989; and his ms letter to the minister, 8 December 1840, on MR 1910; also anon. ms, *Notes sur l'Administration Militaire* 'about 1850', in MR 1979.
94 Captain Berton ms, *Coup d'oeil sur les Conseils de Guerre*, 18 October 1843, in AHG MR 2010; *Sentinelle de l'Armée*, 1 May 1836; *Moniteur Universel*, 1838, p. 159.
95 Many projects in AHG MR 2010; Ambert, *Esquisses*, p. 311; Morand, p. 70.
96 Annual Ministry of War reports, *Comte Général de l'Administration de la Justice Militaire Pendant l'Année*, for 1833–51, from which the statistics are extracted for my Appendix II on Military Crime.
97 Anon., *Notes sur l'Administration*, in AHG MR 1979.
98 Captain Liron d'Airoles ms, *De la Réforme Pénitentiaire*, 20 September 1836, in AHG MR 2010; and reports to the crown, May 1832 and 23 April 1836, in MR 1985.
99 Infantry Committee, 7 April 1842, in AHG Xs 141.
100 Inspection of 3rd Line, 1836, in AHG Xb 628; and Infantry Committee, 30 March 1841, in Xs 141.
101 Infantry Committee, 4 May 1844, in AHG Xs 141.
102 Captain Chatelain's ms plans for a *Maison Modèle de Détention Militaire*, April 1832, in AHG MR 2010; and, for an account of St Germain, *Moniteur de l'Armée*, 14 November 1841. General prison reform at this time is in de Tocqueville and Beaumont, part II, and Raspail.

Chapter 6

1 *Journal des Sciences Militaires*, 1847, p. 92; Captain F. Durand, *Des Tendances Pacifiques* ; Ambert, *Esquisses*, p. 332, 24 April 1836.
2 Laborde, 1818, in Appert, p. 15.
3 Infantry Committee, 23 April 1842 – cf. 16th Line Infantry, which actually did introduce examinations for nco promotions, see inspection, 1834, in AHG Xb 641.
4 *Ibid.*, 1834.
5 E.g. Standard-Bearer Adou's ms, *Exposé de la Situation des Sous-Officiers dans l'Armée depuis 1815 jusqu'en 1830, Suivi d'un Plan d'Études Applicable*

aux Écoles Régimentaires, 1 October 1830, in AHG Xo 12.

6   Bardin's dictionary under 'École'; ms report 28 January 1812, in AHG Xo 18; *Journal de l'Armée*, 1833, p. 270; *Spectateur Militaire*, 1826, p. 338; and Strachan, *Wellington's Legacy*, p. 85 *ff.* for parallel British practice.

7   It is perhaps no coincidence that Mutual Education is still used today for the teaching of drill! Details of the method are in Laborde's speech to Parliament, 24 November 1818, reprinted in Appert, p. 23; and E. Roland, *Méthode Militaire d'Enseignement Primaire*, 2nd edn, Paris, 1856, p. iii, in AHG Xo 18. This method was often called 'oriental' due to its similarity with Muslim teaching – inspection of 25th Line, 1842, in Xb 650.

8   Durand, *Coup d'oeil sur l'Ordre Social*, p. 84.

9   Colonel A. Laborde has a very incomplete dossier in AAG. He appears to have been a noble émigré in the Revolution and compromised under Napoleon. After 1815 he was active in politics and the National Guard. B. Appert was a drawing teacher who turned to prison reform, educational theory and liberal politics. See his *Dix Ans à la Cour de Louis Philippe*, e.g. Vol. I, p. 95.

10 Schemes in AHG Xo 18, and inspections of 8th Line, 1833, in Xb 633, and 15th Line, 1839, in Xb 640. The 62nd Line seems to have used a different method every year between 1832 and 1835; see Xb 687: cf. a ministerial letter of 16 October 1837 calling for unity, in E5, 78.

11 *Moniteur de l'Armée*, 4, 28 July, 26 September 1841, for prizes offered by the minister for textbooks. See also Ambert, *Soldat*, p. 17.

12 Ministry of Education statistics for 1827–29 and 1851–55, in Rémond's atlas, p. 170. Illiteracy was most widespread in the south and south-west of France, least widespread in the north-east.

13 *Moniteur Universel*, 1843, p. 1804.

14 *Ibid.*

15 E.g. *Journal de l'Armée*, 1833, p. 375. At least we can see that Croubois, p. 175, is very wide of the mark when he dismisses regimental education in its totality.

16 *Sentinelle de l'Armée*, 24 September 1836; Lieutenant Renard ms, *Rapport sur les Écoles Régimentaires*, 6 November 1847, in AHG Xo1.

17 Baron Zaeppfel, ms letter to the minister, 9 March 1821, in AHG Xo 12; Marnier ms, *Projet sur la Composition des Régiments d'Infanterie Légère et de Ligne*, 1 June 1822, in MR 2008; H.Calais, *Mémoire sur l'Établissement d'Académies Militaires en France*, January 1834, reprint in MR 2071.

18 See inspections of 52nd Line, 1834, in AHG Xb 677; 19th Line, 1834, in Xb 644.

19 Roland, *Méthode*, pp. iii, 167 : but by 1866 it was clear that his hopes had not been heeded – Captain Aomary, 26 October 1866, in AHG MR 2009. See also Infantry Committee, 14 May 1844, in Xs 141, and 15 June 1849, in MR 2127.

20 Appert, p. 126. See also Sala, p. 51, P.Adou, 1 October 1830, ms in AHG Xo 12.

21 Avril, p. 87; letter from Saumur commandant, 17 December 1846, in AHG MR 2190.

22 Boichot, p. 4.

23 Captain F. Durand, *De la Nécessité de Fonder des Bibliothèques Militaires*, pp. 11–

16; *Journal de l'Infanterie et de la Cavalerie*, Vol. I, Introduction; *La France Militaire*, 1845, No.1.

24 6th Line, 1841–42, in AHG Xb 631; 47th Line, 1840, in Xb 672; 20th Light, 1840, in Xb 713; 3rd Light, 1840, in Xb 697.

25 Le Louterel, p. 90; Infantry Committee, 23 April 1842, in AHG Xs 141, and 1851, in MR 2127; *Journal de l'Armée*, 22 May 1836; Castellane *fils*, Vol. I, p. 231.

26 Cf. La Motte Rouge, Vol. I, p. 136, had access only to the private books of his captain.

27 Estimate based on inspection reports, 1831–45.

28 E.g. in 1845 the 21st Light could not find the thirty-five volumes recommended for the nco course; AHG Xb 714.

29 There is a selection in AHG Xo 1.

30 Laborde stressed the Napoleonic Wars; Appert, p. 30; cf. Gouvion St Cyr's official charts, which dealt with the wars of the monarchy – see Pelet's letter, 3 September 1833, in uncatalogued *Dépôt* carton A 35. For the relationship between passion and armies, see the work of de Rougemont, Caillois and Huizinga in the 1930s.

31 Gorrant ms, 19 June 1840, and de Sailly ms, 11 January 1841, in *Dépôt* carton B 12. Cf. Lamarque's *Nécessité d'une Armée*, p. 99; Pelleport's memoirs, Vol. I, p. 1.

32 Orleans's directive to authors in his AAG dossier; *Spectateur Militaire*, 1826, p. 494; d'Alton's orders to 8th Line, 1833, in AHG Xb 633; Adou in Xo 12; Calais in MR 2071; and – perhaps strangely – the arch-technologist Paixhans, *Constitution Militaire*, p. 125.

33 Orleans's directive.

34 Inspections of 22nd Line, 1842, in AHG Xb 647; 7th Light, 1845, in Xb 701; 12th Line, 1844, in Xb 637.

35 Ordonnances of 24 July and 14 February 1816, in AHG MR 1984; Appert, Vol. I, p. 86.

36 Chambray, *Philosophie*, pp. 87, 92; Commissaire, p. 136.

37 Anon., *Réponse*, in AHG MR 2252; Une Société de Militaires et d'Hommes de Lettres, Vol. I, p. 135; Lamarque, *Esprit*, p. 28.

38 Ambert, *Soldat*, p. 373 and *Esquisses*, p. 503; cf. Guignot ms, *Souvenirs d'un Zouave en Algérie et en Crimée*, 1867, in AHG MR 2008, who wants chaplains re-introduced. For the creation of a 'French ideology' for Algeria see Keller's *Lamoricière*, Vol. I, p. 162, and Bugeaud in Blanc, p. 394.

39 Anon. ms, *De l'Avantage qu'il y Aurait d'Établir dans les Régiments d'Infanterie une École Gymnastique*, 1828?, in AHG collection Mellinet, MR 2004.

40 Hulot's 1841 inspection of 18th Line, in AHG Xb 643. Hulot was associated with light infantry throughout his career and was an adc to Soult from 1803. He was not employed in the Restoration, but became a champion of the *Chasseurs à Pied* in the July Monarchy.

41 Avril, pp. 99–101; and Inspection of 21st Line, 1839, in AHG Xb 646. The inspector of 26th Line in 1836 added 'civilisation' to the list of benefits imparted by dancing (Xb 651).

42 Le Louterel, pp. 80–2; Valentin in *Moniteur de l'Armée*, 20 June 1850; and see Commissaire's experience with his company bully, p. 153.

43 Rogniat, *Considérations*, p. 185; Rapatel's general survey of his 1841 inspections, in AHG Xs 96.

44 Colonel F. Amoros, 1770–1848, gained his rank in the Spanish Infantry before joining the French during the Peninsular War. He was on half pay in France during the Restoration, when he turned to his pedagogic interests: dossier in AAG, and Spivak's article.

45 Correspondence between Caux and Coutard, 1829, and map of the gymnasium, in AHG MR 2004; Grundler's reprinted article on Light Infantry, 29 August 1831, p. 13, in MR 2140; and the problem with detached officers in, e.g., 29th Line, 1831–34, in Xb 654.

46 Correspondence with Amoros, in AHG Xae 19; report to the crown, 15 July 1829, in Xo 18. See also Puvis's 1832 experiences, in AHG Xb 648; and *Journal de l'Armée*, 1833, p. 363 – which in its fifth issue even questions the legality of making conscripts do gymnastics at all.

47 AHG Xb 660. D'Alton rose through the Infantry and Staff and was an inspector from 1815 to 1841.

48 Le Louterel, p. 88; and Infantry Committee general report, 1851, AHG MR 2127. For the danger of accidents when emphasis was placed on individual feats of virtuosity, see Fourcy's 1826 comments in Fririon's AAG dossier.

49 Anon. ms,*Sur les Escrimes de la Baïonette, de la Lance et du Sabre*, n.d., in AHG MR 2009, and AAG dossier of General Aulas de Courtigis, letter of 9 May 1846. Captain J.F.A. Müller was a German cavalryman who settled in France on the collapse of the Napoleonic Empire, publishing his *Théorie de l'Escrime à Cheval* in 1816. Attempts to employ him in cavalry training foundered, however, on his incompetence, litigious temperament or – in one case – dishonesty. He eventually took a post with the Turkish army, but continued to produce self-justifying pamphlets (AAG dossier).

50 Infantry Committee, 29 May 1851 and general 1851 report, in AHG MR 2127; cf. La Motte Rouge's 1838 ms regimental project in Xb 676; and Langermann's ms, *Théorie d'Escrime à la Baïonette Rédigé d'après les Ordres du Ministre*, 1830, in MR 2009. Unfortunately I have been unable to trace further details on Pinette.

51 *Moniteur de l'Armée*, 8 August 1841; Ambert, *Esquisses*, p. 327 *ff.* ; and the singing class in 54th Line, 1843, in AHG Xb 679.

52 Inspection of 28th Line, 1845, in AHG Xb 653.

53 Oudinot's 1847 pamphlet is particularly full and revealing for this whole subject. Oudinot was the son of a Napoleonic marshal who rose through the Emperor's Pages and the Cavalry to become a general in 1824. He was a great traveller, and commanded the Rome expedition in 1849.

54 E.g. anon. ms on gymnastic schools in AHG MR 2004; Marnier's May 1837 *Améliorations*, in MR 2140; Inspection of 7th *Chasseur* battalion, 1843, in Xb 720.

55 Chief Engineer (*Ponts et Chaussées*) Thenard's 1831 ms, in AHG MR 2141; See also Durand, *Coup d'oeil*, and Morand, *De l'Armée*.

56 *Journal de l'Infanterie et de la Cavalerie*, February 1834.

57 *Sentinelle de l'Armée*, 8 May 1836; Clouet, p. 123.

58 *Sentinelle de l'Armée*, 16 April 1836, *Moniteur de l'Armée*, 24 October 1841.

59 Paixhans, *Constitution Militaire*, p. 134; Pelet, 22 February 1834 ms note, in

AHG MR 2038; cf. the opposite view was taken by Roguet, *Vendée*, p. 223 *ff*.

60 Roguet, *Vendée*, p. 239, says that use of the army would overcome seasonal fluctuations in the labour market.

61 Boyer, 25 December 1836 ms report in AHG MR 2038; Charlier ms, *Considérations sur l'Emploi des Troupes aux Travaux Publics*, April 1844, in MR 1962.

62 Anon. ms, July 1834, in AHG E 5, 59; Lamaque, *Mémoires*, Vol. II, p. 212; and *Spectateur Militaire*, 1826, p. 368.

63 Lambertye in *Bulletin des Sciences Militaires*, 1824, p. 229; Castelbajac ms, June 1845, in AHG MR 2140.

64 Anon. ms, *Projet d'un Règlement pour la Colonisation Militaire de la Cavalérie Régulière*, in AHG MR 1989.

65 Tanski ms, *Mémoire sur la Domination Française au Nord de l'Afrique*, 10 August 1835, in AHG H 226; and Bugeaud's *Les Socialistes et le Travail en Commun*.

66 Yacono 'La colonisation militaire'.

67 Rey, *Abrégé Historique des Services et des Travaux de la Légion Etrangère*, 1849, pp. 10, 14, in AHG MR 1844; and Duvivier ms, *Mémoire sur l'Afrique*, March 1838, in AHG H 226.

68 Castellane, Vol. III, pp. 146, 251; Lamarque, *Esprit Militaire*, p. 96.

69 Fabvier to 40th Line, 1841, in AHG Xb 665.

Chapter 7

1 This change is noted in the second paragraph of anon. ms, *Essai sur l'Art Militaire*, in AHG MR 1984: see also my *Forward Into Battle*, chapter four.

2 In his *Journal*, Vol. 3 – and compare Castellane's very similar view of the battle of the Rio Seco, in *his* journal, Vol. I, p. 25.

3 The Prussian *landwehr* was admired by the French left, by royalist ex-émigrés like La Roche Aymon, and by *Dépôt* analysts such as de Caraman – see his 'Essai sur l'Organisation Militaire de la Prusse' in *Spectateur Militaire*, 1828. The standard – scarcely flattering – work on the British was Baron C. Dupin's *Voyages dans la Grande Bretagne* .

4 The original experimental battalion was called *Chasseurs de Vincennes*, after its barracks, soon changed to *Chasseurs d'Orléans*, after its patron.

5 E.g. Mordacq, pp. 53, 63; Chalmin, p. 350.

6 Gouvion St Cyr's *Maximes*, p. 9; Carrion Nisas, *Essai sur l'Histoire Générale*, Vol. II, p. 374; Pelet ms, *Premier Mémoire sur les Manoeuvres de Guerre d'une Division d'Infanterie et d'un Corps d'Armée*, 1826, in AHG MR 2071, pp. 20, 38.

7 Brack's *Avant Postes* and Bugeaud's *Aperçus* are classic cases in point, albeit mutually incompatible, whereas Favé's *Trois Armes* takes the whole principle to extremes.

8 The expression is Bardin's, from his *Dictionnaire*, p. 4979.

9 Bugeaud in Ideville, especially pp. 158–67 for the Alps.

10 Rocquancourt, Vol. IV, p. 40; Morand, p. 145; Gouvion St Cyr, *Maximes,* p. 2. For an exhaustive Second Empire (1865) summary of the best of Napoleonic tactics, see General Renard's paper, translated into English in Public Record Office document WO/33/15, pp. 947–1029.

11 Ardant's career – including a long spell in the *Chasseurs* after the Crimean War

– is well summarised in the prolegomena to his classic *Battle Studies*. For
Trochu see ch. 3, n.29, above.

12   Regnault's article, and compare Castellane, Vol. III, pp. 134, 231 *ff*.

13   The ideal of the Boulogne camp is reflected in, e.g., Thoumas, Vol. I, p. 48
     (following Morand), and in a marked form in the preface to Colin's *La
     Tactique et la Discipline dans les Armées de la Révolution*.

14   Le Louterel, p. 66; Rogniat, *Considérations*, pp. 241–7.

15   Rogniat, *Considérations*, p. 426.

16   *Ibid.*, pp. 88, 122, 376, 411; and, e.g., Chambray, *Philosophie*, chapter two.

17   Rogniat, *Considérations*, pp. 1, 119 for Artillery; p. 94 *ff*. for skirmishers;
     Thiers, *Les Pyrénées*, p. 186 for the isolation of Spanish warfare; and Bugeaud
     in Azan, p. 280, for that of Algeria.

18   AHG Xb 660. Note the importance of close order to this critique, as opposed
     to the open order implied by 'aiming'.

19   Anon. ms – no title or date (but about 1814?), in AHG MR 1979.

20   Anon. ms, *De la Baïonette*, n.d., in AHG MR 1962; Labarre du Parcq, p. 177.

21   Anon. ms, *Quelques Observations sur l'Infanterie*, 1818, in AHG MR 1947.

22   Rogniat, *Considérations*, p. 404. See also Jacquinot de Presle, p. 106; Bugeaud,
     Aperçus, p. 125 *ff*.; Chambray, *De l'Infanterie*, p. 14 *ff*. .

23   Ardant du Picq, pp. 139, 145; Ambert, *Études Tactiques*, p. 427; Le Louterel,
     p. 67. Cf. Trochu, p. 235 *ff*., who condemns this mechanism.

24   *Devoirs du Soldat de l'Infanterie*, wall chart for regimental schools, in AHG Xo
     I.

25   Ternay, p. 354; Chapuis, p. 31.

26   Ambert, *Esquisses*, p. 590.

27   Captain Grand, *Défense et Occupation de la Colonie d'Alger*, Toulon, 1837, p.
     116, in AHG H 226; cf. those who disagreed, e.g. Senior, Vol. II, p. 94, and
     Préval to the Peers, 16 June 1840, in MR 1910 p. 152.

28   *Moniteur Universel*, 1841, p. 164.

29   La Roche Aymon, p. 3.

30   Rogniat, *Considérations*, p. 169; Pelet's *Essai sur les Manoeuvres*, in AHG MR
     2071, p. 8; and Vacca, p. 73.

31   Inspection of 9th Line, 1843, in AHG Xb 634.

32   Jacquinot de Presle, p. 106 *ff*.; La Roche Aymon, p. 111 *ff*.; Le Louterel, p. 9.

33   Capt. Boyer ms, *Quelques Observations sur la Formation de l'Infanterie sur Deux ou
     Trois Rangs*, Strasbourg, 10 September 1833, in AHG MR 2012; Lieut. de
     Taverne, *Essai Historique et Raisonné*, in MR 2011; Duhesme, p. 139 *ff*.

34   Inspection of 1st Line at Toulon, 1836, in AHG Xb 626; 6th Line at
     Briançon, 1832, in Xb 631.

35   Ney's *Études Militaires;* Battalion Commander Swich ms, *Observations sur le
     Règlement de 1791*, Givet, 1825, in AHG Xs 143; General Meunier ms report to
     the Commission on Infantry Manoeuvres, 22 March 1806, in MR 1962.

36   Mallet ms, *Notes et Quelques Observations sur le Règlement de 1791*, n.d. (1825?) in
     AHG Xs 143; General Descars ms report on the inspections of 1821, in Xs
     26.

37   2 April 1846, in AHG Xs 141.

38   Schneider inspecting 6th Light, 1838, in AHG Xb 700.

39   Pelleport, Vol. II, p. 175.

40 E.g. the 'Méthode Legros', invented by a major of the 13th Light Infantry 1844: see his dossier in AAG, and Infantry Committee discussions 6 March, 31 May 1845, 20 May 1847, in AHG Xs 141.

41 Jacquinot de Presle, p. 77; Brack, p. 15 *ff.*.

42 Infantry Committee, 7 May 1842, 25 May 1844, in AHG Xs 141; 7 March 1855 discussion of Colonel Clouard's *Évolutions*, in Xs 138.

43 Capt. Boyer ms, *Quelques Observations*, 1833, in AHG MR 2012.

44 AHG Xs 143; cf. Meunier's submission to a similar commission, ms, 22 March 1806, in AHG MR 1962.

45 Brenier ms, *Observations sur l'Ordonnance de 1791*, 1826, in AHG Xs 143. Brenier, 1767–1832, was the son of a lawyer who was promoted to general in 1799. He served every régime from before the Revolution until 1823 (dossier in AAG).

46 Pelleport, Vol. 2, p. 175.

47 Ms letter to Curial, 6 July 1827, in AHG Xs 143.

48 *Ordonnance du Roi sur l'Exercise et les Manoeuvres de l'Infanterie*, 4 March 1831.

49 Bugeaud, *Aperçus,* p. 125 *ff*; Chambray, *De l'Infanterie*, p. 15 *ff*; and, indeed, de Saxe, *Mes Rêveries*, Vol. I, p. 37.

50 Delorme du Quesney, p. 112; Colonel Marnier's pamphlet, *Améliorations Proposées dans l'Armement et l'Éducation des Troupes*, May 1837, in AHG MR 2140.

51 27 April 1844, in AHG Xs 141.

52 E.g. Duhesme, La Roche Aymon, and Rogniat's *Considérations*.

53 Orleans to the minister on the *Chasseurs à Pied*, 1840, in AHG MR 1947, p. 5; Paixhans's *Constitution Militaire*, p. 41 *ff.*, or Beurmann's reviewer's comment that 'the art of combats becomes a positive art', *Sentinelle de l'Armée*, 1 August 1836.

   Compare Thoumas, Vol. II, p. 631, for a sharp comment ridiculing the idea that the rifle-armed *Chasseurs* had in some way displaced the artillery. De Luna, p. 148, says that some two million shots were fired by the army in the June Days to produce some 5,000 civilians killed (i.e. 400 shots per kill) – plus an unknown number of wounded (perhaps 15,000, making 100 shots per hit?), and 11,000 jailed or deported. Compare this with 75 hits scored at Corunna in 1823 from 6,000 rounds fired from smoothbore muskets, making 80 shots per hit: Bittard des Portes, p. 263.

54 The AAG cahier for the officers of 17th Line Infantry, 1821–41, suggests that of the 43 officers entering from military schools 6 (14%), and of the 174 entering from the ranks 36 (21%), and of the 30 from direct nomination 1 (3%), served in the regiment's *voltigeur* companies – i.e. proportionally more of the dedicated light infantry officers came from the ranks.

55 The Infantry Inspections of 1831–45 seem to show that on average (but with huge variations in individual cases) each man shot ten practice rounds each year with flintlock smoothbores, with an average of 14.3% of 'hits' – taken over all the distances fired. At the extremes, in 1842 the 6th Light Infantry hit the target with only 0.6% of its shots, while in 1844 the 37th Line claimed (although their inspector was incredulous) that they had hit with 70%! More typically the results would fall between 6% and 25% of shots hitting, with only 23 cases (6.2% of the sample) scoring higher, and 30 cases (8.1% of the

sample) scoring lower than those limits.

56   E.g. Delvigne's letter of 8 December 1826; Galimand's ms, *Remarques sur l'Instruction des Corps d'Infanterie;* and Captain Fourmy de Blancheté ms, *Essai sur une École de Tirailleurs*, 1819, all in AHG Xs 143.

57   Conseil Supérieure, 26 December 1828, in AHG MR 2051, p. 7; Infantry Committee, 2 July 1841, in AHG Xs 141; and Orleans's 1840 report in AHG MR 1947, p. 3 *ff.*

58   La Motte Rouge, Vol. I, p. 485 *ff.*; ex-Captain L. Panot, *Cours sur les Armes à Feu Portatives.*

59   Merson's review of Dusaert in *Moniteur de l'Armée*, 15 April 1850; Rémond's *Tactique;* Delorme du Quesney.

60   Delorme du Quesney, p. 135; Ardant du Picq, lithographed *De l'Emploi de la Carabine et des Chasseurs et des Compagnies du Centre*, n.d., in AHG MR 1990.

61   Rémond's *Tactique*, p. 59; Planat de la Faye ms, *Supplément aux Motifs Pour l'Abandon d'Alger*, 1836, in AHG H 226, quoting Pélissier.

62   Marnier, *Améliorations*, in AHG MR 2140, p. 21; Duhesme, p. 145.

63   1854, lithographed copy in AHG MR 2041.

64   Thoumas, Vol. II, p. 452.

65   Engels was enthusiastic – in Chaloner and Henderson, pp. 83–6.

66   La Roche Aymon p. 44; Colonel Lebeau ms, *Observations sur les Avantages de l'Emploi de Quelques Carabines Rayées à l'Armée*, 16 April 1833, and Lt.-Col. Henry ms on *Chasseurs à Pied*, 2 December 1840, both in AHG MR 1962.

67   Beurmann in *Sentinelle de l'Armée*, 1 August 1836.

68   Chef d'Escadron Sol ms, *De la Création de Régiments Speciaux d'Infanterie pour le Service d'Afrique*, 30 December 1835, in AHG H 226; General Lucay ms, *Mémoire sur l'Organisation de l'Infanterie Française en Légions Départmentales*, 1815, in MR 2008.

69   Lithographed *Projet d'Ordonnance* and *Procés Verbal du Comité Central*, 6 August 1832, in AHG MR 2019, and Duc d'Aumale, *Les Zouaves et les Chasseurs à Pied*, pp. 150–1.

70   General Achard, inspecting the 2nd *Chasseurs* in 1845, was scathing about the role of ambition in this context – AHG Xb 717.

71   All the reports on the first formation are in AHG Xb 716.

72   *Chasseurs* were sometimes used as shock troops, in a 'grenadier' role – e.g. La Motte Rouge on Magenta, Vol. II, pp. 73,76.

73   *Sentinelle de l'Armée*, 8 May 1841.

74   Orleans report in AHG MR 1947; 'B.G.', *Théorie Militaire du Pas de Course.* See Carrion Nisas, *Essai*, Vol. II, p. 516 for the speeding up of normal drill paces after 1815, apart from the *pas gymnastique.*

75   Anon. ms, *De l'Avantage &c*, n.d. (1828?), in AHG MR 2004; cf. the deleterious effect on the Line Infantry of imitating the *Chasseurs* – inspection of 37th Line, 1843, in Xb 662.

76   *Sentinelle de l'Armée*, 8 May 1841.

77   Orleans report in AHG MR 1947; Henry ms in MR 1962; and for some of these moral qualities, inspections of 30th Line, 1838 and 1840, in Xb 655.

78   Ardant du Picq, *De l'Emploi*, in AHG MR 1990; and Captain J. de Bellefonds, 'Note sur les Chasseurs à Pied' in *Spectateur Militaire*, Vol. 33, p. 552.

79   Achard to 2nd *Chasseurs*, 1845, in AHG Xb 717.

80 Meetings of 9 April 1842, 9 March 1843, 19 March, and 25 May 1844, 13 March 1845, in AHG Xs 141.

Chapter 8

1 See, e.g., Pelet's notes on the art of war in AHG MR 2073; Colonjon ms, *Quelles sont les Connaissances que doit Posséder un Lieutenant de Cavalerie?*, August 1845, in MR 1989.

2 Instructions for inspectors, 14 July 1821, p. 8, in AHG Xs 24; 28 May 1845, p. 46 *ff.*, in Xs 25.

3 Léonard shows that the eighteenth-century reformers believed that war had just become scientific in their day, while Renan clearly believed the watershed came in 1870–71, when *he* was writing.

4 Chapters *De l'Instruction* extracted from La Roche Aymon's *De la Cavalerie*, Paris, 1828, p. 587, in AHG MR 1956; Clouet p. 2 *ff.* .

5 Pagezy de Bourdéliac ms, December 1826, in AHG MR 1984; anon. ms on regimental schools, 1830, in Xo 12; and renewed debate in the Second Republic – *Moniteur Universel*, 1848, p. 1555; 1849, p. 2414.

6 E.g. Lenglet ms, 26 April 1826, and Boyer, ms, 1 December 1830, *Observations sur la Loi du 10me Mars 1818*, both in AHG MR 1984.

7 E.g. Du Barail, Vol. I, p. 5 for the African cavalry, and Antioche's Changarnier, p. 3 *ff.* for direct entry into the *Garde du Corps*.

8 D. Johnson, *Guizot* p. 127 *ff.* .

9 E.g. Durand, *Des Tendances Pacifiques*, p. 46 *ff.*

10 Report to minister, 16 October 1830, and Report on Military Schools (1829?), both in AHG MR 1954; ms letter from minister to Préval, 15 April 1835, on ncos at Saumur, in MR 1956.

11 Report to minister, October 1830, in AHG MR 1956.

12 Chalmin, *passim*, for the school system. For the St Cyr and La Flèche measures of 1831, Duvergier, Vol. XXXI, pp. 362, 365; and Ordonnance, 31 December 1817, in AHG Xo 1.

13 *Moniteur Universel*, 1849, p. 2414.

14 The civilians were mostly teachers of German or general literature.

15 Dossiers in AAG.

16 The sample is weighted towards those whose AAG dossiers can be traced, and particularly those who taught military subjects. Note however that the generals commanding schools are included in the sample, as well as professors, since obviously the morale and academic tone of such institutions depends largely upon leadership.

17 Thirty-two per cent of the sample came from the Infantry, as compared to 61% of officers in the army as a whole; 16% from the Cavalry as against 20% of the army; 20% from the Artillery as against 10%; 16% from the Engineers as against 4%; 8% from the Staff or Geographical Engineers as against 5% – and 8% of the sample were of unknown origins.

18 Six per cent of the sample of military school staff came from outside the hexagon, as opposed to 13% in the general sample of military authors – see chapter three, above. Eleven per cent of the sample came from the Loire, as opposed to 7% of military authors – but apart from these two cases, the

distribution is broadly similar in the two samples.

19 La Motte Rouge, Vol. I, pp. 69–70; Titeux, p. 200 *ff*.; Ordonnances of 30
    July, 23 September 1814, in AHG Xo I.

20 Castellane, Vol. I, pp. 365–6; Joffrés, *Considérations sur l'École Speciale
    Militaire de St Cyr*, March 1845, in AHG MR 1955.

21 Titeux, *passim.*

22 *Ibid.*, p. 286; Lieutenant A. Bernard, *Souvenirs de la Promotion de l'Empire*, p. 9 *ff*..

23 Titeux, p. 276; ms note (1842?) on St Cyr instruction in AHG MR 1955; and –
    for subsequent revisions – Xo 11.

24 Titeux, p. 345 *ff*.; and ms (1842?) note in AHG MR 1955. Tholosé was an
    engineer who rose through Soult's staff and then the *Dépôt de la Guerre*.

25 Titeux, p. 349 *ff.*

26 As argued by Taverne, in *Essai Raisonné*, in AHG MR 2011.

27 La Motte Rouge, Vol. I, p. 106.

28 Unfortunately I have been unable to trace Chantreau's dossier.

29 Colonel J.T. Rocquancourt was an engineer who started teaching at St Cyr in
    1821, eventually becoming director of studies. In 1848 he taught Egyptian
    officers for a spell, and retired in 1852 (dossier in AHG).

30 Rocquancourt, Vol. IV, p. 627.

31 See Irvine's article of that title.

32 Cf. *Sentinelle de l'Armée*, 1 January 1848, already criticising Rocquancourt for
    his inordinate length. Colonel N.E. de Labarre Duparcq was an engineer
    who started to teach at St Cyr in 1849, becoming director of studies in 1861.

33 Note, however, that Labarre Duparcq also wrote about Bugeaud and
    Clausewitz – who were both especially interested in morale .

34 See the army's official *Annuaires* .

35 See Pinet for the general history of Polytechnique, supported by de la
    Jonquière. For the teaching staff, *Annuaires* and AAG *Célébrités* carton.

36 Pinet's 1894 article.

37 Reports to the crown, November 1814, in AHG Xo 8.

38 AHG Xo 8.

39 Gay de Vernon, *Traité Élémentaire d'Art Militaire et de Fortification.*

40 Gay de Vernon, Vol. II, p 3.

41 E.g. Dusaert's 'Essai sur l'art de la guerre' in *Moniteur de l'Armée*, 5 and 15
    April 1850.

42 See his minute books in AHG MR 1979, 24 November, 15 December 1825.

43 Chambray's *Polytechnique.*

44 This vital consideration was unfortunately lost on those post–1870 critics
    who condemned Polytechnique simultaneously for failing to create genius
    and for neglecting the mediocre.

45 Compare the 1960s story about one of '*les X*' (as the Polytechnicians are
    known, due to their devotion to algebra) who, when he heard his companion
    was suffering from an upset stomach, instantly retorted with the typically
    rarefied question 'Did you eat an acid or a base?'.

46 This envy was shared by foreigners – see the British War Office *Report on the
    Training of Officers for the Scientific Corps*, London, 1857 – although ironically
    this came from the army of which Chambray, in turn, was himself most
    envious.

47 See Chambray's *Polytechnique*, p. 51.
48 *Travail de la Commission Mixte*, 1807, in AHG Xo 12.
49 Chalmin, p. 178 – but note that the rate of turnover of teachers at Metz was exceptionally high.
50 Paixhans, *Constitution Militaire*, p. 84, specifically links criticism of the Metz school to changes in warfare.
51 Report on Metz regimental school, 1850, in AHG Xo 12.
52 Report on Arras regimental school, 1850, in AHG Xo 12.
53 E.g. letter of 24 December 1817 for the Artillery Bureau, in AHG Xo 12, showing how de Feltre controlled these appointments politically – and how Gouvion St Cyr wanted to reintroduce appointment by examination.
54 See report of the staff commission, 1833?, in AHG Xs 139; and cf. Bernard's memoirs from St Cyr, pp. 50, 56, 86, 90–8.
55 Colonel T. Fix, *Souvenirs*, p. 26.
56 Memos by Desprès n.d. (1819?); anon. (Préval?), 1816; and Koch, 1836 – all in AHG MR 1978. See also Pelet's correspondence, 1833–34, in Xs 139.
57 Pelet's note on examinations 1841, in AHG Xs 139.
58 The syllabi are in AHG Xs 139; cf. Fix, p. 23.
59 Ternay, *Traité*, especially p. xlii, for a discussion of the 'rules' of warfare.
60 *Spectateur Militaire*, 1827, p. 491. See also other suggestions for a war school in *Sentinelle de l'Armée*, 8 May 1836, 24 March 1837; also Bardin's dictionary under *École*, and Favé, p. xv.
61 État Major Commission, 1833?, discussing complaints by the engineers, in AHG Xs 139.
62 Duvallier's suggested *Athenée Militaire des Modernes*, January 1831, in AHG MR 2141; Pagezy de Bourdéliac, *Plan Sommaire*, in MR 1984.
63 Series of ms notes on the school in AHG MR 1978, especially minute of 3 July 1818 and Règlement, 4 November 1819.
64 Préval attacked this in his 1834 inspection report, in AHG MR 1956.
65 Final part of *De la Cavalerie*, in AHG MR 1956.
66 Anon. ms (Captain Donop?), 4 January 1830, in AHG MR 1956; cf. lithographed *De l'École Royale de Cavalerie et des Capitaines Instructeurs* (by Captain St Victor?), n.d., in the same carton. Note that La Roche Aymon had himself spent many years in Prussia.
67 Ordonnances, 5 November 1823, in AHG Xo 14, 7 November 1845, in MR 1956; cf. report to the crown, 16 July 1834, and Commission of 24 March 1825, in same carton.
68 Cf. critique of the course by Mussot, ms, *Mémoire sur l'École de Cavalerie*, 1844, in AHG Xo 15.
69 Lithographed *Résumé du Cours d'Art Militaire*, 1862, and anon. ms note on it, both in AHG Xo 14.
70 Captain Jacquemin, lithographed *Recherches Historiques sur les Écoles de Cavalerie en France*, 1 August 1839, in AHG MR 1989.

Chapter 9

1 Quoted in Castellane, Vol. II, p. 498.
2 Guillon, p. 270 *ff.*; Pelleport, Vol. II, p. 169.

3 *Moniteur Universel*, 1831, p. 1963.

4 *Moniteur Universel*, 1841, p. 99 *ff.*.

5 It is ironic, however, that Thiers had himself failed to exploit the subtleties of deterrence while managing the crisis of 1840.

6 Ms, *Receuil des Notes Adressées aux Différents Bureaux du Ministère de la Guerre* 1824–27, in AHG MR 1979. See also his attack on the Intendance in ms, *Rapport au Roi*, 1825, in MR 2010.

7 See 'Caux' in Bardin's dictionary, and Maison's ms, *Rapport au Roi*, in his AAG dossier, for examples of ministers anxious to limit the power of their bureaucrats. Gentil St Alphonse, writing to the Dauphin, 14 June 1829, complained openly of interference in the reports of the Conseil Supérieure – ms in AHG MR 1910, p. 137; and see *Journal de l' Armée*, 7 February 1836.

8 Préval ms, *Examen de la Question du Défiler*, 1839, in AHG MR 1910, p. 131.

9 AAG dossiers, and criticism of Genty and Melchion in *Journal de l' Armée*, 11 September 1836.

10 Préval's ms letter to Orleans, 2 December 1841, in AHG MR 1910, p. 179.

11 However Thoumas, Vol. II, pp. 12, 42 *ff.*, and Odier on administration, show that the best members of the Intendance were quite capable of taking a wider view.

12 Morand, p. 99, wanted to revert to a dual ministry, although General Rostaing opposed it – see his ms, 22 March 1817, in AHG Xs 117.

13 Attempts were made to reintroduce a dual organisation in 1821 and 1836, but proved abortive.

14 The changes may be followed in detail through the official *Annuaires*, and in AHG MR 2015.

15 E.g. Pamphile de Lacroix's *Raisons d'État* (published 1823 after being originally intended for private circulation); Fabvier, *De l' Armée*, and in *Moniteur Universel*, 1851, p. 34.

16 Admiration of the British is in the anon. ms report, 15 March 1821, in AHG MR 2019.

17 For organisations before 1815 see AHG, *Papiers Guibert*, in Xp 4, Xs 116, MR 1944. For the *Conseil d'État* after 1815, see Pelet's ms note on Préval's projected *Rapport au Roi*, 1832, in MR 2070; Pamphile de Lacroix, p. 48; Bardin, p. 1559.

18 St Chamans, p. 319.

19 Préval ms, projected *Rapport au Roi*, in AHG MR 2070; and Maison's in his AAG dossier. See also Ledru des Essarts, 1821, in Xs 26; Préval ms *De l' État des Officiers*, 1828, in MR 1953, and Schramm in the Infantry Committee, 11 May 1844, in Xs 141.

20 Anon. ms, *Note sur l' Institution d'un Conseil Supérieur de la Guerre*, 1849, in AHG MR 2070, and Bardin on Caux. General Caux was the engineer son of the chief engineer, who had worked in the ministry since 1807 – rising to general, *conseiller d'État*, and later (1828) minister. Dossier in AAG.

21 Ambrugéac had retired as a subaltern during the Revolution but served again in 1810 and was made a general by the king in 1815. Dossier in AAG.

22 The members were Marshals Marmont, Molitor and Victor; Generals Ambrugéac, Bordessoulle, Caux (the minister of war), Dode de la Brunerie, Foissac-Latour, Gentil St Alphonse, Girardin, Loverdo, Pelleport, Préval,

Reille, Rogniat and Valée, and Intendant Regnault.

23 The original terms of reference were laid down in Caux's *Rapport au Roi*, 6 March 1828, in AHG Xs 140, cf. ms notes on a memoir submitted to the Infantry Commission of the Conseil, 12 June 1829, in MR 2008, and Marmont's memoirs, Vol. VIII, pp. 197–9.

24 Castellane, Vol. II, p. 276, for a typical conservative view.

25 Its transactions are in AHG Xs 142 and MR 2019, and especially in the official minutes, MR 2050 and 2051.

26 File 2 in AHG Xem 21.

27 Discussion by Pelet in ms report, 12 August 1832, in AHG MR 2070.

28 Préval ms, in AHG MR 1910, p. 1, cf. the ministerial *Moniteur de l'Armée*, 1 December 1841, which rejects a similar view expressed by its rival, the *Sentinelle* .

29 *Journal de l'Armée*, 7 February 1836.

30 Article, 'Des comités et des commissions de la guerre' in *Le Constitutionel*, 19 March 1834, in AHG MR 2070.

31 Pelet, 1832, in AHG 2070.

32 Préval's projected *Rapport au Roi*, 1832, in AHG MR 2070, and his original *Projet de Règlement*, p. 74 *ff* .; Morand, p. 96.

33 Pelet in 1832 in AHG MR 2070; and Xem 21, dossiers 6, 7 and 8.

34 Taverne, in his *Essai Raisonné* in AHG MR 2011, is bitterly opposed to the separation of arm committees.

35 See Fabvier, *De l'Armée;* and Carvalho's ms note on his ideas, 24 December 1845, in AHG MR 2141, dossier 2; cf. the reply to Fabvier by Colonel Lefaivre, 15 April 1846, in MR 1962.

36 AHG Xs 135; MR 2096, 2097, 2098, 1995, 1996, 2076. Maréscot was the son of a noble officer who started his career as an engineer in 1776. He won overnight promotion to general in the early Revolution, helped Napoleon over the Alps in 1800, but was disgraced over the defeat at Baylen and not re-employed until the Restoration. Dossier in AAG.

37 *What Indeed?* we may *well* ask! But in any event see Pelet's *Partie Secrète des Séances*, 29 November 1820, in AHG MR 2097, p. 10. The gunner Andréossy had been Napoleon's chief of staff at *Brumaire*, and held influential posts until helping negotiate the surrender in 1815. In the Restoration he was a liberal deputy.

38 Marshal Dode de la Brunerie was the son of a notary, became a general of engineers in 1809, and was a favoured royalist in the Restoration – but best known for directing the Paris fortifications of 1840. His striking portrait today surveys the magnificent staircase leading into the AHG at Vincennes.

39 Carnot, *De la Défense des Places Fortes;* Paixhans, *Force et Faiblesse;* Rogniat, *Considérations*.

40 *Moniteur Universel* 1841, p. 99.

41 AHG Xs 135; MR 1995–6; and see also the engineer reports on Bitche in Xe 283–4 and Xe 470–1.

42 Haxo, 1774–1838, started his career in the Artillery of the Revolution, but soon transferred to the Engineers. He became a general in 1810, commander of the Guard Engineers in 1813, and one of the leading members of his arm during the Restoration.

43   This actually happened in 1843.

44   The only significant career basis for this division seems to have been the lack
     of any direct command experience among the first three of the five named
     generals: see AAG dossiers.

45   Pelet's collection of documents in AHG MR 2077; and see the dossiers of
     commission members in AAG.

46   Schramm's father was a Swiss sergeant who became a general. A corporal in
     Egypt, the junior Schramm had become an Infantry general by 1813. The
     Restoration did not employ him before 1828, with the result that he enjoyed
     the favour of the July Monarchy and became minister of war in 1850–51.
     Dossier in AAG.

47   For Lamoricière's role see Keller, Vol. II, pp. 9–172. The non-reforming
     tendencies of the other Commission members was all the more disappointing
     in view of their earlier liberal ideas, e.g. Oudinot himself.

48   Pelet's lithographed *Essai sur le Systeme Défensif de la France Modifié par la
     Fortification de Paris et par les Chemins de Fer*, 15 July 1842, in AHG MR 2077.

49   Pelet ms, *Mémoire sur la Répartition des Armées*, 10 October 1848, in AHG MR
     2077.

50   For the debate around the Staff Corps, see AHG Xs 139, MR 1954, 1978,
     1999.

51   Pelet defends this in his ms, *Essai sur les Manoeuvres*, n.d., in AHG MR 2012;
     cf. Lecouturier de Vienne, in *Spectateur Militaire*, 1828, p. 65, who opposes it
     as increasing Staff Corps privileges.

52   AHG Xem 21, dossier 10; and MR 1954.

53   Ms, *Observations sur la Création d'un Bureau d'Organisation et d'Inspection*,
     addressed to the minister, n.d., in AHG MR 2027.

Index

Note: Numbers printed in italic type indicate main entries

Abd-el-Kader, Emir, *37–8*, 40–3
administration, regimental, *91–3*
aeroplanes, 77
'African' officers, *12–13*, 39–40, 45, 54, 61
Algeria, *3–4*, *32–43*, 167–8
  colonisation policy, 21, 49, 87, 110–12, 154
  cultural influences, 19, 54, 107
  operations, 45, 62, 68, 92, 130
  training, 9, 61, 74, 116–18
  weaponry, 78, 80
  welfare, *95–8*, 105
Allent, Chevalier P. A. J., 70, *143*
Allix, General J. A. F., 60, 80
Alps, 30, 40, 116
Alton, General A. D', 109, 124
Ambert, General J., 62, 64, 73, 107, 121
Ambrugéac, General L. A. M. de V., 156
Amoros, Colonel F., 79, *108–9*
anarchy, 9–10, 117, 124
Ancien Régime, 8, 15, 18, 58, 85, 92, 106, 144, *159–60*
Ancona, 30, 150
Andréossy, General A. F., *160–1*
Angoulême, Duke of, 13, *22–4*, 41
anti-semitism, 19, 34
Antwerp, *28–30*, 32, 78, 150
Appert, B., 102

Arab Bureaux, 37
Ardant du Picq, Colonel C. J. J. J., *79*, 117
arms of the Service, 57, 65, 115
assassins, 77, 96
Aumale, Duke of, 42
Austerlitz, 1805 battle of, 8, 118
Austria/Austrian, 4, 30, 103, 112, 150, 168
Aymard, General Baron A., 61, 75

Ballasteros, General F., 24
balloons, 77
Balzac, Honoré de, 55
Barail, General F. C. du, 17, 39
barracks, 5, 9, 47–8, 65, 95–6, 99
battle indoctrination, 109, 121
Baudelaire, Charles, 54
bayonets, 49, 78, 86, 107, 109, 117, 119–21, 126–7, 130
Bazaine, Marshal F. A., 5, 16, 117, 168
Beauchamps, Captain A. H. P. de, 60
Bedeau, General M.-A., 39, 43, 164
Belgium/Belgians, 4, 21, 28–30, 38, 81, 149
Berry, Duchess of, 41, 43
Berthezène, General Baron P., 35–6
Berthier, Marshal L. A., 56
Beurmann, Captain J., 64
Bitche, *161–4*
Blanqui, L. A., 49
Bléton, battalion commander M. A., 60
Boichot, Sergeant Major J., 65–6

Bonapartism, 7, 12, 22, 54, 58, 60, 65, 102, 108, 145, 147, 156, 158, 165
Bosquet, Marshal P.J.F., 39
Bossuet, J.-B., 72
Boulanger, General G., 39
Boulogne,1804–05 camp, 8, 118
Bou Ma'za, *Mahdi*, 42–3
Bourbaki, General C. D. S., 39
Bourbon kings of France, 7, 12–13, 85, 34–5, 47–8, 160–1
Bourdesoulle, General E. T. de P., 24
Bourke, General J. R. C., 24
Bourmont, Marshal L. V. de, 32–5, 56
Boyer, General de Rebeval, 35
Brahaut, Colonel G.N., 153
Brenier, General de Montmorand, 124
Britain/British, 5, 22, 25, 27–8, 38, 60, 77, 102, 108, 115, 121, 125, 155
Broussais, health inspector F., 95–6
Buchet, General J.-B., 122
budget for defence, 8, Appendix I
Bugeaud, Marshal T. de, 13, 38–46, 78–9, 116–17, 125, 127, 168
Blow, H.D. von, 57, 60
bureaux in ministry of war, 77, 133, 151–66
Byron, Lord, 25, 130

Cadiz, 4, 24, 34
Caesar, Emperor Julius, 59, 69, 72
Calais, H., 64
Canrobert, Marshal F. de C., 39, 41, 88, 168
Caraman, General V. M. J. L. R. de, 163
Carbonari, 22
'career open to talent', 16–20, 93–4, 101, 133–6
Carnot L., 8, 161
Carrion Nisas, General M. F. H. E., 60
cartography *see* topography
Castellane, Marshal E. B. F. de, 4, 61, 75, 98, 109, 117, 168
Caux, General Vicomte de L.-V. de B., 25, 155–6
Cavaignac, General L. E. de, 14, 37–9, 43, 168
censorship, 18, 64

Chalmin, Commandant P., 65
Chambray, General G. de, 60, 142
Changarnier, General N. A. T., 38–9, 41, 43
Chantreau, P.N., 139, 146
chaplains, 95, 106–7
Charles, Austrian Archduke, 56
Charras, General, 39, 43
Chassé, General Baron D. H. de, 28–30
Chasseurs à Pied, 61, 77–9, 87–8, 107, 109, 115–17, 123, 125–30, 158, 168
Chateaubriand, F.-R. de, 54
chess, 75, 117–18
children, 62, 86
circus performers, 107
Clarke, Marshal H. J. G., 157
class, social, 7, 10, 15–17, 53, 65, 90, 133, 135–8
Clausewitz, General Carl von, 6, 8, 20, 55–6, 59, 140, 149, 160
Clauzel, Marshal B., 35–9
Clermont Ferrand, 46
Clermont Tonnerre, General J. G. A. de, 124, 142, 151
Clouet, General A. L. A., 60
colonels, 73, 76, 90–1, 98–9, 103, 106, 109
Combes, Colonel, 78, 168
Commissaire, Sergeant S., 66
committees of arms: Artillery, 80–1, 157–9
Cavalry, 156–9
Engineers, 157–9, 163
Gendarmerie, 158
Infantry, 75–6, 89–90, 99, 123, 126, 156–9, 164
Staff, 157–9
committees of Defence, 154, 159–66
common sense, 116, 122–4
Commune de Paris (1871), 3, 10, 45, 48
Comte, Auguste, 54
conscription *see* recruitment
Conseil Supérieure de la Guerre, 13, 92, 153–6, 157–60, 164, 168
Considérant, Victor, 80
Constantine, 38, 40, 43
Cosmography, 70–1, 103, 138, 145
Cossacks, 54, 77

counter-insurgency, 3, 21, 43–50, 53, 118

coup d'état, 3, 12–13, 14–15, 43–4, 60, 145

Courtigis, General Aulas de, 164

Coynart, Captain, 81

crime, 98–100, Appendix II

Crimean War (1853–6), 4, 13, 21, 28, 62, 116, 127, 130, 168

Curial, General P. J. B., 124

Damas, General Baron A. H. M., 151

Damrémont, General C. D. de, 39–40

dancing, 88, 108

Daudet, 54

debts, 16, 91

Delvigne, Lieutenant H. G., 64, 78–9

Departmental Legions, 7, 128

Dépôt de la Guerre, 61–2, 72, 81–2, 106, 145, 154–66

Desmichels, General, 37–8

digging, 107, 110–13, 144

discipline, 62, 79, 86–91, 96–111, 119–20, 135, 137, 140–1, 144, 169

disease, 22, 25–8, 34–6, 40, 86–91, 95–6, 112

Dode, G. de la Brunerie, 82, 160, 163–4

dogs, 86

Doisy, Captain, 72

Dreyfus, Captain Alfred, 19, 55, 169

drill, 8, 73–5, 85, 88, 94, 116, 118, 122–5, 129–30, 145–6

drink, 17, 86–9, 95–6, 111

Drouet D'Erlon, Marshal J. B., 37

Ducastel, ex-gunner, 80

duelling, 18–19, 108–9

Duhesme, General P. G., 56, 59

Dumas, General Mathieu, 60

Durand, Squadron Commander P. F. F., 61, 72

Dusaert, Colonel L. E., 49

embastillement, 47

'empty battlefield', 114

Espinay, Marquis d', 80

exercises, tactical, 74

Fabvier, General C.-N., 14, 22–5, 119, 159

Favé, Colonel I., 71, 81, 136, 142

fencing, 78, 88, 107–9

Ferdinand, king of Spain, 22–5

Férussac, Baron de, 63

Fézensac, General R. A. P. J. de, 59

Fix, Colonel T., 145

Flèche, École de la, 136–7

Foreign Legion, 30, 36, 128–9

Forey, Marshal E. F., 39

fortification, 57, 75, 80, 110–14, 138, 140–3, 145, 149–50, 159–64

Fourierism, 61–2

Foy, 10, 14

Franco-Prussian War (1870–1), 3–5, 12, 16, 28, 32, 69, 93, 117, 138, 150, 165, 168

Franc-Tireurs, 4

Frederick the Great, king, 70

freemasonry, 19

Fririon, General Baron J.-F., 63

Garibaldi, General Giuseppe, 30–2

Garraube, General J. A. V., 79

Gassendi, General J. J. B. de, 57, 143

Gaulle, Acting Brigadier C. de, 55

Gay de Vernon, Colonel S. F., 57, 136, 141

generalship, 5, 68–76, 114–15, 120

Genty, Captain, 153

Gérard, Marshal E. M., 16, 28, 136, 138

German army *see* Prussian army

girls, 17, 86–9

Gouvion St. Cyr, Marshal L., 59, 94, 122, 157, 165

Grande Guerre, la, 6–7, 12, 21, 49, 53, 150, 161, 167

Grandmaison, Colonel L. de, 70, 169

Gravelotte, 1870 battle of, 5, 32, 41

Greece, 4, 21, 25–8, 33–4, 38, 96

Grimoard, 57

Guadeloupe, 9

guards, 78, 102, 128, 147, 155–6

guerrillas, 33–42, 48–9, 79, 118

Guibert, Count Hyppolyte de, 6, 57–8, 85, 122, 155

Guilleminot, General A.-C., Count, 22, 27, 68, 160

Guillin, monsieur, 78

Guizot, F., 36, 103
gymnastics, 79, 87, 107–10, 126, 129, 148, 169

half pay, 17, 60, 67, 79–80, 151, 156
Halleck, General 'Old Brains', 56
Hamley, Sir E. B., 56
Harispe, General J.-I., 89
Haussman, 45
Hautpoul, General A.-H. d', 136
Haxo, General N., 30, 78, 82, 163, 168
heavy artillery, 30, 77, 79–81
historians/history, 3–4, 6, 72–3, 106, 138
Hitte, General J. E. D. de la, 34
Hoche, General L., 49
Holland, 28
horses, 19, 42, 60, 112, 147–8
Houdetot, General C.-I. de F., 129
Hugo, Victor, 54–5
Hulot, General J. L., 129
Humbert, Chef d'escadron E., 148
Humboldt, Alexander, 149

Ibrahim Pasha, 25
India, 5, 117
industry, 16, 19, 77, 92, 110–12, 141, 160
Inkerman, 1854 Battle of, 118
inspectors, 73, 76, 89–90, 101, 103
intendants, 93, 95, 153, 156–8, 165
inventors, 77–82, 115
Italy, 4, 8, 30–2, 130, 149
Itier, Colonel, 64, 78

Jacquinot de Presle, Captain C., 63, 148
Jamin, General J.-B., 88
Jena, 1806 Battle of, 8, 118
Jomini, Baron A. H., 6, 55–8, 60, 69–70, 73, 139–40, 145–6, 167
July Revolution (1830), 3, 7, 12, 34, 40, 43–7, 136

Koch, General J. B., 58, 63, 137, 145–6, 168

Labarre Duparcq, Colonel N. E. de, 140

Laborde, Colonel A., 102
Lacuée Cessac, General J. G. de, 57
Ladmirault, General L. R. P., 39
Lamarque, General M., 10, 14, 49, 60, 63
Lamartine, A. de, 54, 121
Lamoricière, general C. L. L. J. de, 13, 39, 43, 45, 78, 151, 164, 168
Lancaster, Joseph, 102
Langres, 161
Laplace, P. S., Marquis de, 54, 70–1, 142
Larrey, surgeon Baron, 95
Lauriston, Marshal, J. A. L., 14
Le Boeuf, Marshal E., 39
Lecamus, Captain C. L. F., 137
Lechevalier, artillery officer, 80
Le Couturier, Colonel, 60
Le Flô, General, 39
Lenglet, Captain E. H. F., 71
levée en Masse see Nation in Arms
libraries, 72, 105–7, 144, 169
Liddell Hart, Captain B. H., 69
light infantry *see* Chasseurs à Pied
Ligne, Prince C. de, 57
limited War, 6, 12, 21, 30, 32, 53, 149–50, 160
Liskenne and Sauvan, 73
'literature', 54–5, 62, 138, 141
Lloyd, General H., 57
logistics, 22, 25–8, 34, 39–42, 47, 91–3
Loi St Cyr (1818), 7, 11
Loi Soult (1832), 7, 11,
Louis Philippe, king, 28
Lyautey, Marshal L. H. G., 39, 169
Lyon, 34, 42–4, 61, 65

MacDonald, Marshal E. J., 102
MacMahon, Marshal M. E. P. M. de, 39, 168
MacNamara, Robert, 70
Madagascar, 4
Maginot, Corporal A., 150
Maison, Marshal N. J., 18, 25–7
Maistre, Joseph de, 55, 121
manuals (including 'regulations'), 73, 90, 98, 105, 137–8, 143, 145, 147–8
  Artillery, 57, 80
  Cavalry, 78

Field Service, 73, 97
Fortification, 57
Infantry Drill, 57–8, 79, 90,122–5, 139
Staffwork, 57
Maoism, 39
Marbot, Baron M. de, 59, 63
Maréscot, A.-S. de, 160–4
Marmont, Marshal A-F. L. V., 16, 44–5, 56, 59, 80, 157
Martineau, Intendant, 153
massacres, 36, 40–2, 45–6
Maudit (or Mauduit), Captain Hippolyte de, 64
Maupassant, G. de, 54
maxims, 59, 72, 122, 139
medical officers, 95–6
Melchion, Intendant d'Arc, 153
Melegnano, 1859 Battle of, 118
Merson, Squadron Commander L. F., 64
mess, officers', 16
Metz, École de, 30, 81–2, 135, 137, 143–4
Michaloz, artillery officer, 81
military Art, 62–3
military Press, 6, 18, 57, 60–7, 94, 105
military schools, 16, 18, 65, 73, 97, 133–48
military vocabulary, 86–7, 90–1, 97–8, 169
Mina, General Espoz y, 24–5
Minié, Chef de Battalion C. E., 79
ministers of State, 14
ministers of war, 13–14, 17, 39, 90, 115, 151–66
ministry of war, 13, 61, 68, 73, 151–66
mobilisation, 5, 11, 30, 68, 160–5
Molènes, Paul de, 54, 62
Molitor, Marshal G. J., 24, 156
Moltke, General H. von, 20
Moncey, Marshal B-A. J., 24
Montgéry, Captain, 79
Moore, General Sir John, 86
morality, 87–8, 101, 105–10, 117–18, 139–41
Morand, General C. A. L. A., 56, 59–60, 85, 122

Morocco, 42
Motte Rouge, General J. de La, 78, 139
Müller, Colonel, 109
Mussot, Colonel P., 64
mutiny, 14–15, 17, 19–20, 22, 35, 44, 109, 119, 167

Napier, General W. F. P., 56
Napoleon I, Emperor, 3–4, 8, 33, 41, 56, 68, 72, 93, 118, 123, 128, 136, 139, 141, 154–5, 167
Napoleon III, Emperor, 3–4, 12, 14, 32, 39, 43, 81, 128, 142, 150, 168
Napoleonic warfare, 5–6, 8, 21, 58, 62, 73, 92, 106, 116, 118, 120, 122, 126, 143, 146, 168
National Guard, 9–10, 44–8, 54, 161
nation in arms, 6–8, 10, 150, 163
navy, 14, 25–7, 33–4, 77, 80
Nazism, 19, 41, 86
ncos, 17, 93–5, 97–8, 101, 103, 119, 135–6, 146–7, 159
Neigre, General, 30
Ney, Marshal M., 56, 58
Niel, Marshal A., 39
nobility, 7, 15–16, 19, 101, 109–10, 150, 167
Noblot, Captain E. P. J., 60
nostalgia, 9, 36, 88, 96, 110, 169
nuclear strategy, 150

oath of loyalty, 14–15
Odier, Sous-Intendant F. A., 145
oilskins, 87
organisation, 68, 80–2, 91–3,133–66
orientalism, 16
Orleans, Duke of, 13, 37, 61, 74, 106, 129, 166, 168
Oudinot, General Duke, 30–2, 164
Ouvrard, contractor, 22, 92

pacifism, 106, 110
Pagezy de Bourdéliac, Captain, 72
Pailhès, General A., 137
Paixhans, General H. V., 30, 79–80, 161, 168
Papal States, 13, 30–2, 39
paperwork, 90, 94

Paris, fortifications, 47, 60, 80, 111–12,
    114, 150, 161–3
    military authorities, 14, 37–8, 61,
        89, 130, 137
    military institutions, 81, 144, 165
    opinion in, 3–4, 38, 40, 54, 109, 129
    revolutions, 10, 42–8
    writers, 56, 66
parliament, 10, 14, 36, 55, 67, 151, 155
Pascal, Blaise, 71
pay, 8, 15–16, 19, 60, 94–5,
Pelet, General J.-J., 59, 61, 63, 68, 145,
    157, 160–6, 168
Pélissier, Marshal A., 42, 39
Pelleport, General V. de, 124
penal reform, 15, 88, 90, 97–100, 112
Peninsular War (1808–14), 4, 22–4, 49,
    116–17
pensions, 18, 94
Pestalozzi, J. H., 108
Petitet, officer-author, 153
phrenology, 15
Picq, Ardant du *see* Ardant
pilgrimages, 32
Pinette, fencing master, 109
Piobert, Captain G., 81
Pius IX, pope, 30–2
Poland, 19
Polybius, 72
Polytechnique, École, 54, 61, 70, 135–
    43, 144–6
positivism, 39
Préval, General C. A. H. de, 61, 73, 97,
    153–4, 156–8
primary education, 69, 87, 94, 101–7,
    135, 144, 169
printing, 47, 81
prizes, 108, 111
professionals *see* regular troops
promotion, 16–18, 62–7, 73, 78, 91–3,
    98, 101, 104, 114, 126, 147
Prussian army, 5, 10, 20, 68–9, 74–5,
    82, 86, 115, 118, 120–1, 147–9, 155,
    166, 168
psychology, 46, 86, 88, 95–8, 108, 116–
    23, 127
public works, 62
Puissant, Colonel L, 82

Puvis, Battalion commander, 60
Pyrenees, 22–4, 30, 89
pyrotechnology, 81, 143

railways, 8, 81, 110–11, 165–6, 168
Randon, Marshal J. L. C., 16, 39
razzia, 39, 41–2, 129
recruitment, 3, 7–11, 110
regions of France, 66, 137, 167
regular troops, 7–10, 117, 120–2, 128,
    139, 150, 153–4, 161, 167
regulations *see* manuals
Reille, Marshal H. C., 16
religion, 19, 53, 87, 96, 107, 123, 141
'replacement', 7, 95, 98
reserves, 8–10, 114
retirement, 67, 94
revolution of 1848, 3, 7, 10, 43–7, 164,
    168
Richemont, General Baron C. de, 137
Riego, General R., 24
rifles, 78–81, 125–7
riots, 3, 9, 17, 43–50, 114, 137, 139,
    141, 167
Roche Aymon, General C. de la, 147–
    8, 168
rockets, 33, 77, 79–80
Rocquancourt, Captain J. T., 139–40,
    148, 168
Rogniat, General J., 60, 120, 161, 163
Roguet, General (*père*), 44
Roguet, General C. M. (*fils*), 45–6, 48–
    9
Roland, E., 103–4
Roman Catholic church, 19, 39, 102,
    106, 150
romantic movement, 62, 72, 95, 100,
    107, 124
Rome, 4, 19, 21, 30–2, 151
Rostolan, General, 129
Russia, 4, 25, 27, 55–6, 74, 112, 168

St Arnaud, Marshal A. A. J., 13, 39,
    116, 127–8, 168
St Chamans, General O. de, 45
St Cyr, École Spécial, 54, 81, 117, 135–
    40, 141–5, 147
St Cyr, Gouvion *see* Gouvion

St Simonianism, 39, 42, 49, 61, 102,
112, 141, 169
sapeurs pompiers, 113
Sarragossa, 1808 siege of, 44, 161
Saumur, École de, 135, 137, 145, 146–8
Savary, General, Duke of Rovigo, 36–
7
savings, 95
Saxe, Marshal M. de, 57
Scharnhorst, General G. von, 8, 59
Schneider, General A.-V., 27, 124
Schramm, General J. P. A. de, 164
science, 49, 56, 67–73, 76–7, 95, 101,
105, 107, 115, 133, 135, 141–4, 146–
7, 159, 161, 167
Scott, Sir Walter, 49
Sedan, 1870 Battle of, 3, 10, 32, 41,
53
Seillère, contractor, 33
Senegal, 4
'sensuous tremors', 121
Sherman, General W. T., 41
sieges, 24–5, 27–30, 32–5, 75, 150, 159,
160–4
singing, 88, 109–10
Slim, Field Marshal Bill, 59
socialism, 10, 19, 49, 80, 86
Solferino, 1859 Battle of, 41, 168
Soult, Marshal-General J. de D., 13–
14, 16, 18, 37, 59, 64, 74, 103, 128–
9, 136, 152, 157
Spanish War (1823), 4, 8, 11–12, 21–5,
33, 38, 41, 149
Staff Corps, 59, 65, 68, 76, 81–2, 115,
144–6, 151, 154, 157–67
staff school, 135, 144–6
Staouëli, 1830 Battle of, 33
statistics, 71, 81, 98, 136, 154
steam guns, 77, 161
steamships, 79
Stendhal, 54–5, 114
strategy, 10, 49, 56, 67, 71, 73–6, 78,
146, 150–1, 159–4, 166–7
Suchet, Marshal L-G., 40, 49, 59, 102
Sun Tzu, 70
Suvarov, Marshal A., 121
Sweden/Swedish, 112, 146
swimming, 87, 96, 107

Tabarié, Captain, 153
tactics, 58, 67, 71, 73, 75, 114–30, 167
Tamisier, Captain, 79
tanks, 77
Taverne, Captain E. J. N., 97
telegraph, 28, 81, 165
Tempelhof, G. F. von , 57
Ternay, Colonel C. G. d'A. de, 58,
146
Thiers, A., 12–13, 36, 40, 47, 54, 61,
150–1, 161–4, 168
Thiery, Captain, 81
Thiroux, Captain C.-V., 81
Tholosé, General, 138–9, 142
Thouvenin, General L. E., 81
Thucydides, 69
Thuillier, Colonel, 81
Tolstoy, L., 121
topography, 75–6, 81–2, 88, 103, 116,
138, 140, 145–6
Tourreau, Captain J. C. P. C. de, 64
towns, 19, 86
Trézel, General C.-A., 25–7, 37, 89
Trochu, General L. J., 4, 60, 117
Tunisia, 35
Turco-Egyptian army, 25–8, 33–4, 39

uniforms, 65, 79, 92, 96, 129
universities, 20, 71–2, 108

Vaillant, Marshal J. B. P., 32
Valazé, General E. Dufriche de, 63,
163
Valée, Marshal S. C., 33, 40–1, 80,
160
Valentini, 57
Vauban, Marshal S. le P., 28, 49, 59,
161
Vaudoncourt, General Baron F. F. de,
60, 63
Vegetius, 72
Vendée, 4, 43, 48–9, 111, 161
veterans, 8, 11, 17, 73, 112, 119
Veuillot, Louis, 32
Victor, Marshal C-V., 22, 36
Viénot, drill instructor, 139
Vigny, Alfred de, 4, 54–5, 62
Voirol, general, 36–7

wall charts, 104–5
Warner, E., 56
war school *see* universities
washing, 96
Waterloo, 1815 Battle of, 3–4, 12, 21,
     22, 33, 37, 41, 55, 85, 114, 167
Wellington, Duke of, 116–7, 121

Willisen, K. W. von, 56
Wilson, Colonel Sir Robert, 24

Yusuf, Captain J., 36, 38

Zola, Émil, 55
Zouaves, 39, 78, 128, 168